Don't Use A Chainsaw In The Kitchen
A How-To Book
From Shot To Table
And Beyond

Dedicated to my Mother, Virginia Stevens,
My Grandmother, Velma Miller
And my Dad, who taught me
How to make pie crust,
James Stevens

Copyright 2012
Publisher: R. E. Stowell
177 Simpson Way

Fairbanks, Alaska 99712

Rosalyn Stowell

All Rights reserved.   Except for use in any review, the reproduction or utilization of this work in whole or in part in any form by any electronic, mechanical or other means, now known or hereafter invented, including xerography,   photocopying and recording, or in any information storage or retrieval system, is forbidden without the written permission of the author or her heirs.

The autobiography at the back of the book is a totally biased, opinionated version of my life, told strictly from my point of view.

Table of Contents

Hints & Tips

If you are using only whole wheat flour and want your cakes to turn out as though you were using all white bleached flour, exchange one quarter of the measure of flour with corn starch.

A good sugar-free snack for children can be made by using frozen bananas as popsicles. Peel banana, push stick or plastic fork or knife into it, freeze on a cookie sheet until firm.

For a not-so-sugar-free snack, dip frozen bananas into chocolate syrup or melted chocolate for a chocolate coated pop. Store in freezer until ready to eat.

Use brown sugar in place of white sugar when making cinnamon rolls, for a nice caramel flavor. Drizzle a bit of white corn syrup over the bottom of the pan before placing cut rolls in pan, for a sticky roll.

Use zucchini, cut in strips and slightly cooked to reduce moisture content, in place of noodles in lasagna. Use eggplant the same way.

Pierce small whole winter squash with a small knife, bake whole until almost tender, cut in half and remove seeds, brush with butter or margarine, return to oven and cook until tender. This makes it much easier to cut squash.

Use cooked winter squash in recipes calling for pumpkin. The flavor is the same and they are much easier to handle. May also use cooked, pureed carrots in place of pumpkin, or cooked sweet potatoes. About the only time pumpkin can't be substituted, is making Jack O'Lanterns. Carrots just don't quite pass it off, children notice, right away. They are the pits to carve, too.

Brown Sugar - 1 cup white granulated sugar + 1 T. molasses = 1 cup brown sugar

When reconstituting dry milk powder, add a drop of vanilla to the liquid mixture. It will improve taste.

If you are mixing dry milk to drink, and don't mind the added calories, add 1 T. unsalted butter per quart of mixed milk. Whiz in the blender until well blended.

When making cookies, spread the dough in a raised edge cookie sheet and bake for bar cookies. Saves a lot of time and you can burn the whole batch at one time instead of pan by pan.

Make cheesecake filled cupcakes easily by mixing I 8-ounce package cream, 3 T sugar and 1 T lemon juice. Fill cupcake cups half full of cake batter. Place I T. cheese mixture on top of batter. Bake as directed for cupcakes.

Use the same cheese mixture and drop by tablespoonfuls over cake batter and leave or swirl as for marble cake. Bake as directed for cake. Makes a wonderful surprise flavor in each slice of cake.

To add smoked flavor to hamburger, mix a few drops of liquid smoke in the meat before forming patties. Mix some smoked BBQ sauce with the meat for even more of an outdoor flavor.

If you wish to use less sugar or are using artificial sweeteners, improve flavor and enhance sweetness by using more vanilla and/or cinnamon in the recipe.   Chopped dates and raisins add sweetness, also.

HOMEMADE CURRY POWDER

Place 1 T cumin seeds

   6 black peppercorns

   2 dried chilies or 2 t. red chili flakes, may add more to taste

   1 t. fennel seeds

   6 whole cloves

   1 3" cinnamon stick in small dry skillet.   Toast over medium heat, shaking the pan frequently, about 3 minutes or until spices become fragrant. Let cool, then grind in a small grinder, food processor or mortar and pestle. Store in airtight container.

GRAVY TIPS

   If your gravy isn't as thick as you like, add some instant potatoes to it.   Or use instant potatoes to thicken broth for gravy.

   Use instant potatoes to thicken soups, it works very well.

   If gravy or sauce isn't as brown as you wish, caramelize a teaspoon of sugar over heat until it turns dark brown.   Stir the gravy with the spoon until gravy reaches desired color.   Soak any remaining sugar from spoon in hot water.   As sugar browns, it loses it's sweetness.

   Another method of adding color to gravy, is to use a few crystals of instant coffee or use strong coffee for part of the liquid.   Adds an elusive flavor that compliments the meal.

SWEETENED CONDENSED MILK (Substitute)

   Combine 3/4 cup sugar, 1/3 cup evaporated milk and 2 T.   margarine or butter in saucepan.   Heat only until sugar is dissolved, stirring constantly.

BURGER TIP

When making hamburger patties, add finely chopped or ground ham or corned beef to the meat before forming.   Mix well.   Adds a different flavor to a plain hamburger.

EGGS

For anyone that may not know, the BEST way to make "hard-boiled" eggs is in the OVEN! Place the eggs in a muffin tray so they do not move around, turn the oven to 325 degrees, pop in for about 25-30 minutes and remove! Not only are they tastier, but they also are much easier to peel!

ANGEL FOOD CAKES

An easy way to make Angel Food Cake using a one step mix without a whisk or mixer is to use a can of soda pop.   Root Beer makes an excellent cake.   Mix thoroughly with a fork, the mix will foam up.   Pour into an ungreased tube cake pan and bake according to the package directions.

Always make sure utensils are grease free and do not use plastic when making Angel Food Cake.   Always invert the pan when you remove cake from the oven, to allow it to cool.   Cake may fall if you don't.   Balance hot cake pan on the neck of a bottle, if the pan don't have legs.   Remove from pan after cake is thoroughly cooled.

To make a chocolate Angel Food Cake, add 2 rounded T. of unsweetened cocoa powder to the dry mix and mix well before adding liquid.   Proceed with directions for making the cake.

Beer Pancakes taste very similar to Sourdough Pancakes. Just use beer in place of liquid when making batter. A complete type pancake mix, using beer in place of liquid works very well.

Everyone tired of plain old pancakes for breakfast? Add any of the following or combine flavors, in the batter before cooking. Peanut butter, chopped apples, cinnamon, nutmeg, raisins, chopped nuts, chopped dates, and dried chopped fruit, ¼ cup oatmeal, ¼ cup bran. Try any of these added to cooked cereals also, children love it.

When baking, try to have the ingredients at room temperature. This can have an affect on the finished product.

Coconut milk can be made by extracting the liquid from the coconut meat by squeezing the pulp dry through a cheesecloth. An inferior product can be made by soaking dry coconut in water or milk and then squeezing dry.

To chop raisins and sticky fruits, heat the knife or food chopper.

To blanch nuts, cover with cold water, bring to a boil, set aside and let soak until the skins wrinkle, drain, cover with cool water and slip the skins off between your fingers.

Don't crowd the frying basket or kettle when deep frying. Don't use butter as it burns too quickly.

DEEP-FAT FRYING TEMPERATURES

360 to 375 degrees, F ....Uncooked mixtures, doughnuts, shellfish

375 to 385 degrees F ....Cooked mixtures with coatings

385 to 395 degrees F ....French-fried potatoes, vegetables, etc.

Keep herbs and spices well covered and out of the light, if possible, (dark containers or in a cabinet).   The flavor of dried herbs may be brought out by soaking a few minutes in hot water, then cold.   Use the soak water in the recipe if possible.

TRAVEL COOKING

If traveling with children, prepare hot dogs as you drive by wrapping securely with 2 or 3 layers of tinfoil and "cooking" on the engine.   May mix meatloaf, shape, surround with vegetables and "cook" the same way.   Place package so it won't fall while traveling, stop and turn it over at least once, to thoroughly cook through.   Food must be wrapped well, with seams sealed, so food doesn't leak onto engine and so engine oil doesn't spoil the food.   Flat packages cook quicker than bulky, thick ones, so plan accordingly. You may wish to fix individual meals, to cook more quickly.   Children enjoy this very much.   May even fix pot roast this way, when you get confident.

SUGAR BEET SUGAR
Instructions
Things You'll Need:
• A pound or more of sugar beets
• A large pan
• Colander
1. Wash and scrub the beets to remove any dirt or residue.
2. Chop small or shred the beets.

3. Place the beets into a large pot and add enough water to keep them from sticking. Cook until the beets are soft and are losing their color.

4. Strain the beets, reserving the juice. Freeze the cooked beets for Borscht, cakes or dispose of, if desired.

5. Put the juice back on the stove and let it simmer until it reaches a thick, syrupy consistency. Stir constantly. The syrup should be similar in thickness to honey or corn syrup.

6. Remove from heat and let cool. As the syrup cools it will begin to crystallize. Cover with a dish towel or cheesecloth and let sit overnight.

7. Remove the crystallized beet sugar from the pan. Pound or otherwise break into small sugar crystals.

8. Use as you would store-bought sugar. Store as you would any sugar.

Tips & Warnings

• Beet sugar will not be pure white like store-bought sugar. It will still have a tinge of color.

• Beet sugar is better for you nutritionally than refined white sugar.

KEEPING BERRIES

Berries are delicious, but they're also kind of delicate. Raspberries in particular seem like they can mold before you even get them home from the market. There's nothing more tragic than paying $4 for a pint of local raspberries, only to look in the fridge the next day and find that fuzzy mold growing on their insides. Well, with fresh berries just starting to hit farmers markets, we can tell you how to keep them fresh:

Wash them with vinegar!

When you get your berries home, prepare a mixture of one part vinegar (white or apple cider probably work best) and ten parts water. Dump the berries into the mixture and swirl around. Drain, rinse if you want (though the mixture is so diluted you can't taste the vinegar,) and pop in the fridge. The vinegar kills any mold spores and other bacteria that might be on the surface of the fruit, and voila! Raspberries will last a week or more, and strawberries go almost two weeks without getting moldy and soft. So go forth and stock up on those pricey little gems, knowing they'll stay fresh as long as it takes you to eat them.

MAPLE SYRUP FROM POTATOES AND SUGAR

-Peel 6 medium sized potatoes, add 2 cups of water and boil until but one cup of fluid remains.

-Remove the potatoes--use for something else.

-Let the potato water cool--do not add any more water to it.

-Bring to boil again, while slowly adding one cup of white sugar and one cup of brown sugar.

-Let cool after it has dissolved.

-Bottle the syrup and set it aside for a few days...important to let it sit awhile to develop its flavor!

Medical advice is hearsay only

MAKING TINCTURES

Fresh Herbs

Take enough chopped-up herb to jam a glass jar full, add enough 95 % alcohol to cover, close tight lid tightly, let sit in a cool dark spot for 2-4 weeks, strain, bottle, label.   80 proof vodka works, too.   Helps to shake it every couple of days, too.   80 proof may spoil while making if not watched carefully.   100 proof is better for fresh herbs.

Dried Herbs

Take enough crushed-up herb to jam a glass jar full, add enough alcohol-water-mix to cover, close tight lid tightly, let sit in a cool dark spot for 2-4 weeks, strain, bottle, label.

90 or 95% alcohol is best, but is not available very easily in most areas.   The 80 proof is only 40% alcohol, so pay attention to keeping it cool and dark while making and store in cool dark conditions.   A dark glass bottle is best for storing.

Here is a natural recipe for a form of Vapor rub:

Vapor Rub

1/2 teaspoon eucalyptus essential oil

1/8 teaspoon peppermint essential oil

1/8 teaspoon rosemary essential oil

1/8 teaspoon clary sage essential oil

1/4 cup olive oil (I personally think that coconut oil work better, because it is a thicker base and doesn't seep through socks.)

Mix ingredients together in a glass bottle (not plastic as the essential oils will bleed into it making the rub less effective) and shake or mix well.

Massage onto feet before bed for a bad cough.

I have heard that using a blue glass bottle to store it in is better.

Note: coconut oil doesn't store as well as olive oil after opening

To stop night time coughing in a child (or adult as we found out personally), put Vapor Rub generously on the soles of your feet, cover with socks, and the heavy, deep coughing will stop in about 5 minutes and stay stopped for many, many hours of relief. Works 100% of the time and is more effective in children than even very strong prescription cough medicines. In addition it is extremely soothing and comforting and they will sleep soundly.

HEALING TONIC FOR STOMACH

For a general, overall healing - get some ginger root, slice off a 1/8 inch piece and peel it, place in boiling water, allow to steep for a minute or two. (Nuke water with root in it if you have a microwave). Drink twice a day. If you have frequent stomach upsets - do this regimen for a year. This will also heal other things, over time. You may find yourself not needing Tums, Rolaids, Previcid, or Prilosec, eventually. If you cannot access ginger root - dried ginger will work - use a half teaspoon to start. Be prepared, it doesn't absorb in water as well. Feel free to add a dollop of LOCAL honey. It you eat LOCAL honey, you will develop immunities to the pollen of plants where you live.

ELECTROLYTES
World Health Organization Oral Rehydration Solution Recipe

1/2 tsp. Table Salt
1/2 teaspoon(NaCl) Salt Substitute .(Mortons salt replacement)
Baking Soda 1/2 tsp. salt substitute (KACL)
2 Tablespoons Table Sugar
1 Qt. + 2 tablespoons Clean water

Mix and store in a clean container.
Remake after 24 hours if not refrigerated
Keep cool
** Adding extra sugar can worsen diarrhea.
Sip as tolerated.

AND

GIVE ZINC TO DECREASE AND STOP DIARRHEA FLUID LOSS
• For infants less than six months old, give Zinc 10 mg once
daily for 10 days.
• For children six months and older, and adults, give Zinc 20
mg once daily for 10 days.
• You can get Zinc tablets at the clinic. You can dissolve the
tablet in the ORS if they can not swallow tablets.

OR

1 (1/4 ounce) envelope unsweetened flavored drink mix (enough for 2 quarts)
• 1/2 teaspoon table salt (sodium chloride)
• 1/4 teaspoon salt substitute (potassium chloride; eg. Morton Salt Substitute)
• 1/4 cup sugar
• 1/4 cup granular fructose (substitute 1/4 cup plus 2 tbs. corn syrup)
• ¼ cup glucose
• 1/2 teaspoon citric acid (can substitute 2 tbs. lemon juice)
• water, to make 2 quarts

DANDELION ROOT HEALTH BENEFITS **Medical advice is hearsay only**

* Dandelion root extract is unique, and is one of the only things found to help with chronic myelomonocytic Leukemia and it is rumored effective in treating Breast Tumors
* Detoxification of vital organs : Because of the diuretic abilities of dandelion root, it is beneficial for flushing out the Liver, Kidneys and Gallbladder. İt works great to purify the blood and cleanse the system. This also makes it a good herb for fighting infections.
It is also used for Arthritis, Osteoarthritis , Gout and Rheumatism
* Dandelion tea actively ameliorates disease—it is a potent disease-fighter—and helps the body heal, helps boost immunity and Heart Disease, and age-related Memory Loss.
* Treating Anemia : Because of the high content of iron in dandelion root, it is beneficial for building red blood cells in the body to treat anemia.
* Treating Diabetes : Dandelion root has been shown to lower blood sugar levels in patients. In Europe, it's used to treat Type-1 and Type-2 diabetes.
* Digestive System : Dandelion root, when made into a tea, is beneficial for relieving constipation, flatulence and fullness.
*Treating High Blood Pressure : Dandelion root is a natural Diuretic. When combined with its high potassium content, it is an effective treatment to lower blood pressure.
* Dandelion tea helps reduce High Cholesterol.
* High Nutritional Value : Dandelion root contains vitamins A, B-complex, C and D as well as the minerals Iron, Zinc and Potassium. This combination of vitamins and minerals also makes dandelion root a High Antioxidant Food.
* Mood Enhancer : Due to the high amount of vitamin B-complex, dandelion root can help to stabilize mood and Treat Depression.
*Dandelion root is also used to treat skin disorders such as Acne, Eczema and Psoriasis.

* It is very beneficial to Menopausal Women
* Laxative : Dandelion root is also a mild laxative and is used to help with regularity.
* Dandelion tea helps with weight control—especially with Weight Loss.
(Composting spent dandelion tea Blossoms, Leaves, and/or Roots, after drinking your dandelion tea, improves soil composition.)
(There are very few side effects linked to using dandelion root. Allergic Reactions to the herb have been reported. People taking prescription lithium, a diuretic, medication to lower blood pressure or medication to lower blood sugar should not take dandelion root. Women who are Pregnant or Breastfeeding should consult their doctor before taking this herb.)

ORANGE CLEANER
Orange peels, vinegar in a quart jar, let sit for 10 days or so...strain out the liquid and use as an all-purpose cleaner. Easy, cheap, natural, smells good!

HOME MADE POTASH
As per the instructions found at the Caveman to Chemist website (some potash was manufactured).
This was done by starting with wood ash made in a wood-burning stove. Mixed hardwoods were used and the ash was collected from the ash grate. 250 g of ash were placed in a glass bowl with 2500 g of hot tap water (approximately 50°C/120°F). This was stirred to mix thoroughly, then allowed to settle for 12 hours.
The bowl now contained a sandy-looking precipitate, a small quantity of charcoal floating on the surface, and some fairly clear but slightly colored liquid. 1250 g of the colored liquid was withdrawn from the bowl and placed in a stainless steel pot.
The liquid in the pot was brought to a roiling boil. It was boiled until all liquid had evaporated and only a greyish residue remained. This residue was scraped out of the bowl. A total of 22 g of residue was obtained.

Pearlash (potassium Carbonate)
On this side of the Atlantic the early colonists were blessed with hardwood forests as far as the eye could see. Aside from being a logical building material and fuel, hardwoods provided another important resource, ashes. Ashes were a major export two hundred years ago, both to Canada and Britain. They were valuable for sweetening gardens and providing lye for making soap. They were also a source of potash and its derivative, pearlash, another creative leavening agent.

To make pearlash, you first have to make potash which itself is made from lye. To make lye, you pass water through a barrel of hardwood ashes over and over until an egg can float on the residue. (To make soap you boil this "lye water" with lard or other fat until it is thick, pour it into molds and harden it into cakes.) To make potash, you evaporate lye water until you have a solid.

Pearlash is a purified version of potash. It is an alkaline compound which will react with an acidic ingredient such as sour milk, buttermilk or molasses to produce carbon dioxide bubbles, the very same thing that yeast produces. Pearlash was used primarily in the seventeenth and eighteenth centuries but because of its bitter aftertaste, it not only did not replace yeast but was eventually replaced by "saleratus." However, if you have no leavening agents and a lot of time on your hands, you may wish to try making and using this.

Super Soap Bubbles

1 quart dishwashing liquid

1 gallon distilled water

1 cup glycerin

Mix, let set 24 hours or more for best results.

Super Duper Soap Bubbles

4 parts glycerin

2 parts liquid soap

1 part corn syrup

Mix gently, wait at least 24 hours before using.

For a Super Bubble maker, round out a metal coat hanger, wrap with string or pipe cleaners. Put bubble mixture in shallow flat pan to dip bubble maker in. Saturate well and gently swoop hanger through the air.

PLAYDOUGH (For the kids)

Mix 4 cups flour, I T. alum, ½ cup salt, set aside. Mix together, stirring constantly, 3 T. cooking oil, 2 cups boiling water, enough food color to make it look as dark as final color you want. Add to dry mix. Knead until smooth, Keep in well sealed container. Zip-close bags are fine. Does not need refrigerated.

MODELING CLAY

2 cups plain or pickling salt

1 cup flour

1 teaspoon Alum, powdered, if desired for drying

1 2/3 cup water

Food Coloring

Combine all ingredients in a saucepan. Cook over medium heat, stirring constantly, until mixture is very thick, about 3 to 5 minutes. Cool slightly. If too sticky, add more flour. Add food coloring to make desired color. Store in airtight container in the refrigerator. If drying, place in 200 degree F oven for 1 to 2 hours until dry or firm to the touch.

SLIME

2 cups School Glue
2 cups water, divided
Food coloring
1 t. borax
Combine glue, 1 ½ cups water and food color of choice. In separate bowl, dissolve borax in ½ cup water. Add to the glue solution. Watch the slime form. Do not mix. Just lift the slime out and have fun. Store in airtight container. Slime is very sticky on fabrics or paper. Otherwise it easily peels off surfaces. If it gets in fabric, soak in water until it dissolves.

STEPPING STONES

½ cup salt, ½ cup flour, ¼ cup (give or take a bit) water. Knead until dough forms. Flatten out into a square or circle about ½ inch or more thick. Make impression, hand or foot of child, Bake at 200 degrees F for 3 hours.   Make one every year to show the changes in your child's life.   Make a stepping stone path in your flower garden.

GRAFTING
You don't need grafting for apples, all you need is a fresh cutting and some rooting hormone. If you don't want to purchase rooting hormone, just grind up the bark from a handful of weeping willow branches and soak it in water for a few days. Make a fresh angled cut on your apple tree cutting and soak the cut end in the water overnight, then plant it in starter. Cut whatever leaves you have on the cutting in half and keep the plant misted and watered for a few weeks while it grows it's own roots.

WEIGHTS AND MEASURES

3 teaspoons = 1 Tablespoon	1/4 cup flour = 1 ounce
4 Tablespoons = 1/4 cup	4 cups flour = 1 pound
5 1/2 Tablespoons = 1/3 cup	250 degrees F = 120 degrees C
1 cup = 8 fluid ounces	275 degrees F = 135 degrees C

1 cup = 1/2 pint

2 cups = 1 pint

2 pints = 1 quart

4 quarts = 1 gallon

2 gallons = 1 peck

4 pecks = 1 bushel

1 liter = .264 U.S. gallon

1 liter = .220 Imperial gallon

1 quart, dry = 1.101 liters

1 quart, liquid = .9463 liter

1 ounce = 28.35 grams

1 pound = 16 ounces = .4536 kilogram

1 pennyweight = 24 grains

20 pennyweight = 1 Troy ounce

12 Troy ounces = 1 Troy pound

300 degrees F = 150 degrees C

325 degrees F = 165 degrees C

350 degrees F = 175 degrees C

375 degrees F = 190 degrees C

400 degrees F = 205 degrees C

425 degrees F = 220 degrees C

450 degrees F = 230 degrees C

475 degrees F = 245 degrees C

500 degrees F = 260 degrees C

To convert Fahrenheit degrees into Celsius, subtract 32, multiply by 5 and divide by 9, reverse to convert Celsius to Fahrenheit, - multiply by 9, divide by 5 and add 32.

At sea level, the boiling point of water is 212 degrees Fahrenheit, 100 degrees Celsius. The freezing point of water is 32 degrees F., 0 degrees C.

CAN SIZES

No. 303 = 2 cups

No. 2 = 2 1/2 cups

No.2 1/2=3 1/2Cups

No. 3 = 5 ¾ cups

No. 10 = 12 to 13 cups

COMPOSITION OF AND
NUTRITIVE VALUE OF ALASKAN GAME MEATS
(Mammals) - 100 Grams
Compiled from latest available tables (see footnotes A,B,U.)

Item	Moisture	Calories	Protein	Fat	Calcium	Phosphate	Iron	Vitamin A	Thiamin	Riboflavin	Niacin	Source Of Analysis
	%		Gms.	Gms.	Mg.1	Mg.	Mg.	2I.U.	Mg.	Mg.	Mg.	
Beef, (comparison)	54.7	323	16.5	28	10	152	2.5	60	.07	.150	4.0	A
Caribou, raw	70.0	130	27.2	1.2	18	280	2.9	187	.182	.520	4.7	U
Moose, raw	72.4	123	25.1	2.5	10	219	2.7	650	.074	.027	5.0	U
Moose Liver	73.5			4.3				96,000				B
Reindeer, raw	70.1	117	26.6	1.2	16	280	2.9	187	.186	.770	4.7	U
Black Bear, raw	71.2	148	18.6	8.2	3	139	6.1	261	.160	.680	3.2	U
Polar Bear, raw	70.3	130	25.6	3.1	17	40	6.1	1,400	.023	.573	4.0	U
Beaver, raw	46.2	480	14.3	39	15	262	2.9	176	.061	.310	1.9	U
Beluga, raw	72.5	107	24.5	0.5	7	270	16.6	335	.070	.400	6.8	U
Muskrat, raw	73.4	101	22.4	1.3	25	220	7.6	2,820	.095	.372	6.2	U
Oogruk, raw	69.6	110	26.7	0.4	10	199	11.6	1,480	.168	.267	5.9	A
Rabbit, raw (wild)	73.0	129	21.6	5.0	12	226	3.2		.030	.060	6.5	U
Seal, raw	67.5	143	28.3	33.0	17	245	19.8	1,050	.135	.452	7.0	U
Seal, liver, raw	74.2	115	18.0	3.2	13	285	13.7	36,600	.180	3.020	8.4	U
Seal, Oil	0	900						4,860				U
Cooking Oil		884		100.0								A
Ground Squirrel, raw	75.4	115	10.1	3.8	2	168	4.5	230	.095	.372	6.2	U
Walrus	65.1	200	19.2	13.6	18	123	9.4	550	.180	.346	3.2	U
Whale, Baleen	73.0	138	23.9	1.6	17	212	14.6	330	.138	.550	7.4	U

100 Grams = almost 1/2 cup
1 MG = Milligram (1000 milligram = 1 gm)
2 I.U. = International Units

A - Table 1, Composition of Foods, 100 Grams, Edible Portion, Handbook No. 8, U.S. Department of Agriculture 1963
B - Table 87, Composition of Alaskan Foods, 100 Grams, The Alaskan Dietary Survey, 1956-1961 by Heller and Scott,
U.S. Department of Health, Education and Welfare, 1967
U - Unpublished manuscript by Christine Heller, Nutritionist, Arctic Health Research Center, U.S. Department HEW,
Anchorage, Alaska
When several analyses were given, an average is stated here.

Meat and Fish Care

What to do after the shot

or cast

Caring For Meat

First, you kill a moose.   May substitute any other large edible animal for this ingredient.   Immediately remove the skin, always making sure to cut with the direction of hair growth.   This cuts down on the amount of loose hair re-attaching to the skinned carcass.   If possible, clean hands and knife often. Especially after touching the hair or fur.   This will lessen the possibility of contaminating the meat with offensive odors or flavors. If you are unable to skin the animal immediately, at least take the time to remove the scent glands (look like calluses) located on the inside of the legs.   Remove enough skin out around each one that you do not accidentally cut into one and mess up the meat that way. This will improve the quality of the meat.   Disconnect the legs at the knee joints.   Also disconnect the head from the body.   I use a utility knife with quick change blades for skinning, gutting and butchering.   Never have to sharpen and easy to change out blades without loosing the screw.   Skin the animal, cutting along the lines shown in the skinning diagram.   Carefully cut the skin around the rectum.   Loosen the bowel from surrounding tissue, tie tightly with a piece of string.   May remove testicles with the skin, as you skin the animal or skin over them and leave attached to the body.   If it is a game animal in season, regulations may require leaving them attached to the body as proof of sex.

In case you are wondering, I usually skin before gutting because I know once the gut cavity is open and the scent wafts out over the air waves, there will be a bear along soon to contest ownership. I also usually skin one side first, then cut off the legs and strip out the backstrap on that side, removing them to about 100 feet from the future gut pile. Then I turn the animal and skin and remove legs and backstrap on the other side.   It is much easier to turn it with parts removed than to try turning a whole moose by yourself.   A bear will head to the gut pile first, then check out the meat, so even if a bear does show up, I may be able to take most of my meat without an argument.

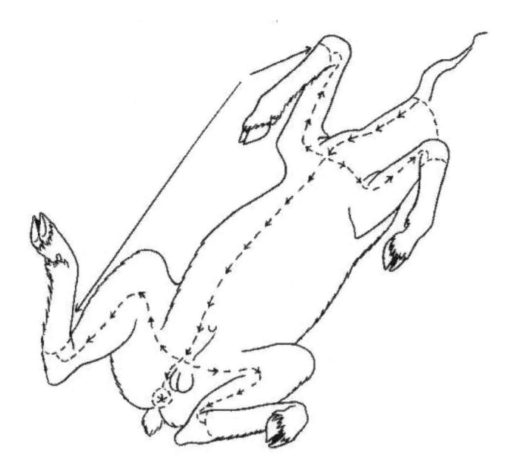

After skinning the animal, position it on the skin to keep the meat clean. If your animal is small enough, just open the gut cavity along the center line you cut to skin it, from   the breastbone to the pelvic bone, tying off the urinary tract, also.   Then turn the animal on it's side and pull the guts, liver, heart and lungs out.

If you are working on an elk or a moose, try cutting along the lines shown in figure 2.   Cutting from the center of the breastbone, along the ribcage, then the loin to the edge of the ham and down to the pelvic bone, using your hand inside as a guide and to keep the guts pushed away from the knife blade as you cut.

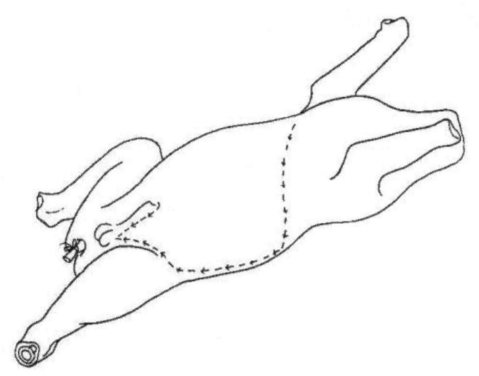

Figure 2

Roll the intestines out, carefully cutting any connective tissues.   Pull the esophagus down with the stomach. Carefully remove bladder.   Remove lungs from the ribcage.   May remove the kidneys or leave attached to the inside of the back.   Remove the heart and liver from the gut pile.

If the animal is very fat, remove the fat from the intestine and from around the kidneys.   Keep it clean and save it to render for lard, making soap or making candles.

If you are planning on making your own sausage casings, once the guts are out and the meat is away from the gut pile, cut a long section of gut free and squeeze out the contents. Later, when you are near water, you can wash this out and scrap the inside clean. You can do the same for the stomach, if you want to make tripe.

When you are removing the liver, be sure and remove the gall bladder also. This is a narrow dark green sac and should be removed carefully.   Although in days gone by, several tribes of Native Americans and some old time Mountain Men used gall for seasoning by dipping their knife blade in it before slicing off a choice bite of meat.   Most modern palates consider meat ruined if accidentally contaminated by gall. Mine included.   Some people add the lungs to the meat to be ground for burger and sausage.   It adds nutrients and is okay as long as no one sees you doing it.   If they do, you won't have to worry about them dropping in for dinner.   You may wish to split the skull and recover the brain for fried brains or scrambled eggs with brains or even to use for tanning.

The testicles may be saved for Rocky Mountain Oysters. Most of these are acquired tastes.

The most important thing is to keep everything clean and to cool the meat as soon as possible to prevent spoilage. Do NOT soak in the nearest stream to cool as this will promote souring of the meat. The exception being, if you have heavy duty plastic bags to place the meat in so the water doesn't touch it and an ice cold stream and no alternative handy. Remove all gunshot damage as it starts spoiling quickly. A large can of black pepper liberally sprinkled on the meat will help repel insects. Good sturdy game meat bags are good, also. The farther you are from the road, the larger the animal will be.

BUTCHERING

Once you get all this meat home, hang in a cool dry area and loosely cover to prevent flies from blowing it and to allow the meat to cool completely and if you are so inclined, age a little bit. Aging is truly only allowing the meat to start spoiling a little bit so it is more tender and personally, I don't do it. If you already know how you want to proceed or what you wish to make from all of this good meat, then get right on it.

Game meat makes great sausage, jerky and excellent roasts, steaks and burgers. The fat can be used in many ways. Personally, I trim all the fat off the meat I intend to eat. The fat is the first part to turn rancid and also carries any off flavors that may have contaminated the meat even if it is just early rut. I place all the fat saved into a nice cool clean area to take care of right away. Fresh is much better for making soap or just rendering to use in other ways. I usually coarse grind the fat to make it render faster.

I also peel all of the membrane off the outside of each muscle group on the meat as I cut it up. I totally dissect the quarters. I don't see any reason to freeze or can the bones. I do save the bones and roast some to a rich brown to add to the rest for making a rich stock and then can the stock for future soup. If I am in a hurry, I peel the large muscles of the membrane, wrap in plastic wrap, then waxed freezer paper and freeze. Then when I thaw it, I can either have a lovely roast as is, or cut it across the grain for steaks. Partially thawed is very easy to slice in uniform slices for steak or to make jerky.

I usually separate the backstrap pieces and the eye of round piece of each hind leg, that is the piece of muscle that looks like a backstrap and is just as good for steaks. These both make delicious chicken fried steaks in cream gravy.

HEADCHEESE

The head, internal organs, ribcage and assorted small pieces should be taken care of immediately. The head should have been skinned at the time of butchering, if you are going to use it. Clean it well, removing the tongue, eyes (unless you like them) and if you haven't already, the brain. Cut the skull into pieces small enough to fit into a large kettle, cover with water and boil several hours for Headcheese. If you wish to add the tongue meat to the headcheese, boil separately until tender. Peel the white layer off and discard, chop remaining meat into small pieces and add to the meat that has been removed from the cooked skull. Season the broth and meat mixture to taste with salt and pepper, boil 15 minutes more to further reduce the broth. Pour the mixture into pans, when cool, slice and serve without further preparation. It will thicken as it gets cold. Instead of pouring into pans, you may pour into pint wide-mouth jars, to within ½ inch of top of jar. Place lids on, process in pressure canner at 10 pounds pressure for 75 minutes. Store in cool place. Simply slide out of the jar, slice and serve. If you want to be sure it will jell firmly enough, add a couple of teaspoons of plain gelatin soaked in cold water to the hot broth and stir well to make sure it is well dissolved through the mixture. Then proceed as above.

BRAIN

Soak the brain overnight in enough water to cover, with 1 Tablespoon salt and 1 teaspoon baking soda added. Soak testicles in this solution, also, after peeling the membrane from the outside. If very large, slice into ½ inch slices, first. Brain and testes slice much easier if partially frozen first.

KIDNEYS

Kidneys should be cleaned <u>before</u> soaking. Peel membrane from the outside of the kidney. Cut kidney in half, carefully remove veins and surrounding darker tissue. There won't be much left but it will be tender and similar to chicken liver in flavor. The remaining meat should be the same lighter color as the outside of the kidney. Soak overnight in lightly salted water with ½ teaspoon baking soda added.

LIVER & HEART

The Liver and Heart should have the membrane peeled from them. Also all the large veins should be removed. The Heart should have all the fat and cartilage and heavy vein walls removed. At this point, heart liver and kidneys may be frozen. Quality is best if used fresh or if frozen, use within 1 month. Freeze covered in water to preserve quality.

RIBCAGE

The ribcage should be wiped with a damp cloth to remove any hair or leaves or whatever that may have adhered to it. Personally, I use a sawzall and cut the ribs into narrow strips across the bones, then parboil until tender and BBQ. Depending on the animal and time limits, I sometimes remove all the meat off the bones and add to the pile to grind for hamburger or sausage. A moose will yield about 50 pounds of meat in the grind pile if you opt for the deboning. The cut ribs can be packaged and frozen, I just don't like using up freezer space for bones.   If I debone, I save the bones and add to the stock pot.

NECK

I like making the neck into a roast or two.   Then I remove all the meat and grind for mincemeat or plum pudding or to make really good sandwich spread. For sandwich spread, grind the cooked meat, add chopped onion, pickle and dressing and scoop onto a slice of bread.   Add cheese, lettuce or whatever your heart desires for a very good sandwich.   The bones go into the stock pot. Some bones are roasted while I make a roast, to add flavor and color to the stock for canning later.

A game animal may be cut into the familiar cuts you usually buy in a store or it may be boned out.   I separate the chunks into individual muscle groups, each muscle peeled of it's membrane covering and sliced across the grain into smaller tender steaks.   If an animal has any off flavors or is slightly tough, this is the best way to handle it.   Off-flavors are usually in the fat or membranes, so removal improves tenderness and flavor.   I prefer this method of meat cutting, even with a good tender animal.   It doesn't take long to catch on to separating the muscle groups and more of the animal can be cut into tender tasty steaks. The small end pieces can be added to the grind pile for burger or sausage or used as bite-sized finger steaks.   If your steaks seem more like boot leather than steak, you may decide to can most of the animal.   An hour and a half at 10 pounds pressure will tenderize the toughest animal.

TANNING SOLUTION

If you want to try your hand at tanning some animal hides, a good tanning solution can be made as follows.   In a wood or glass or plastic container, stir 1 gallon warm water with 1 pound rock or pickling salt until salt is dissolved.   Slowly add 4 ounces (½ cup) 40% sulfuric acid, available at service stations as battery acid.   Always pour the acid into the water, never pour water into acid.   Use only non-metal utensils as metal will change the chemical nature of the solution.   It doesn't do the metal any good, either. Increase the recipe as many times as necessary to make enough to thoroughly cover whatever skins you are tanning.   Wear rubber gloves, unless you don't mind slightly toughening your own skin.   Every day, stir and rearrange the hides in the solution, to assure even pickling.   This is actually a pickling solution but makes a cured hide very well.   Check skins by making a small slit next to the edge of the skin and check for color.   As the hide pickles, it turns white.   In a thick hide, the white works slowly towards the center, leaving a pink line, until pickling is complete.   Skins can not be left too long in this solution, so don't worry about leaving them in it until you can dry and soften them.   It is best to over pickle than to under pickle as then they spoil.   Use baking soda to kill the acid if spilled or splashed.   After pickling is complete, thoroughly rinse hides in cool water, then add baking soda to the rinse water and rinse some more.   Hang hide to partially dry, then shake and stretch out on a flat surface.   Warm a good hide oil to a comfortable temperature and spread thoroughly over entire flesh side of the hides.   Fold outer edges to the middle and roll the hide up from the neck edge toward the tail.   Next day, start stretching and pulling the hides to soften as it dries.   This makes good hats, mitts and boots as long as it is for a dry climate.   Moisture will make the hide return to it's former unpickled state to a certain degree and you   will have to rework the hide.

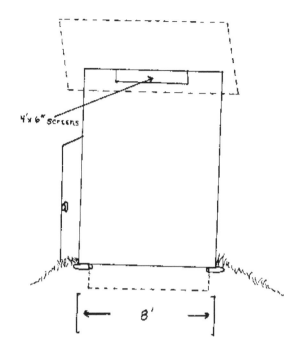

4' x 6" screens

8'

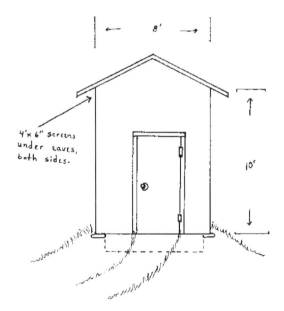

8'

4' x 6" screens
under eaves,
both sides.

10'

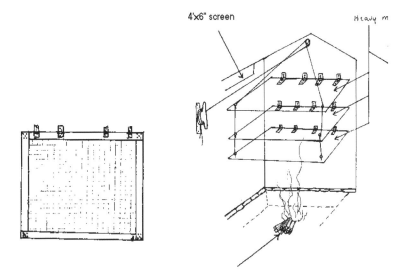

If you wish to cure some of the meat or to make jerky from some of it, you should start as soon as possible after butchering. Curing will not improve poor quality meat, so shouldn't be considered. A smokehouse is a nice addition to the homestead and adds a pleasant flavor to a wide variety of meats and fish. (But not at the same time.) A smokehouse for smoking cured meats should be about 8 ft. square and 10 ft. tall. There should be small, screened vents, about 6 inches by 4 ft. under overhanging eaves of the roof.

This allows circulation without much smoke loss. We placed hooks in the ceiling to hang meat from for aging and placed hinged racks 3 and 4 ft. down from the roof. This way the racks may be folded down while hanging meat and may also lower one side to remove the finished product. It also makes turning small pieces much easier, and evenly distributing the meat over the racks. The door should be tight fitting to keep smoke in and bugs out. This type of smokehouse should never have a hot fire built in it, and is not suitable for fixing fish, if you wish to eat the fish without further cooking. I prefer to dig the floor level down about a foot or below the vegetation line in the soil, to lessen the chance of unplanned fire. This can really liven up a dull day, but can ruin a lot of good food. When you wish to smoke something, start a small fire with a bit of paper and dry kindling. After the fire has started, add wet or green wood. Peeled alder, peeled birch or peeled aspen should all make a very good flavored smoke. Do not build up a big fire, all you need is a good smudge of smoke all the time. Most meats have the required amount of smoke in 1 to 3 days, such as ham, bacon and such. Jerky may require more time to dry properly. If the weather is too cold, the smoke does not penetrate the meat.

The best weather for smoking is nice, dry days and cool nights. The smokehouse temperature should be maintained between 80 to 100 degrees F. Any higher and the meat will start to cook and the fat to render, much cooler and it will take a long time for your meat to reach the desired degree of smoke. Resinous woods should not be used as they are usually too strong and leave a film of resin on the meat. After the meat reaches the desired smoke, let the fire go out and the meat cool on the racks. This may take a day or so, but this way the meat develops a dry surface and resists spoilage.

There are two basic types of cure, dry cure and brine cure. Dry cure is usually used for hams, bacon and jerky. Brine cure is used for corned meat, (beef or game), cured tongue, birds (game birds, turkey, chicken) or even pork chops, for a treat.

Any type of meat may be cured and/or smoked. This is limited only by your imagination and available meats. Some cheeses are made into quite a delicacy by smoking for a few hours. Turkey, duck, chicken, grouse or goose is a very special treat if smoked from a couple of hours to overnight, depending on size, before cooking, even without being cured first. small birds and animals dry out if not watched carefully, while smoking, especially if the skin is removed, so you may have to baste with liquid or cook in liquid to assure tender, juicy meat.

Jerky usually has better flavor and keeping qualities when all of the fat has been trimmed from the meat before curing and smoking. Very cold, or partially frozen meat slices into thin strips easier than room temperature meat does. Slice the meat in thin strips, across the grain of the meat, for the nicest jerky. Of course, you may just chunk it up and keep your teeth in shape by gnawing on it when dry. It cures and smokes more uniformly if all the strips are of the approximate same size and thickness. Of course, if you just can't resist sampling the product early, then it's nice to have a few very tiny slices on the smoking tray to taste. When the jerky is still quite pliable and a bit too raw for most folks' taste, is a good time to remove several pieces. Slice these strips into very thin slices and freeze for later use as "chipped beef". Make a good cream gravy, add a handful of thin slices and some sauteed mushrooms, and you have a real taste treat.

BASIC DRY CURE

4 lb. Brown Sugar   Mix these dry ingredients together, being

2 lb. plain or pickling salt   sure to use plain salt, not iodized. You

1/2 lb. Black Pepper   may store this mix in a glass jar.

This is the best cure for jerky that I've ever tried.   I also use it for ham, bacon and shoulders being cured.   I do not like to use saltpeter, and all it does is retain the red color of the meat.

ANOTHER BASIC DRY CURE

5 lb. plain salt   Mix the ingredients, being careful to distribute
4 lb. white or brown sugar   the saltpeter evenly through the salt.
3 oz. saltpeter   May store in glass containers until ready to
use. Use 1 1/4 to 1 1/2 oz. of Basic Dry Cure per pound of ham and about 1 oz. per pound for bacon.   For jerky, place thin layer in bottom of container, place layer of meat slices, sprinkle with cure mix, and continue until all the meat is covered in a thin layer of mix.   For jerky, overnight is usually a sufficient length of time to cure.   For hams or shoulders, rub 1/2 of cure on the meat, packing more onto the large end of meat.   On the third day, add more cure, and again on the tenth day, being careful not to knock off any of the salt.   Rub the cure on the meat side of bacon slabs, and stack on top of each other.   When I didn't have crocks to place meat in, I have used large cardboard boxes, lined with clean plastic, to cure the meat in.   For hams, allow 2 days per pound of meat.   For bacon, 1 1/2 days per pound or 7 days per 1 inch of thickness.   The meat should be kept between 38 to 45 degrees F. while curing.

After the meat has cured, remove from the dry pack.   Brush the lighter cuts to remove salt.   Hold them under refrigeration or in a cold place (36 to 40 degrees, F.) until the heavier cuts are cured.   If you do not desire a smoke flavor, hang the meat in a cold place at least a week, more is better. If you want to smoke the hams and bacon, soak the meat in water, hams i1/2 to 2 hours, bacon 1/2 hour. Hams and shoulders should be placed in stockinet covers to help retain their shape. Put a strong cord through the shanks and hang to dry from 1 to 3 weeks. Bacon holds shape best if a wooden skewer or clean, galvanized wire is forced through one end and hung by a cord from this skewer.

Scrub the hung meat with a stiff brush and water. This will give it a brighter color while smoking. Let it dry overnight to avoid streaking. A wet surface will not take on an even color.

Place the meat in the smokehouse, either hanging or laying on the racks, so that no pieces touch. start your fire as described earlier in the book. Open the smokehouse ventilators to let moisture escape. May close the vents on the second day, but is not necessary. smoke the meat until it reaches the color you like best. Usually two days of smoking is enough. You do not need a dense cloud of smoke to do the job, a thin haze of smoke is just as effective. Be careful not to overheat the meat. If the weather is cool or cold, and not damp, the meat may be left in the smokehouse for storage and removed as you use it. The meat should be kept dry at all times or it is likely to mold. If mold has just started, it may be removed by wiping meat with a cloth soaked in vinegar. Although some molds are of benefit to mankind, they do not enhance the looks or flavor of meat.

Cut meat in pieces about 6 inches square and uniformly thick. Meat to be cured should be cooled as quickly as possible and started immediately after butchering as possible. Meat that is not really fresh may sour before it is cured. Thaw meat thoroughly that is frozen, before curing. Weigh the meat. For each 100 pounds, use 8 lbs. plain salt (not iodized). sprinkle a layer of salt 1/4 inch deep in bottom of crock, wooden barrel or clean plastic container. Pack meat pieces closely together, one layer deep, sprinkle more salt. Alternate layers of meat and salt, covering the top layer of meat with considerable salt. Let the salted meat stand overnight, in a cool place. In the morning, make a brine of 4 lbs. sugar, 2 oz. baking soda, 4 oz. saltpeter dissolved in 1 gallon of lukewarm water, per 100 pounds of meat. Add 3 gallons of cold water, pour over meat. Pour part of the brine over meat, as soon as meat starts to shift, put clean weights on it to hold it in place. Pour remaining brine over meat, being sure that all meat is under the brine. Weights may be a clean board with gallon jugs full of water on it or clean rocks, not limestone, as it has a tendency to dissolve in the brine. Iron will rust, so mostly just use common sense in deciding what the weights should be. If any meat is not under the brine, the meat and the brine will spoil quickly.

Hams and bacon may be cured, using the brine cure method. Hams may require quite a bit more time in the brine, though, so be sure to leave in solution long enough.

When you are curing meat in a brine cure, a white scum will form on top of the brine. This is normal and no cause for alarm. However, "ropey" pickle is caused by bacterial action and if not rectified in time, may cause the whole batch to spoil. The brine becomes stringy, sticky or slimy. It will drip from the fingers like syrup and possesses an offensive odor when warmed. If this occurs, the meat should be taken from the brine immediately. and each piece scrubbed with fresh water. Then boil the brine, skim, add 4 Tablespoons of baking soda for each 100 pounds of meat. Allow brine to cool thoroughly before repacking the meat in it. Also, scald the container again, before repacking. An even better idea is to make new brine to pack the meat in. Do not make the new brine quite so strong as the original and do not leave the meat in it quite so long. This is not certain to save the meat. The only certain way is to keep everything perfectly clean to start with and keep the temperature under 40 degrees F. throughout the cure. Then "ropiness" will not occur.

If you do not wish to work with large batches and are not even sure you would like the finished product, but want to try a little bit. You can cure individual cuts of meat in the kitchen. Use either fresh or freshly thawed meat. You may cut the recipes down that have been given in this book, or you may wish to buy a meat curing mix. If you are using one of the mixes given in the preceding pages, you may wish to add a small amount of liquid smoke flavoring to it for added flavor. Check your refrigerator with a thermometer to be sure the temperature is under 45 degrees F.

To use as dry cure, rub all surfaces of the meat with the cure mix. Place in a plastic bag, close the open end and refrigerate.

To use as a brine cure, add to water, mix thoroughly and pour over meat placed in a glass bowl or jar, crock or enameled container. May use plastic dish, also, but flavors may permeate the plastic. Weight the meat down, to keep it submerged in the brine. Cover the container and put it in the refrigerator or any cool, dry place under 45 degrees F.

When cure is complete, remove meat from plastic bag or other container, wash in cool water, dry and use at once or may be stored a few days in the refrigerator. If the meat becomes sticky, rub the meat with salt until the stickiness disappears, wash it in cold water, dry, refrigerate and use within the next couple of days.

For roasts, use 3 Tblsp. cure mix to 1 pound of meat. Allow 3 or 4 days for mild flavor, 6 to 10 days for a full-cured roast. For chops or steaks, 1/4 to 1/2 cup mix to 1 cup water, 6 to 8 hours to cure, or overnight if extra thick. Chicken, duck, or game birds, 1/2 cup mix to 3 cups water, leave in brine 8 to 12 hours. Turkey or goose, 1 lb. mix to 3 quarts water, up to 10 pound bird, about 3 days. To 16 lb. bird, 4 days, larger birds, 5 days.

FISH require a bit different handling than other meats, but the most important to remember is, it MUST be fresh.

Scale and dress freshly caught fish, remove heads but leave collarbone attached. Wash thoroughly. Rub salt or vinegar to help remove slime. Be sure to remove dark vein down the backbone. Split fish to the back skin, but not through it. Large salmon may be cut all the way through the back skin and the backbone removed. Leave both sides attached at the tail to hang the fish by. If the fish is really large, slice from the flesh side, through to the skin, about every inch. This is a traditional method of curing fish and you may have seen pictures in magazines of racks of fish cut this way, drying along riverbanks in Alaska. There's a good reason for this, it works. If fish are caught and cleaned in the evening for smoking the next day, let them stand in the brine overnight. As they are dressed, place them in a non-metal container, in brine made of 1 1/2 cups salt (non-iodized) to 1 gallon of water. When all the fish are dressed, remove them from the brine. Lay them flat, flesh side up, in a non-metal container and salt each piece, using same salt in a shaker. Cover with waxed paper and store in the refrigerator or a very cool area overnight. In the morning, drain and rinse fish and let excess moisture drip off for at least 15 minutes before placing over smoke.

If you catch and smoke the fish the same day, clean and place in brine made of 4 cups salt to 1 gallon of water. Leave in brine 1/2 to 1 hour, depending on size and thickness of fish. Remove from brine, rinse in cold water. Drain about 10 minutes and let hang about 1 hour in well ventilated area. They are ready for smoking. If humidity is high, it may require a longer drying period to form a dry glaze on the fish before starting to smoke.

String fish on wire just below the collarbone. This holds them flat and increases the capacity of your smoker. If you don't have many, they may be laid flat on the wire racks. Clean racks well after using, so your next batch of meat doesn't have a fishy flavor. Place the fish so they do not touch each other.

For cold smoke, follow the directions for hot smoke, but do not use the high temperature at the end. Continue smoking until the fish are quite dry if you wish to store them without canning or freezing. Fish smoked this way require cooking before eating, to be safe. I know some people do not cook dried fish, but I'm not one of them.

Fish strips may be made from your fish by filleting the fish, the cutting the fillets into narrow strips, leaving 2 attached at one end to hang them over the racks. Drop the strips into a weak brine made of 1/2 cup non-iodized salt and 1 cup brown sugar to 1 gallon cool water. Let set about 1 hour, drain and allow to hang until a nice glaze forms on the meat. This is called a pellicle, and if you allow it to form before you start smoking, the finished product will be much nicer looking. No white fat deposits will form on the surface.

You might like a Teriyaki marinade for some of your salmon strips or for a few of the fillets. A simple one is made by combining 1 cup soy sauce, 1 1/2 cups brown sugar, 2 T. minced fresh ginger and 3 cloves minced garlic. Leave the strips in the marinade until the flesh starts looking slightly candied. Stir often and keep very cold. Two or three days is not too long. This is also a good recipe for Teriyaki jerky. The meat may be held a week in solution before smoking or drying. After draining the strips, sprinkle with lemon pepper or garlic pepper for added zip.

SAUSAGE may be made from any meat, not just pork. Most game meats are improved by adding pork fat for sausage making, but beef fat may be used. If the game animal has no odor to the fat, you may use the fat from your animal, but this usually isn't a good idea. Sausage requires 1 part fat to 3 parts lean meat for a standard sausage. More fat makes it shrink too much during cooking, less fat makes hard patties that do not brown easily. Either cut the meat and fat into small chunks, or coarsely grind it. Spread it out in a thin layer on a clean countertop or table. Sprinkle the seasonings on and work through the meat. Grind the meat again., using the 1/8 or 3/16 inch plate. You can experiment with all types of meat for sausage. If you have a large supply of any animal available, be adventurous. Rabbit meat, cut from the bones, pork fat added, makes a delicate sausage. With beef fat added, it is a bit more robust. But it is delicious. Bear, moose and caribou all make very good sausage. If you have any favorite recipe for sausage, try them all. Following are some different seasonings you may like to try. Never use iodized salt.

For 25 pounds of meat

1 cup salt

3 T. ground black pepper

½ T ground or flake red pepper

3 T ground sage (optional)

OR

1 cup salt

2 T ground sage

2 T ground black pepper

1 t dried sweet marjoram

1 T sugar

1 t mace

1 t ground or flake red pepper

1 cup flour

For 4 pounds of meat

5 t salt

4 t ground sage

2 t ground black pepper

½ t ground cloves OR 1 t nutmeg and 1 t sugar - may omit cloves and nutmeg, just use sugar

The above recipes are for a regular breakfast style sausage, to form into patties and fry or broil. However, they may be stuffed into casings and used as link sausage, or stuffed and lightly smoked before cooking. The following recipes are each for <u>10 pounds of meat</u>.

PEPPERONI

10 T salt

2 T sugar

½ t sodium nitrate (saltpeter)

1 T red pepper

1 t allspice

5 t ground anise seed

1 pint cold water

BOLOGNA

1 pint ice water

½ t sodium nitrate (saltpeter)

1 T ground white pepper

2 T paprika

1 T nutmeg

1 t allspice

1 t onion powder

8 T salt

2 cups non-fat dry milk (dry)

Keep ingredients cold while mixing and stuff into casings. Dry and smoke the Pepperoni. Cook Bologna after stuffing, in 160 degree F water until internal temperature is 152 degrees F. chill. Smoke 3 hours in 115 to 120 degree smoke.

BASIC BREAKFAST SAUSAGE (Base for Several Sausages)

<u>For 20 pounds of meat</u>

1/3 cup salt

6 T ground black pepper (yes, that is 6)

1 cup brown sugar

   Mix all ingredients very well. May use as patties, or stuff into casings for sausage links. Using this same basic recipe, you can make any of the following variations by adding the listed ingredients to the above recipe. Experiment! Use any combination that sounds good to you, being sure to write it down as you do it so you can do it again, if you like it. This basic mix is also good just to grill and serve as burgers for wild game meat.

HOT LINKS
Add:4 to 6 T crushed red pepper flakes and 2 T granulated garlic
Stuff into casings for Hot Links or make patties for a tasty treat.

ITALIAN HOT SAUSAGE
To the Hot Link Additions and Basic Recipe, add:
 2 T crushed Italian seasonings, 1 T crushed Oregano, 2 t crushed Anise seed
and ½ t liquid smoke (optional)
Stuff into casings or use as bulk sausage in recipes.

ITALIAN SWEET SAUSAGE
Add to the Basic Recipe:
1 T minced garlic
2 T crushed Italian seasonings
1 T crushed Oregano
1 t each, crushed Anise seed & Coriander seed
½ cup white or brown sugar
Stuff into casings or use as bulk sausage in recipes.

WIENERS   fine grind after mixing
1 pint ice water
½ t sodium nitrate (saltpeter)
4 T paprika
6 T dry ground mustard
1 t ground black pepper
1 t ground white pepper
1 t ground celery seed
1 T ground mace or coriander
1 t garlic powder
8 T salt
4 T dextrose (may use sugar)
2 cups non-fat dry milk, dry
Mix well and stuff into casings, twisting in hot dog sized links.

BRAUNSCHWEIGER ½ liver, ½ meat and fat, fine grind after mixing. Mix at least 15 minutes.

½ t sodium nitrate (saltpeter)

7 T salt

5 T onion powder

½ t allspice

1 T ground white pepper

½ t ground marjoram

1 t nutmeg

1 t ginger

1 t ground sage

1 t ground cloves

3 T dry ground mustard

1 pint ice water

Cook after stuffing, in 160 degree F water until internal temperature is 152 degrees F. chill. Smoke 3 hours in 115 to 120 degree smoke.

The sodium nitrate may be omitted from these recipes, but the finished product will not have the red or pink color of store bought products.   In the sausage recipes, if you do not wish to use sugar, you may substitute half as much honey or fructose for the whole amount of sugar called for.   The flavor will be a bit different, but still good.   If you do not have access to sausage casings, you may make some from good quality cheesecloth doubled or muslin. I have not tried this, have been told it works.   Since it is almost impossible to stuff sausage in a manual meat grinder without at least three and preferably four hands to do everything that needs done at once, I don't know how material casings would work.   Maybe better, they wouldn't be so slithery.

PLAIN ITALIAN SAUSAGE

15 pounds meat and suet

2 ounces salt   (8 T)

1 cup smoked salt

1 ounce ground black pepper (4 T)

1 ounce ground coriander (4 T)

¼ ounce mace (1T)

Mix with hands at least 15 minutes. A small amount of ice water may be added to make mixing easier. Pack into a pan and cool overnight. Grind through smaller plate of grinder once or twice. Stuff into casings. Boil in plain water until sausage floats, cool. Instead of stuffing, may use as bulk sausage.

LIVER SAUSAGE

Cook about 4 pounds of meat scraps until almost tender. Remove veins and membrane from about 5 pounds of liver, slice liver into thin trips. Place in scalding water for 10 or 15 minutes. Grind meat and liver with coarse plate. Add enough broth the meat was cooked in to make texture soft but not wet. Add 4 ounces (½ cup) smoked salt, ½ ounce (1 T) ground black pepper, 1 t red pepper, 1 t ground sage and 1 t allspice. Mix well, as if you were kneading bread dough, stuff into casings and simmer in hot water until sausage floats. Plunge into cold water and chill thoroughly, drain.

SUMMER SAUSAGE

Grind together 4 lb. pork, 12 lb. game meat (moose, deer, caribou, bear, whatever) add 3 heaping t. meat tenderizer, 3 t. ground black pepper, 3 t. whole mustard seed, ½ cup smoke salt, 1 t. liquid smoke. Mix thoroughly. Let stand in cool place overnight, covering to prevent drying on top. Stuff into casings, tie shut and let stand in cool place overnight, don't freeze, smoke for about 4 hours, let smoke draw in overnight, smoke again for 4 hours, let stand one day. Store in freezer until used. Boil slowly or fry to cook.

HEADCHEESE WITHOUT THE HEAD

4 pork hocks, 4 venison shanks (moose, caribou, deer, whatever you have). Cut as much meat as possible from the bones and chop into small pieces. Put meat and bones into a large kettle, cover with water, add salt pepper, chopped onion and chopped garlic cloves to taste. Cover, boil slowly until very well done and meat falls from the bones. Remove bones from broth, cut off any remaining meat, return meat to broth and discard bones. Boil until liquid is reduced by half. Pour into loaf pan and cool well. When cold it slices well and is very good in sandwiches.

JELLIED MOOSE NOSE (Head Cheese, sort of)

Cut upper jawbone of moose just below the eyes. Skin as much as possible, put in a large kettle of scalding water and parboil 45 minutes. Remove and cool in cold water. Pick off any hairs like pinfeathers from a bird. Wash thoroughly. Place in fresh water with onion, crushed galic cloves and 2 to 4 ounces pickling spices. Boil gently until tender, cool overnight in the broth. Remove bone and cartilage. The bulb of the nose is white meat, the thin strips along the bone and jowls is dark meat. Slice or chop the meat thin and pack in jars, heat the broth to boiling and cover meat with the broth, clean rims, place lids on jars and process. Wide mouth pints work best so you can slide the contents out to slice and serve without heating. Process pints at 10 pounds pressure for 75 minutes. Adjust for altitude.

PICKLED TONGUE

Cook 5 or 6 deer tongues or 2 or 3 moose tongues until tender in salted water, cool slightly and peel off white skin and trim end. Slice and place in jars, not packing tightly. Make pickling solution by boiling 1 pint vinegar, 1 pint water, 1 T. whole mustard seed, ½ t. mace, 1 t. whole cloves, 1 t. whole allspice, 1 bay leaf, 1 t. peppercorns and salt to taste for 10 minutes. Pour over tongue slices and let stand in cool place for a week. Instead, you may process in pressure canner as for soup mix.

This pickling solution may be used over fish, also. Parboil fish that has been salted overnight, lat stand in solution a few days. Very good.

RULLEPOLSE (MEAT ROLL)

Split flanks almost to the edge, open like a book, or cut a piece of muscle as though you were shaping a jelly roll to make a large flat piece of meat out of it. Cut meat scraps into small strips, mix with salt, pepper, chopped onion and ginger to taste. Spread mixture on the flank or meat piece, roll, wrap tightly with twine, place in brine solution until ready to use.

To make brine: use enough water to cover meat roll, add salt until peeled raw potato floats, add 1 t. saltpeter to each 2 gallons water. Boil until salt is dissolved, cool, add meat, weight to keep from floating.

To use: soak roll in cold water overnight. Boil in fresh water 2 hours. Place in a loaf pan with weight on top to shape, until cold. Slice and use as sandwich meat.

LIVER

Remove membrane from outside of the liver and all large veins. Slice liver in ½ inch thick slices. Roll the slices in flour to coat while heating skillet on high with a small amount of grease in it. Quickly sear one side of the liver, turn heat down, turn the meat and add salt and pepper. Cover skillet and cook over medium heat just until done, there should still be a slight pink tint to the center of the slice. Do not overcook liver. The flavor gets strong and the texture gets hard and dry.

KIDNEYS

Clean kidneys BEFORE soaking. Remove outer membrane and slice in half. Remove all white or darker red tissue and veins. All that remains should be the same color as the outer meat part. Soak overnight in water with baking soda added. Drain, roll in flour and prepare as for liver.

STEAK AND KIDNEY PIE

Slice steak and drained kidneys after soaking, into bite sized pieces. Saute with onion until almost done. Dice potato, prepare gravy in the drippings from sautéing the meat. Mix meat, onions and potatoes, place in baking dish, top with biscuit dough crust, slash vents, bake at 400 degrees F until crust is browned and done.

ROCKY MOUNTAIN OYSTERS   (May substitute Brains)

As soon as possible after butchering or neutering, peel the membrane from the testes. Soak overnight in salted water with 1 t. soda added. Drain and rinse after soaking. If they are large, slice into ½ inch slices. Dip in flour, then in milk and then in cracker or bread crumbs. Fry in hot fat or oil until browned on both sides, serve. Brains should be handled the same way.

BRAINS AND EGGS

Peel and soak brain the same as the testes in the recipe above. Slice into cubes, beat eggs, heat lightly greased skillet, fry cubes until color starts to change. Add eggs and a dash of milk, lightly scramble, salt and pepper to taste and serve.

Once you have caught a fish, it is important to clean it right away. Bleed the fish and gut it, being sure to remove the dark vein along the backbone. The faster the fish is cleaned and cooled on ice or cooked, the better the finished product will be.

FISH SAUSAGE

If you have a large supply of fish and would like to try something different, make some sausage from the fish. Make sure you have all of the bones and skin removed before grinding the flesh. Follow your favorite sausage recipe, using the ground fish in place of the venison or pork. Salmon is very good in sausage and most people can not tell fish sausage from any other sausage. Use the fish sausage in spaghetti or tacos or just fry or broil patties for a unique burger. Any fish should work well for sausage, as long as the fish is fresh Nothing can improve fish that has been handled wrong, just as any food needs to be kept cool or frozen as soon as possible. Late salmon have less fat & taste best. A mild flavored fish is also very good for sausage.

SALMON QUICHE

Beat 2 eggs with a fork, add 1 pound ground salmon, 1 cup grated cheddar cheese, 1/2 t. garlic powder, dash Italian seasoning and 1/4 t. salt. Mix well, pour into an unbaked pastry shell. Bake at 350 degrees for about 50 minutes or until browned and set.   May add mushrooms, onions, or other vegetables if you like.

SALMON BITES

Cut boneless salmon into bite-sized pieces. Make batter of half cornstarch and half hotcake mix, adding 1 T. season salt, 1/4 t chili powder, 1/4 t celery salt and 1/2 t pepper. Add enough water to make thin batter. Mix well.

Coat salmon pieces with flour, dip in batter and deep fry until browned. Serve with dipping sauces, hot mustard, tomato & horseradish or tartar sauce.

Never overcook fish. By the time it flakes with a fork, it is usually overdone. Fish should just feel firm to the touch. When making soups, add the fish minutes before serving.

BAKED SALMON

Clean salmon, removing insides and head. Place under a hot broiler until the skin starts to lift and remove, roll skin off and do the other side the same. Place some onion slices and if you like, some lemon slices inside the belly cavity. Cover the top side of the skinned salmon with heavy cream and return to broiler. Broil until the cream is browned and bubbly and carefully turn the salmon and spread heavy cream on the other side. Return to broiler and brown the second side, also. By this time, the fish should be completely cooked and ready to serve.

SMOKED SALMON SPREAD

Drain and flake 2 cups cooked salmon, removing any bone and skin. Combine flaked salmon with 8 ounces softened cream cheese, 1 T. lemon. juice, 1/4 cup minced onion or chopped green onion, 2 t prepared horseradish (optional), and 1 T. liquid smoke. Mix well, chill several hours. If using canned salmon, bone and skin can be mashed into it.

POOR MAN'S LOBSTER (Halibut or any mild white fleshed fish)

Cut halibut into small strips, not over 1 inch thick, set aside. Bring to a boil, 1/2 gallon of water, ¼ cup salt and ¼ cup sugar. When mixture boils strongly, dump in all the fish at once.   When it floats, it's done. remove from water immediately.   Do not overcook, it will toughen.   Serve with melted butter.

May use other firm white fleshed fish, but I prefer halibut, myself.

BEER BATTER HALIBUT

1/2 cup minus 1 T. corn starch, ½ cup flour, 1/2 t. salt, 2 T. season salt, 2 t. garlic powder, and an 11 or 12 ounce can of beer.   Mix all ingredients together, mixture should be the consistency of cream.   Add more beer if too thick. Cut halibut into 1 ounce chunks or long strips, dredge in flour, then dip in batter.   Deep fry until they float, or about 3 minutes.

BROILED CRAB LEGS

Using the large leg sections, carefully cut away the softer inner side of the shell.   A very sharp knife, used carefully does this with a minimum of bloodshed on the cook's part.   Melt some butter, add I clove minced garlic, 1 T. minced celery and 1 T. minced onion, brush on crab meat and broil until hot. Serve with the rest of the melted butter mixture.

LASAGNA

Brown 1 pound hamburger, 2 minced cloves of garlic, 1/2 cup diced onion, then drain off fat.   Add 8 ounce can tomato sauce, I can tomatoes, 1½ t. salt, 1/4 t. pepper, 1 t. oregano and 1/2 t. Italian seasoning, simmer 15 minutes. Cook 8 ounces lasagna noodles or one recipe homemade noodles cut wide, in salted water until almost tender and drain.   Starting with a thin layer of sauce, layer alternate layers of noodles, ½ pound grated medium cheese (mozzarella, cheddar, Monterey Jack) 1 pound cottage cheese or ricotta, ½ cup parmesan or Romano cheese and sauce, in that order, ending with a dusting of parmesan.

Bake at 350 degrees F until bubbly all through. Allow to set at least 5 minutes before slicing and serving. This can be made ahead and reheated. It may be frozen after assembly, also.

POTATO PIES   or Stuffed Potatoes

Scrub 6 large baking potatoes, cut off 1/2 inch of the top, reserving top. With a sharp spoon, hollow out, leaving 1/2 inch shell.   Chop 2-3 cups leftover meat finely, add 1/2 cup finely chopped onion and finely chopped potato from what was scooped out.   Moisten with gravy or broth, season to taste.   Stuff the potato shells, replace the tops, place in greased pan.   Bake 1 hour at 350 degrees, basting occasionally with butter.

BARSSILIA

Cut into bite-sized pieces, 2 pork chops or steaks, 1 lb. boneless lean ham, 1 chopped onion, 2 cloves garlic, crushed, and cook until golden brown.   Add 1 T. brown sugar, 1 t. salt, 1/2 t. tumeric, 1/4 t. cayenne, 1/4 t. oregano, a dash of saffron, I large green pepper, cut in strips, 1/2 cup water, 1 T. vinegar, 2 T. chopped pimento and simmer 45 minutes.   Serve over hot cooked rice.

MOCK OYSTERS

Mix 1½ pounds ground lean meat, 1 cup canned tomatoes, 1 egg, 12 saltine crackers, crumbled and salt and pepper to taste.   Shape into small patties and fry in shallow hot grease.   Serve hot.

SLOPPY JOES

Brown 2 pounds hamburger and 2 diced onions, drain fat.   Add 2 T. vinegar, 2 T. Worcestershire sauce, 1 T, diced green pepper and 3/4 cup catsup.

Simmer 20 minutes. Butter 8 buns and toast on hot dry griddle, spoon sauce onto buns.

STUFFED FLANK STEAK

Sauté 1/2 cup chopped celery, 1/2 cup chopped onion, 2 T. chopped green pepper, and 1 T. chopped parsley in 2 T. fat until almost tender. Add 1½ cups soft bread crumbs, 1 t. poultry seasoning or sage, 1/2 t. salt and 1/4 t. pepper. Add as much broth or water as necessary to make dressing hold together. Split a 1 pound flank steak almost to the edge and open like a book. Spread stuffing over opened steak, roll and tie at intervals with string. Heat 2 T. fat in skillet, brown meat roll on all sides. If skillet has large enough cover, use skillet, if not place in casserole with 1½ cups broth or water and cover. Bake at 325 degrees for 2 hours. Thicken juices with 2 T. flour mixed with 2 T. butter or margarine. Remove string, slice as a jelly roll and serve with the gravy.

SWISS STEAK

Trim fat from 1 ½ pounds steak, cut in serving pieces. Pound flour, salt and pepper into both sides of steak. Brown in hot fat. Place meat in baking dish, cover with 2 medium onions, sliced, 2 green peppers, sliced, and I can of tomatoes and juice from frying meat. Cover and bake at 350 degrees for 1 hour, uncover, and bake another hour or until meat is tender. May be prepared ahead of time.

CAJUN ROAST

Large turkey-sized roasting bag, large pan to bake in.

8 or 9 pound rolled roast, or any boneless roast (8 cloves garlic, 8 green onions and

4 green chilies)   Save green onion tops to add later.   Poke holes in roast and insert cloves of garlic, green onions and chilies.   Cut green onions off flush with outside of roast.

Cover roast with salt and crushed red peppers.   Place 2 T. flour in roasting bag, shake well, smooth flour on bottom of bag, placed in large pan. Add roast, 2 pounds mushrooms, 8 medium potatoes, 8 carrots, 1 cup chopped green onion tops (from green onions pushed down into roast and tops cut flush with outside of roast), 1/2 cup parsley, 1/2 cup water, 1 T. celery seed, 2 cups wine, 2 T. soy sauce, 1/2 t angostura bitters.   Pour the liquid carefully into the bottom of the bag.   Seal bag, Poke holes in top of bag -with a fork. Bake at 325 to 350 degrees until roast reaches required degree of doneness. If you are using game meat for this recipe, you may wish to wait until the last hour of baking to add the vegetables.   Most game meat should be cooked well-done.   If not using roasting bag, use a good tight fitting roaster pan and lid.

FAMILY MEAT LOAF

In large bowl, combine:

1 ½ pounds ground meat, 2/3 cup quick-cooking rolled oats, 1 cup milk, 1 t. salt, dash of pepper, ¼ t. poultry seasoning, 2 eggs, 1 t. Worcestershire sauce, 1 small onion, diced, Put in a 9 x 5 inch loaf pan.   Prepare glaze: ¼ cup catsup, 2 T. brown sugar, 1 t. mustard, dash of nutmeg, mix well and spread evenly over the meat loaf.   Bake uncovered at 350 degrees for about 1 ¼ hours.

Any ground meat may be used for meat loaf, it does not have to be beef.   Even ground rabbit meat makes a pretty good meat loaf. If meat is extremely lean, you may add a tablespoon or two of butter or oil to the mixture,

IF you wish to can just a jar of meatloaf and raw pack the mixture into the wide mouthed pint jars, wipe the rims and do not put on the lids, bake in the oven until the meat registers well done with a meat thermometer in the center of the pack. Have your lids ready and the water boiling in the pressure canner. Remove one jar at a time wipe rim again and put on the lids, place immediately into the hot water and again, after filling and putting lid on the canner, proceed for the longest time given for meat processing in your canner book. I usually process at 10 pounds of pressure for 90 minutes for pints.   Or precook in miniloaf pans and while still hot, pack and can.

TIPSY HAM OR ROAST

1 ham, not precooked or canned, or one roast.   1   bottle   your favorite type of whiskey.   Large syringe.   Someone to keep an eye on the cook.

Fill syringe with whiskey, inject into the ham or roast in several different spots, enough that it almost squirts back at you.   Bake, covered, in 250 degree oven; 10 hours for ham, 8 hours for roast.   Season ham with cloves, if you like. Salt and pepper roast as you usually would.

Variations: Inject real maple syrup into ham, instead of whiskey. Inject melted butter into a turkey before roasting, may add a little whiskey. The alcohol content evaporates during baking, so don't worry, no one but the cook should be affected by the whiskey.   If the cook doesn't drink, then there's no potential problem.

HAMBURGER PIE

Brown 1 pound of hamburger, add 1 chopped onion, 1/2 cup chopped celery and 1 clove garlic, minced.   Cook until onion is tender.   Add one can or 2 1/2 cups chopped tomatoes, 1 can drained string beans, 1 can drained whole kernel corn, 1 8-ounce can tomato sauce and 1/2 cup uncooked rice.   Bring to a boil, stir through to distribute rice, pour into large baking pan.   Make a batch of biscuit dough, roll or pat out 1 inch larger around than the pan the meat mixture is in. Place biscuit crust over meat mixture, pressing over edges of pan to hold in place.   Cut vents for the steam to escape, brush crust with milk and place in 350 degree oven.   Bake 30 minutes or until crust is browned and done.

Variations:

Add 2 T. chili powder to hamburger mixture, sprinkle 1 chopped green chili over mixture, before adding crust.   Add sautéed onion and grated cheese, 1/2 cup each, to biscuit crust.

MOCK CHICKEN FRIED STEAKS

To 1 pound of any ground game meat, add 1 raw egg, 2 slices of bread and 1/4 cup milk or water.   Mix very well, but not until mushy.   May beat egg, bread and liquid well, before adding meat.   Form into 1/2 inch thick patties. Coat with flour, dip in milk or water, then into fine bread or cracker crumbs. Allow to set for 5 to 10 minutes, brown in 2 T. hot oil on each side,   season with salt, garlic and pepper to taste.   Serve with cream gravy.

I usually use a coarsely ground game meat for this recipe.   Bear, moose or venison works very well.

CAMPFIRE ROAST

One large boneless piece of meat. Pierce deeply with a knife, adding jalapeno peppers, green onions or cloves of garlic here and there over the whole roast. Rub the surface with salt and pepper. Either wrap the whole roast in several layers of aluminum foil, sealing well, and bury under the campfire or fire pit. Add several inches of dirt, pull the coals back over and build up the fire a bit. Allow it to die down for the day while you are hunting. OR, rub flour over the entire surface of the roast and brown in a hot Dutch Oven in a small amount of oil or grease. Cover with a tight fitting lid and cook slowly until done. This can be buried under the campfire also if you are careful not to loosen the lid so dirt gets into it. Serve in the evening after the days' hunt or work, with hot Bread-On-A-Stick that each person cooks over the campfire.

GARBAGE (variation of Shepards' Pie, one of Kara's inventions)
    You can use almost any leftovers you may have on hand for this dish, hence the name, Garbage.
1 lb ground beef
2 large cans Beef Vegetable Soup
1 can string beans
1 can corn
2 garlic cloves, minced
1 diced medium onion
Brown beef and onion, drain and add garlic. Mix in other ingredients and place in a
Medium baking pan.
Make up about 2 cups of mashed potatoes. May use leftovers. Cover the top of the meat mixture with the mashed potatoes. We usually season the mashed potatoes with ranch dressing (dry) and garlic. Cover the potatoes with grated cheddar cheese   and bake until bubbly and cheese is well melted.
VARIATION: If you have more mashed potatoes than filling for the amount of people you are feeding, make a "crust" of the mashed potatoes in the baking dish, then fill with the meat mixture and top with more mashed

potatoes.   The "crust" will brown nicely if you coat the baking dish with butter before adding the potatoes.   .

KARA'S WELFARE CHEESESTEAKS (Cheap and very good)
1 pound ground meat, chopped onion, chopped green peppers, jar of cheese dip.   Brown the burger, drain, add the onion and peppers and cook until just done. Add the cheese dip.   Spoon into rolls and eat.   May use nacho cheese dip.

KLUBE

Fry and set aside: 2 pounds cut up boneless pork chops, 12 oz pork sausage and 1 medium onion, diced.

Peel and grate: 8 medium potatoes and 1 large onion.   Add 4 beaten eggs, 1 ½ t. sugar, ¼ t. pepper.   Gradually add enough flour to make dough that will hold it's shape.   Using a small amount of the meat mixture as the center, form dough into 3 inch balls.   Carefully drop the balls into boiling water.   Cook about 75 minutes, stirring very gently once in a while to make sure they don't stick and burn to the bottom.   Add enough of the cooking liquid to the remaining meat mixture to make a sauce or gravy to serve over the cooked balls.   Serve piping hot.

BUTCHERING CHICKENS

If you are butchering your own chickens for the first time, have lots of water boiling before you kill the chickens.   My Dad held the chicken by the legs and chopped their heads off on the chopping block.   Then he held them until they quit flapping. A friend hung them over the clothesline and slit their throats to bleed them out.   I shoot the heads off with a 22.   Whatever method used, remove the heads and allow them to bleed out as soon as possible.   Hanging over the clothesline allows them to flap without bruising the flesh as it does if you chop off the head and let them flop around on the ground.   Have a large kettle of very hot water handy and plunge the whole bird into it and back out. This makes the feathers easier to pluck. Hold the legs and pluck away from you for easiest plucking. After plucked, use either a rolled piece of newspaper, lit, to singe the hairs off the bird, still holding it by the feet. Then cut off the lower leg-foot section at the joint below the drumstick. Then proceed to gut and dismember or leave whole, depending on what you are planning on doing with the bird. Remove the crop in front of the breast section and discard along with the other bits and pieces in the neck. Cut the skin carefully from the end of the breastbone, around the vent and carefully insert your hand and pull everything out. Use your finger to dislodge and remove the lungs from the ribs on each side. If this is a hen, you may have eggs in various stages of development. They can be added to the broth made from bones and assorted other trimmings. Above the tail, there is an oil gland that needs to be carefully removed without getting any on the meat. I cut back far enough and gouge out the whole thing. Remove the heart, liver and gizzard from the gut pile. Trim the heart and liver, carefully split the gizzard down through the dark muscle part to the sac inside that contains the grit and food being digested. Cut carefully so you don't puncture the sac. Peel the sac out whole and trim the 2 openings into the gizzard so no gut material contaminates the meat. If you are doing several birds, you might want to make broth from the feet. I know, sounds gross. DON'T let the kids see you making this. Scald the feet and slip all the skin and toenails off. Cover with water and simmer a couple of hours. This actually makes very good broth. I can't bring myself to eat the feet, but my Mom and Grandmother enjoyed them very much. I discard them after making broth. My pets enjoy them very much. I usually debone most of the chicken, removing the skin from the breast, cut down along the breastbone and peel the meat out on each side. Pull the breastbone free from the rest of the bird, bend the body back to break the backbone apart at the end of the ribs and cut to separate into 2 sections. Cut the wings free from the backbone. Bend the ribs back so they break free of the backbone and slide a knife under and pull the ribs away from the meat. This makes the back into a nice piece for frying. Cut the drumsticks free by bending the leg back and cutting across the dimple made at the joint. Pull the thigh back and cut lose at the hip joint. Sometimes I debone the thighs, also depending on how I plan to use them. I usually put the skin, excess fat, breastbone, ribs, neck, lower backbone and wings in a pot with some onion, celery and parsley to simmer for broth. Most birds can be butchered and cleaned in the same manner or just skin some of them if they are too hard to pluck.

HONEY CHICKEN

Marinade chunks of chicken thigh fillet with 2 T. cornstarch, 1 t. minced garlic, ½ t. salt, ¼ t. pepper, 2 T. lemon juice, and 1 T. sesame oil overnight. When you are preparing the meal, in a bowl mix honey and a couple Tbsp of butter or water with a pinch of salt and microwave until lukewarm. Basically you want to dilute the honey so that it coats the chicken when its done cooking. Set this aside. Make a batter from ½ cup flour, 1 t. baking powder, ½ cup corn starch and about 1 cup, more or less, water, making sure its not too runny but not too thick- about the consistency of melted ice cream. Dip the chunks of chicken in this batter and deep fry. Drain on paper towels, and when they are almost all done frying heat the honey up in a pan with the butter or water and then when its hot pour some of it in a bowl, followed by the chicken chunks. toss to coat. Place them on a serving platter and sprinkle with sesame seeds. Serve over rice.

CHICKEN MANICOTTI (My daughter's invention, thanks, Kara)
    Precook 2 chicken breasts.   Dice, set aside.   Precook Manicotti shells, drain, rinse, set aside.   Mix 1 quart ricotta or cottage cheese, diced chicken, 2 eggs together.   Stuff noodle shells and place in lightly greased pan.   Pour pint of Alfredo sauce over and sprinkle with grated white cheese of choice.   Bake at 350 degrees F. until bubbly, allow to set 5 to 15 minutes before serving.

STIR FRY GARLIC CHICKEN   Serve over hot rice
Slice raw chicken breast into thin bite sized pieces, half frozen slices easiest. Set aside.   Slice whatever fresh vegetables you have on hand or like into small uniform pieces.   I usually use onion, broccoli, celery and bell peppers, some bok choy is good, also.   Mix 1 T. cornstarch, 3 T. soy sauce, 2 t. minced garlic in a cup, add enough water to make almost 1 cup total, set aside.   Heat skillet or wok with very small amount of oil until hot and add the chicken, stirring to cook quickly, add the veggies halfway through the chicken being cooked and just before the vegetables are almost done, stir in the liquids after stirring well. Stir and cook until liquid turns fairly clear and thickens.   May add a few drops of sesame oil as you remove from heat and stir through for Sesame Garlic Chicken.

CHICKEN CHEESE ENCHILADAS
Make Cheese Sauce, melt ¼ cup butter, blend in ¼ cup flour, dash of salt and paprika. Add 2 cups milk and stir until sauce thickens and bubbles around the edges.   Blend in 1 ½ cups cheese.   Add 1 cup shredded cooked chicken to half the cheese sauce, set aside.
12 tortillas, ¼ cup cooking oil, 10 ounce can either green or red enchilada sauce.   Heat tortillas in the oil for about 5 seconds on each side, dip in the enchilada sauce, spoon the cheese sauce with chicken in the center of each and roll up.   Place seam side down in baking dish.   Combine remaining cheese sauce and enchilada sauce and pour over filled tortillas.   Bake at 350 degrees F. for 25 minutes.

ENCHILADA SAUCE
Ingredients
- 1/4 cup vegetable oil
- 2 tablespoons flour or corn flour
- 1/4 cup New Mexico or California chili powder

- 1 (8 ounce) can tomato sauce
- 1 1/2 cups water
- 1/4 teaspoon ground cumin
- 1/4 teaspoon garlic powder
- 1/4 teaspoon onion salt
- salt to taste
- Optional - add 1 teaspoon cocoa powder, mix with other dry ingredients
- OR   Pinch of cinnamon and ½ teaspoon sugar

Directions

Heat oil in a skillet over medium-high heat. Stir in flour and chili powder, reduce heat to medium, and cook until lightly brown, stirring constantly to prevent burning flour.

Gradually stir in tomato sauce, water, cumin, garlic powder, and onion salt into the flour and chili powder until smooth, and continue cooking over medium heat approximately 10 minutes, or until thickened slightly. Season to taste with salt.

ROASTING A TURKEY OR OTHER BIRD WHOLE

Pluck any remaining pinfeathers and singe if needed for little hairs all over the bird.   Make sure the lungs and oil sac at base of tail have been removed. Remove all the excess fat from inside and around the neck area.   Rinse the bird and pat dry.   Loosen skin over the breast and unless the bird is a very fat bird to start with, spread soft butter over the meat under the skin.   Add the seasonings you like on whatever type of bird you are roasting.   Instead of butter, you can place strips of bacon under the skin.   If using a roasting bag, follow the instructions for that.   If using a roasting pan with a wire rack in the bottom, place the bird on the rack and a cup of water or wine in the pan under the bird.   Cover tightly with the roaster lid and bake in a 350 degree F. oven until the leg moves easily when wiggled or the juices run clear if the meat is pierced deeply.   Remove the cover for the last ½ hour of roasting to brown the skin.   Remove the bird from the oven and let set at least 10 minutes before carving to allow the juices to settle in the meat.   Pour off the pan drippings and skim excess fat off.   Use a roux of butter and flour to thicken the juices for gravy to serve with the meat.   For a low cal gravy, use flour or cornstarch and water instead of the butter/flour roux.   A chunk of ice brushed over the top of the pan drippings will harden up the fat for easy removal.

SOAP

You may wish to make soap from the fat you have from butchering. You should read the entire section on making soap before trying it the first time. You may add or use other fats that you have saved from cooking, as long as it is not burned. Animal and vegetable fats and oils combined make a superior soap. This is a good way to use fat that you do not want to save for cooking but do not want to throw away. The essential ingredients for soap making are clean fat, pure uniform lye (purchased from a store, although directions for impure, not-so-reliable lye making will be given, later) and water. Best results are obtained using soft water whenever possible. Snow melt or rainwater are perfect. If water is very hard, soften by adding a small amount of lye and letting it stand three to four days. Remove the hard particles which settled to the bottom. Utensils needed for a small batch of soap are enameled or granite ware or glass. For large batches an iron kettle may be used. Never use copper, aluminum, tin or zinc as the lye solution attacks these metals. For stirring, use a large graniteware spoon or wooden spoon or ladle. Shallow cardboard boxes or wooden boxes may be used for molds. Line boxes with damp cloth or damp heavy paper. When soap is hardened the entire "cake" can be removed from the mold by simply lifting the cloth or paper.

Miscellaneous refuse fats and meat fryings (usually rancid) should be washed by adding equal amounts of water and bringing to a boil. Remove from heat, stir and carefully add cold water, one quart to every gallon of hot liquid. The cold water precipitates foreign substances and the clean fat comes to the top. Remove the fat when it is firm. Some fats require a second washing to remove all odors. To sweeten small amounts of rancid fat, add five cups water and one cup vinegar to every six cups of fat. Boil for fifteen minutes and set aside to cool, when cold, skim off fat. A method of clarifying slightly burned or dirty grease is by melting, straining through a cloth and then frying a few small pieces of white potato in it until it ceases to crackle.

To remove additional fat from cracklings left after making lard, add one tablespoon of lye to each gallon of cracklings, cover with water and let cook for about two hours. Remove from heat, add a large amount of water and let stand. A layer of clean fat will harden on the surface, which is ready for soap making. Discard the cracklings as they are unfit for human consumption after this treatment.

CAUTION IN HANDLING LYE. When working with lye, particularly when dissolving it, stand well back so as not to inhale the fumes. Protect hands by wearing rubber gloves or handle material with paper. Should any of the lye solution get on your skin, apply vinegar to the affected part immediately and rinse thoroughly with plenty of clean water. NEVER leave lye where it might be reached by children. It is a very good idea to set up a stove or fire outdoors to do your soap making on. Always be sure to have adequate ventilation, in any case, when making soap.

HARD SOAP - COLD PROCESS
6 pounds clarified fat
2 1/2 pints soft water
1 can lye, about 12 oz.
2 Tablespoons borax
1/2 cup water
1/2 cup ammonia
Dissolve the lye in the 2 1/2 pints of cold water in a graniteware or glass container. As the lye dissolves the mixture becomes hot. Let cool to 70 degrees Fahrenheit or room temperature before using. Melt grease in a crock or kettle of iron or enamelware. Mix thoroughly with an enamel or wooden spoon and let cool to about 105 degrees F. or until the path of the spoon is plain in the mixture as it is stirred. Continue to stir slowly and steadily in one direction as you add the lye mixture in a slow thin stream. Continue to stir until all the lye has combined with the fat and the mixture is like thin honey. Mix the borax and 1/2 cup water until dissolved, add the ammonia and stir into the soap mixture, still stirring in one direction only. Perfume may be added at this point, if desired, such as rose oil, spice oil or citronella. The mixture now quickly becomes thick and syrupy and should be poured gently into the mold. Cover the mold with a blanket or carpet and set in a warm room until hard. Most soaps may be removed from the mold in a few hours. The blocks should then be cut into cakes with a string, knife or fine wire, stacked in a warm dry place,

free from drafts and allowed to cure for several weeks. The longer soap ages, the better it gets.

HARD SOAP - BOILING PROCESS

Recommended for rancid grease. Preliminary step; dissolve 1/2 cup lye in 4 quarts water, add 8 pounds grease, stirring constantly, bring to a boil, remove from heat, let stand 12 hours. Skim the fat, discard the water and impurities left in the kettle. The fat is now ready for soap making.

8 pounds clarified fat

2 cans of lye, about 24 ounces

4 gallons water

Dissolve the lye in the water and add the fat, stirring until the fat is entirely melted. Place on stove and boil slowly for 2 hours. Remove from heat to stop boiling or turn the heat down to just below boiling for another 30 minutes. The mixture, by this time, should be the consistency of heavy molasses.

Then add following:

½ cup borax

½ cup tepid water

½ cup ammonia

Dissolve borax in tepid water, add ammonia and stir into mixture, stirring one direction only. Add scent at this time. Pour mixture into lined molds and cover with carpet or blanket and set in warm room for at least 24 hours. Remove from molds and cut into desired size cakes. Stack in a dry place, free from drafts, where it will not freeze, and allow to age. The soap will have a cheeselike texture at first, but will harden upon standing several weeks, months is better. For use in a washing machine, make soap jelly by shaving 8 ounces of soap into 2 quarts water. When completely dissolved, store in a jar and use as needed.

MAKING LYE FROM WOOD ASHES

To make this lye, a simple leach pit can be arranged by placing a barrel or tub a few feet above ground on a rock or wooden platform. Plastic buckets work well, also. Bore several small holes in the bottom of the tub, bucket or barrel, cover these holes with small rocks. Fill the tub, bucket or barrel with hardwood ashes, preferably oak, but apple wood, birch, alder or aspen should all give a nice white soap. Pour hot water over the ashes, slowly, let it leach slowly through, catching the liquid in plastic buckets. It isn't good for metal buckets or containers. The longer it takes the water to drain through the ashes, the stronger the lye will be. The water should be poured over the ashes a second time, letting it drain through again. This will give a stronger lye. The lye water should be strong enough to float a fresh raw egg, still in it's shell. If it isn't, pour it through again.

OLD FASHIONED SOFT SOAP

Heat the lye water you have just made. In another container, glass or graniteware, melt the fat you wish to make soap from, with enough lye water to prevent burning. Continue to add lye water until the mixture is thoroughly combined, using a wood or graniteware spoon. When enough lye water has been added, the entire mass will be uniformly clear. To test, take a small amount from the center of the kettle, place on a piece of glass and allow to cool. If the soap continues to be clear, it is ready. Add scent if desired. Pour into molds and proceed as other soaps. Soap may be too soft to hold it's shape so can be stored in glass jars, crocks or plastic containers.

SUGGESTIONS AND TIPS ON SOAP MAKING

When too much lye is used, a hard flinty soap is formed that crumbles when shaved. Soap should have a smooth velvety texture that curls when shaved. Greasy soaps show a lack of lye. Always stir slowly and evenly in one direction only, Hard vigorous stirring will cause separation of fat and lye. If grease comes to the top of the soap, it may be slowly heated by placing on an oven door and stirring until it thickens and looks like honey. Needless to say, the oven should be on, to give a bit of heat, while doing this. If the boiling process has been used and the soap, when cut, shows a darker color at the bottom, more water was needed in the blending process.

It is recommended that all soap making be done outdoors or in an open sided shed. My Grandfather made molds for the soap that were used by my Grandmother, my Mother and the neighbors.

Practices makes near perfect. If half olive oil is added in place of part of the fat called for, this makes a good hand and bath soap. You may also add lanolin for part of the water. Practice with different scents and develop your own fancy bath soap.

CANDLES

Use extreme caution when working with the hot fats. Be sure no small children or pets will be around the work area. Read the complete section on making candles before beginning.

Use freshly rendered lard from the animal you have butchered. Rancid fat will make a foul smelling candle when you burn it.

FOR CANDLES

Use:

5 pints lard

1 pint beeswax (You may use up to 50% beeswax)

1 teaspoon alum

1 cake Camphor (just for a pleasant odor)

This will make about 3 dozen candles, depending on long and big you make them. You may use aromatic oils in place of camphor, but some have an unpleasant odor while burning so you may wish to test a small amount first.

SALTING THE WICKS

The wicking needs to be soaked in salt and dried. Most people doing this project will run into the problem that their wick burns out in 10 - 20 minutes. To match and even out perform commercial wicking, just add salt. Salt prevents the cotton from charring too early so you can burn your lamp for an hour or two without any adjustments."

To salt the wicking:
1. Cut your wicking from cotton cloth.
2. Put your wicking in a bowl with a little water.
3. Pour table salt over the wicking.
4. Squeeze the wicking dry and then dry further on a tray. You can bake it dry in an oven at 200F for 20 minutes or just let it dry overnight. It will be crusty with salt but that's good and the wicking will still be reasonably flexible.

PRIMING WICKS

Measure enough wick for 2 candles and about 4 inches extra, before cutting. This gives you enough extra to hang the candles between dips, without touching. Heat fat mixture to 160 degrees F. (71 degrees C.) Turn off the heat. Fold the wick in half, hold by the middle and dip in fat 1 minute. This removes moisture and air and makes your candles burn better. Remove wicks and straighten with damp fingers. Hang to cool. A broom handle or dowel placed across the backs of 2 chairs can be used to hang the wicks and later, the candles as you dip them. The space keeps wicks and later, candles, from touching and sticking while cooling.

DIPPING

Have the fat mixture at 160 degrees F in a container at least 2 inches taller than the length of the finished candle. A large coffee can or juice can makes a good holder for the fat mixture. Always have a thermometer in the fat mixture, not the hot water bath surrounding it. A candy thermometer is ideal. A double boiler is handy for melting the fat mixture, a large pan of water works well, too. Any container used for candle making will probably be ruined for any other use. Dip the primed wick about 3 seconds, allowing 1 to 3 minutes between dips. On the last dip, increase the fat temperature to 180 degrees F (82 degrees C) for a smoother surface. You can add some color to the last dip, also. Before the finished candle cools too much, trim the base flat. You may trim the bottom during dipping and put the trimmings back into the pot, if the candle requires a pointy bottom.

All work surfaces should be damp, including hands. Wax doesn't stick to moist items.

For a fancy effect, before the candle hardens, place on a smooth damp surface, roll with a damp rolling pin, leaving candle about ½ inch thick, starting about an inch up from the base and tapering to about ¼ inch thick at the tip. Immediately hold upside down with one hand by the base and starting at the flattened section by the base hold with thumb and forefinger of the other hand. Pull candle slowly upwards, sliding between thumb and forefinger and turning steadily.   Repeat for a more extreme twist to the candle.

Always let candles cool at least one hour before lighting.

Problem	Cause	Repair
Lumpy surface	First dip too fast	Roll on smooth surface while still warm
Spits while burning	Water in candle	Pour off melted wax & relight or remelt
Cracks while rolling	Uneven temperature	Redip until pliable

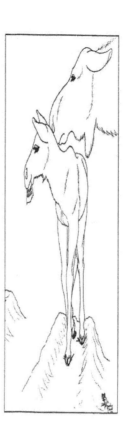

Early Season Gardening For Alaska Or Any Cool Climate Area.

VEGETABLES FROM SCRATCH

Before we leave our cabin, in the Autumn, we try to rototill and hill up at least 1 or 2 rows in the garden. We plant all of our garden in raised rows, about 18 inches high, 18 inches wide at the top, with edges raised a couple of inches higher to hold water in the row.

Usually we make our first trip to our cabin and garden spot in early April. Most of the time I have to brush the snow from the top of the raised row I intend to plant. Sometimes I pour boiling water down the row to thaw enough soil to cover the seeds. I plant 2 or 3 rows on top of each raised row. The center row to remain in place and the 2 side rows to transplant starts to the rest of the garden in late May. These seedlings start better then the ones I start in the house and transplant outside, later. A little bit of everything is started at this time. Lettuce, radishes, turnips, broccoli, cauliflower, cabbage, collards, kale, bush beans, dwarf peas, onion sets, bok choy, zucchini, yellow squash, vegetable marrow, spaghetti squash, acorn squash, cucumbers, beets and carrots are all planted through the snow. 1 gallon plastic milk jugs with the bottoms cut out are used as hot caps over each hill of squash and beans.

Only one or two feet of row is planted to each variety at this time. Interior Alaska can have snow and frost every month of the Summer, although it is unusual. The record low for the month of May is 1 degree below zero F. The record high for May is 90 degrees above zero, F.

After planting, a minimum of 2 layers of plastic is placed over the entire row, plastic jugs and all. The plastic is held down by logs, rocks, loose dozer parts and assorted strange things that have turned up over the years as we've worked the garden plot. During the Gold Rush in the early 1900's, this was the site of a roadhouse. Later it was mined, now it is a very prolific garden.

As we make additional trips and the soil shows up through the snow, the assorted weights holding down the plastic is replaced with soil to make a good barrier against voles. If the voles get too bad, I have put traps under the plastic so no other small animals or birds will be killed.

About the second week of May, I pre-sprout all the large seeds (peas, beans, corn and squash) before the main planting. Sprout by soaking overnight in lukewarm water at room temperature. Drain and rinse several times every day to prevent souring, especially of corn, and to prevent drying out. Handle with care as soon as the root shows, to prevent breakage.

Sprouted seeds do not rot from cold, wet soil. Their growth may slow considerably, though. By pre-sprouting, the garden is in production from 1 to 2 weeks earlier, which can mean the difference between success and failure of a crop. All of the garden can usually be planted by May 20th. This is for Interior Alaska, near Fairbanks. The raised rows help the soil warm faster, and plastic over the rows speeds warming and early growth. Every little bit helps. If there is plastic over the rows of beans, they must be watched carefully and the plastic removed before the foliage touches it. The plants will still produce, but the foliage will have a rust appearance. The tender plants with milk jug mini-greenhouses, have the caps removed during the day and replaced at night. This works very well for all squash and cucumbers, tomatoes and eggplant. Remove milk jugs when full of foliage and danger of frost is passed.

The milk jugs and all plastic are removed by the first of June, and we start picking small outer leaves from lettuce, thinning early onions and radishes for small salads. Since the onions are poked tightly together along the outer edges of the raised rows of cabbage, cauliflower and broccoli , I pull every other one as we start using them through the Summer.   These early salads are really appreciated after a long cold Winter.

All wood ashes go into the garden, sifted on each row.   This is good for the soil and repels root maggots, which are about the only pest we have in the garden, of the usual garden variety of pests.   There are the unusual pests - moose, bears and such, but not much repels them.

All the weeds that are pulled go into the "stink barrel".   This is just a large barrel of water, rotting weeds and non-meat kitchen scraps, that is used to water the garden with.   Once a week, ideally, once a month, closer to reality. In other climates a compost heap would take care of this, but we do not have the correct organisms or climate for a successful compost pile.   Try not to get any of this water on anything you plan on nibbling while weeding.   The odor isn't grand and tends to spoil the appetite.   It does wash off, though.   If the rain isn't sufficient and you must haul water, as we do, the raised edges again come in handy on the rows. It not only holds the plastic above the young plants early in the season, but also keeps the water where it's needed on the plants, not wasted between rows on the weeds.   About once a month, if I remember, I mix fish fertilizer and water everything with it.

Once in a while a cow moose with calves will wander into the garden. So far, the most damage they have done is their huge footprints mashing things. The calves are curious and will go down the rows pulling   all the tags I placed to mark each variety planted.   A mama moose is as dangerous as a mama bear so I am not about to tell her that her darling shouldn't do that.   A calf moose has the loveliest eyes, large melting brown, with long, long lashes.   They are so adorable with the tiny body and incredibly long legs.   Such a darling baby sure does grow into an awkward looking adult.   I think a moose is   ungainly looking when just standing there, but when they are moving silently through the woods or browsing in a pond, they are magnificent. They do appear to have been assembled by committee, though. Bulb-like nose, shoulder hump, huge ears and long legs with slender hind quarters, that's a moose.

Very few years are favorable for the corn to reach maturity. However, every year I can depend on enjoying the immature ears, using them as miniature corn. Just pick the immature ears whenever you want a treat and before the cob begins to toughen. The whole thing tastes like the fresh corn and is sweet and crunchy. They add a nice touch to soups and stews, even if they are canned. They are great, pickled, also.

As the squash reach maturity, the yellow or white ones seem to intrigue bears. It's not that they like them, they just don't know what they are. The bear wanders up and down the rows, taking one bite out of each squash, then spitting it out. Then he hightails it through the fence, if I step outside. Gardening in Alaska can be exciting.

If you are planning on canning your garden produce, remember, the sooner it is canned after picking, the better the finished product.

DRYING FRUITS AND VEGETABLES

If you do not have a dehydrator, you may still dry foods. The oven, set on low or with a pilot light lit, and the door propped open a bit, will work. So does a fiberglas or stainless steel window screen hung above a heating stove. Regular window screen may rust onto your drying food and ruin it.

It is best to cut the food into uniform-sized pieces or slices so that everything on the rack dries at about the same rate. As the food gets drier, it should be turned, then as it dries more, stir it occasionally. As mine dries, I move the almost dried to one side of the screen and add more food. There can be food in several stages of drying, all on one large screen over the heater. Be sure and have the screen high enough that the food doesn't cook. If your heater gets as hot as my old barrel stove does, at the cabin, this is a real possibility. The front edges of the screen are on hooks that I can undo to lower one edge and care for the drying food.

Most vegetables retain a better quality if partially precooked before drying. Fruit does not require treatment, unless you wish to sulfur some for eye appeal. I don't, but that is a personal preference.

Vegetables NOT requiring blanching are - horseradish, celery, mushrooms, okra, onions, parsley peppers and pimentoes.

Vegetables requiring 2 or 3 minutes blanching. Sliced asparagus, green or yellow snap beans, broccoli, sliced cabbage, carrots, cauliflower, cut or corn-on-the-cob, eggplant, peas, spinach and other greens, winter squash cut into 1/8 inch strips, summer squash cut into 1/4 inch strips and tomatoes cut into 3/4 inch slices.

Vegetables requiring 7 or 8 minutes of blanching. Halved brussels sprouts, potatoes cut into 1/4 inch strips or 1/8 inch slices.

If you want some of your fruits, such as apples, pears & apricots to stay light colored without sulfuring, blanch 2 or 3 minutes. This looks pretty, but does give a slightly cooked flavor to the finished product and it won't taste as sweet.

ITALIAN COLESLAW

Layer the following in a bowl, 1 medium cabbage, shredded, 1 medium onion, sliced thin.   Sprinkle 1 cup minus 2 T. sugar over the cabbage. In a saucepan. Combine 1 cup cider vinegar, 1/4 cup cooking oil, 2T. sugar, 1 t. salt, 1 t. dry mustard and 1 t. celery seed and bring to a boil. Pour over cabbage and cover. Let stand 4 to 6 hours. Mix well and serve. Will keep well.

WTLTED LETTUCE

Clean and dry 2 large bunches leaf lettuce, tear in bite-sized pieces into bowl, season lightly with salt and pepper, add 2 t. sugar and 2 sliced green onions. Fry 4 slices bacon crisp, crumble, set aside. Add 1/4 cup cider vinegar and 2 T. water to bacon drippings, heat to boiling, pour over lettuce. Toss until wilted and evenly coated. Add crumbled bacon and 2 sliced hardboiled eggs. Makes about 4 servings.

POTATO SALAD or MACARONI SALAD (Use cooked pasta in place of the potatoes)

Combine 4 cups cold boiled potatoes, sliced or diced, 1 cup thinly sliced celery, 1 medium onion, minced, OR 1 cup chopped green onions, 6 hard-boiled eggs, sliced, 1 large dill pickle, chopped, ½ cup chopped black or green olives, ¾ cup sour cream or mayonnaise, mustard to taste. May add a bit of pickle juice to thin dressing. Sprinkle with paprika and serve.

POTATO SALAD #2
Combine 4 cups cold boiled red potatoes, sliced or diced, ½ cup minced onions, ½ cup bacon bits or crumbled cooked bacon, ¾ cup sour cream and 1 t chopped dill weed.

AUNT TOOT'S BEAN SALAD
1 can each, green and yellow string beans
2 cans red kidney beans
2 cans green lima beans
2 cups sliced onions

   Prepare dressing of 1 clove crushed garlic, I cup salad oil, 2 cups sugar OR 1½ cups granulated fructose. 2 cups cider vinegar, mix well until sugar is dissolved, pour over drained beans. Keeps well if kept cool.

COLESLAW

Mix 1 t. salt with one medium cabbage, shredded fairly fine. Let stand at least 1 hour. Press out as much moisture as possible. Add 1 grated carrot, 1 small onion, finely diced and 1 chopped green pepper to the cabbage, mix and add dressing of 1/2 cup mayonnaise or salad dressing or sour cream, 2 T. vinegar, 1 T. sugar, 2 t. prepared mustard, 1/2 t salt or less and ¼ t. pepper. Mix well and refrigerate until ready to serve, stir again and sprinkle paprika over top for garnish.

COPPER PENNIES SALAD

   Peel and slice about 2 pounds of carrots. Slice about the thickness of pennies. steam until almost tender, drain and cool. Mix with 1 sliced green pepper and 1 sliced onion. Combine 1   10 oz. can condensed tomato soup, 1/2 cup oil, 1/2 to 1 cup sugar, depending on your taste, 3/4 cup vinegar, 1 t.

dry mustard, 1 t. Worcestershire sauce and 1/2 t. pepper, mix well, until sugar is dissolved.   Pour over carrots, stir and let sit an hour to blend.   Serve.

For a different flavor, omit Worcestershire sauce and add 1/2 t. dill seed, or 1 t. fresh chopped dill weed.

SAUERKRAUT SALAD

Combine 2 cups well drained sauerkraut, 1 medium green pepper chopped, 1 medium onion, chopped, and ¼ cup chopped pimento.

Dissolve 1 ¼ cups sugar in ½ cup of vinegar, add ½ cup oil and mix well. Pour over kraut mixture and mix well.   Cover and keep cool.   Keeps well.

CREAMY CUCUMBERS

Thinly slice 1 large cucumber, sprinkle with 1 teaspoon salt and let stand 30 minutes, drain.   Combine ½ cup sour cream, 2 T. cider vinegar, 2 drops pepper sauce OR 1 t. hot horseradish, 2 T. chopped chives OR green onion tops, 1 t. dill weed and a dash of pepper.   Pour over the drained cucumber slices.   Chill about 30 minutes. Serve.

CUCUMBER CHEESE SALAD

Dissolve large package of lime flavor gelatin in ¾ cup hot water.   Add 8 oz. softened cream cheese, 1 cup of sour cream or mayonnaise, 1 t. horseradish and ¼ t. salt.   Beat until smooth.   Add 2 T. lemon juice, mix well, chill until partially set.   Shred 1 large cucumber, drain and slice ½ cup green onions or mince ½ cup onion.   Stir cucumber and onion into partially set gelatin mixture, chill in 3 cup mold until firm.

SPINACH   SALAD

Dice 5 slices bacon, brown and reserve. Make dressing of 2/3 cup oil, 1/3 cup sugar, 1/3 cup catsup, 1/3 cup red wine vinegar (may use cider vinegar), 1/3 Cup finely chopped green onions and 2 t. Worcestershire sauce. Wash and chop spinach

May add bean sprouts and sliced water chestnuts with spinach.

WALDORF SALAD

In bowl, combine 2 cups diced tart apples, 1 T. sugar, ½ t. lemon juice and dash of salt. Add 1 cup diced celery and ½ cup coarsely chopped walnuts. Whip 1/2 cup whipping cream, add 1/4 cup mayonnaise, gently fold into apple mixture.

May add 1/2 cup mini-marshmallows or 1 cup seeded grapes.

May use 1/2 cup sour cream in place of the whipped cream for a different flavor Add one can drained fruit cocktail, also, and the mini-marshmallows.

MUSTARD

Mix 1 cup vinegar and 4 ounces dry mustard, let stand overnight. Beat 2 large or 3 small eggs and 1 t. salt, add to mixture- Cook in double boiler until thick. Let cool, Beat or fold in 1½ cups mayonnaise. May add 1 T. horseradish.

MAYONNAISE

Mix 1 t. salt, 1/2 t. dry mustard, 1/4 t.   paprika and dash of cayenne. Blend in 2 egg yolks, add 2 T. vinegar and mix well Add salad oil, 1 t. at a time, beating with mixer, until 1/4 cup has been added. Add 1 3/4 cup more oil, in increasing amounts alternating last   1/2 cup with 2 T. lemon juice.   Beat in 1

T. hot water to cut oil appearance- Makes 2 cups.

(MAYONNAISE-BASED DRESSINGS) May substitute sour cream for mayonnaise

THOUSAND ISLAND
1 cup rnayonnaise, 1/4 cup chili sauce, 2 hard-cooked eggs, chopped, 2 T. each, chopped green pepper and chopped celery. 11/2 T. minced onion, 1 t. paprika, mix well.

BLUE CHEESE
½ cup mayonnaise, ½ cup sour cream, 2 oz. crumbled blue cheese, dash of nutmeg, mix well. May add 2 T. grated onion,, ½ t. garlic powder.

FRUIT DRESSING
1 cup marshmallow creme, 1 T. each lemon and orange juice, whip until fluffy, fold in 1/2 cup mayonnaise.

FRUIT DRESSING #2
1 cup mayonnaise, 1/4 cup cranberry juice, mix well.

(OTHER DRESSINGS)

FRENCH DRESSING
Combine in jar, 1/2 cup salad oil, 2 T. salad vinegar, 2 T. lemon juice, 1 t. sugar, 2 t. salt, ½ t. dry mustard, ½ t. paprika and a dash of cayenne. Shake well before using.

ITALIAN DRESSING
Combine in jar, 1 cup salad oil, 1/4 cup salad vinegar, 1/2 t. salt, ½ t. white pepper. 1/2 t. celery salt, 1/4 t. cayenne, 1/4 t ^{d}ry mustard, I minced clove of garlic and dash of pepper sauce. Shake well before serving.

RANCH DRESSING MIX
2 T, each, dried parsley flakes, Season salt & Accent (optional). 1 T. each,

garlic powder, onion powder, & black pepper, ground.   Add 2 packages dry, unsweetened Kool-Aid lemonade mix.   Store in airtight container.   Using equal parts buttermilk and mayonnaise, use 1 t. mix per 1 cup of liquid ingredients.   May add more mix to taste.

ORIENTAL DRESSING
1 cup salad oil, ½ cup sugar, ½ cup catsup, ¼ cup rice wine vinegar or cider vinegar, 2 t. Worcestershire sauce, 2 T. minced onion, 1 t. soy sauce, scant 1/8 t. sesame seed oil.   Shake well before serving.   Makes a good marinade, also.

HONEY DRESSING
1 to 2 T. olive oil, 1 T. honey, 2 T. lemon juice, dash of salt or soy sauce.

MAPLE SYRUP DRESSING
¾ cup olive oil, ¾ cup wine vinegar, 6 T. maple syrup, ½ t. salt or soy sauce, 1/8   cup dry mustard, ¼ cup minced onion, ½ t. garlic powder.   Shake well.

GARLIC BREAD SPREAD
6 cups shredded Mozzarella Cheese (at room temperature)
1 1/2 cups grated Parmesan Cheese
1 1/2 cups grated Romano Cheese
1 Tbsp coarse ground black pepper
1 cup minced garlic
1 cup Extra Virgin Olive Oil
2 tsp freshly squeezed lemon juice
In a large mixing bowl, add 3 cups Mozzarella Cheese and half of the remaining ingredients. Using a large spatula, fold until all is blended. Repeat with remaining ingredients. Put into sterilized pint Mason jars. Put on sterilized lids and bands. Keep refrigerated. Refrigerator life is only about two months.
Makes about 5 - 6 pints

ROSE PETAL VINEGAR
2 cups white wine vinegar (heat to near boil)
1 cup rose petals (white ends removed)
3 or 4 whole cloves

Gently crush the petals to bruise a bit. In a sterilized canning jar, place the rose petals and cloves. Pour hot vinegar over top, roughly mash the petals with a wooden spoon and seal. Set aside for 10 days at room temperature and in the dark. Shake once a day. Strain vinegar and discard the cloves and rose petals.

HUMMUS   1
1 16oz can chick peas (garbanzo beans)
1/2 cup sesame seeds
3 tbsp lemon juice
1 clove garlic
cayenne pepper to taste
black pepper to taste
parsley to taste
1. Put chick pea liquid, garlic and sesame seeds in blender on high.
2. Add chick peas and lemon juice. Blend until creamy.
3. Add cayenne pepper, black pepper and parsley. Blend for a second to mix in.

HUMMUS   2
1 (12 oz.) can garbanzo (chick peas) beans
1 clove garlic
2 tbsp. extra virgin olive oil
2-3 tbsp. tahini sauce (sesame paste)
juice of 1 small lemon
1/2 tsp. salt

Drain 1/3 of the water from the can of garbanzo beans into a small bowl. Set aside for later use.
In a blender, mix together the garbanzo beans with the remaining can water and the rest of the ingredients.
Blend for 1-2 minutes until a smooth, slightly fluid paste is formed.

If desired, add small amount of the saved can water and blend to create a more fluid consistency.

CHICK PEA DIP - HUMMUS   3
1 (1 lb.) can chick peas, drained
1/4 c. vegetable oil
3 tbsp. lemon juice
1 lg. or 2 sm. cloves of garlic
Salt and pepper to taste

Put all ingredients into blender. Blend on high speed until smooth. Chill in serving dish. Serve with raw vegetables.

BAKED BEAN CASSEROLE

Navy or Great Northern beans are usually used for baking, although other types or combinations make a great pot of beans. Sort and wash 1 lb. dry beans, cover with cold water in a kettle with room for expansion. Bring to a boil and boil for about 3 minutes to soften skins. Remove from heat, drain, cover with more water and let soak for a few hours or overnight, making sure there is enough water to keep the beans covered. Drain, add fresh water, drain again, cover with fresh water and simmer until tender, about 1 hour. Transfer beans to Dutch oven or bean pot, saving juice to add as needed. Add ½ pound of chopped ham, bacon or salt pork, 1 large chopped onion, ½ cup brown sugar, 3 T. molasses, 1 t. salt, (unless you used salt pork) and ½ t dry mustard. Stir gently to distribute ingredients. Add enough of the bean liquid to just barely cover beans. Cover and bake slowly for 4 to 5 hours, 300 degree oven is fine. Check occasionally, adding more bean liquid or water to prevent drying out. Uncover container during last hour of baking.

SCALLOPED ONIONS

This dish may be made 1 day ahead, covered and refrigerated until 30 rninutes before serving. Bake an additional 15 minutes to thoroughly heat.

Peel 2 pounds small onions, (best done under running water to prevent tears) cover with salted water and cook 5 minutes or just until tender. Drain.

Melt ¼ cup butter or margarine in saucepan, add 1/4 cup flour, blend until smooth. Cook 5 minutes but do not brown. add 2 cups milk, slowly, stirring constantly, add 1/2 t. salt and ¾ t. pepper. Stir in 1 cup grated Cheddar cheese (may use any cheese you like, actually), stir until melted. Add ¼ cup chopped pimento pepper and ¾ cup chopped parsley. Mix well, pour over onions in a casserole dish. Mix 1/2 cup bread or cornflake crumbs with ¼ cup soft butter or margarine, sprinkle as a border around the edges.   Bake in 375 degree oven for 25 minutes.

ONION SHORTCAKE (actually very good)

Melt 2 or 3 T butter or margarine, add 2 or 3 large sliced onions and cook until golden and tender.   Make shortcake of:

1 ½ cups flour

2 t. baking powder

1/2 t. salt

3 T. shortening

parmesan cheese (optional)

Add enough milk to the above ingredients to make a stiff dough. Spread out dough in greased 8" x 8" pan. Pour onions on top of   batter. mix 1 small egg with ½ cup sour cream, pour over onions, bake at 350 degrees about 25 minutes.

CORN PUDDING

Combine 3 eggs, 2 cups drained cooked or canned whole kernel corn, 2 cups milk, ½ cup finely chopped onion, 1 T. melted butter or margarine, 1 t. salt and 1 t. sugar.   Pour into greased casserole.   Set in shallow pan filled within 1 inch of top with hot water.   Bake at 350 degrees F for 40 to 45 minutes.   Let stand 10 minutes at room temperature, center will firm up.   Serve.

FRIED SQUASH BLOSSOMS

Pick only the outer portion of the squash flower; leaving the center and stem on the plant, or only pick the flowers without small squash on them. Rinse flowers lightly and pat dry. Make a batter of beaten egg with enough flour added for body. Dip flowers in batter and fry in hot oil, turning once. Season to taste and serve.   For extra crunchy, use cornstarch.

May also dip slices of squash in the batter and fry. Slice the squash quite thin for a delicate taste treat. Try other vegetables, also.

SWISS ONION PIE

Chop 5   medium onions and saute in butter or margarine until golden and tender. Mix 1 pint small curd cottage cheese, 1/4 pound grated Swiss cheese; 3 eggs. slightly beaten; 1/2 cup milk, ½ t. salt, ½ cup cracker or bread crumbs,   together.   Add sautéed onions, pour into unbaked pie shell.   Bake at 375 degrees F.   for 30 to 35   minutes; until golden brown and filling is firmish. Let pie sit for 10 minutes before serving.   Filling will firm up as it cools.

SUMMER SQUASH CASSEROLE

Cook 6 cups sliced squash (yellow., zucchini or your favorite), with ½ cup chopped onion in small amount of water until well blanched. Drain.
Mix 1 can cream of chicken soup with 1 cup sour cream; stir in the squash and onion mixture, 1 cup shredded carrot. I 8-oz. package herb seasoned stuffing mix combined with ½ cup melted margarine, spread ½ of stuffing in bottom of baking dish. Spoon vegetable mixture on top. Sprinkle rest of stuffing over

vegetables. Bake at 350 degrees for 20 to 25 minutes.   I like to add a cup of shredded cheddar cheese to this while mixing, then sprinkle some on top before baking.

GHEVETCH

Mix together and place in 9 x 13 baking dish,   1 cup thinly sliced carrots; 1 cup green beans, ½ cup sliced celery; 1 cup diced potatoes. 2 medium tomatoes quartered, 1 yellow squash, sliced; 1 zucchini, sliced, 1 large onion, sliced, 1 head cauliflower, broke in pieces, 1/4 cup julienne strips green bell pepper and red pepper, ½ cup peas. Make sauce of following ingredients and pour over the vegetables. 1 cup beef bouillon, ½ cup olive oil; 3 crushed garlic cloves, 2. salt, 1 bay leaf, crumbled, ½ t. savory; ¼ t. tarragon. Cover tightly with foil. bake about 1 hour, 5 minutes; stir occasionally. 1 cup of mushrooms may also be added to the vegetable mixture This is a good way to use a little bit of almost everything in the garden, or leftovers.

ONION   PATTIES

Mix together ¾ cup flour, 2 t baking powder, 1 T sugar (optional)1 t salt, 1 T cornmeal and ½ cup dry powdered milk.   Stir in enough cold water to make a thick batter.   Add 2 ½ cups finely chopped onions and drop by teaspoonfuls into hot grease.   Flatten patties slightly as you turn them, fry until browned and serve.

STUFFED   ZUCCHINI   - CABBAGE - GREEN PEPPERS

2 medium zucchini or 1 large or 4 small cabbage heads   or   4 green peppers. Split zucchini   in half, lengthwise, remove entire core of cabbage, loose heads work best, or remove tops around shoulders of peppers. Steam vegetables until almost as well-done as you like that vegetable. I don't precook the peppers at all. While vegetable is steaming, make stuffing. Brown ½ pound hamburger, add ½ cup chopped onion, cook until tender, drain fat from pan. Add 1 can tomatoes (about 1 ½ cups) chopped, 1/2 cup chopped celery, 2 T. tomato paste or 1 8 oz. can tomato sauce and 2 cups cooked rice. Salt and pepper to taste, may add garlic salt. Cook quickly to reduce any liquid so mixture will hold together. Remove centers of zucchini, leaving 1 ½ inch shell, chop center and add to stuffing, mound stuffing into zucchini shells, top with shredded cheese and bake. Place cabbage upside down in dish, pull out center, stuff and bake. Fill peppers with stuffing top with cheese and bake each until cheese melts. KARA'S ALTERNATE STUFFING.   Use cooked diced chicken, diced onion added to cheesy rice while it is cooking.   Add the chicken and mound in the green peppers. Halfway full, add a piece of your favorite cheese, finish filling and add more grated cheese on top.   Bake just until cheese is melted and bubbly.   Pepper shell should still be crunchy and just hot.

GREEN BEAN CASSEROLE

Drain 2 cans, about 4 cups, green beans or use leftover green beans. place in casserole dish, alternating with layers of undiluted mushroom soup and grated cheddar cheese. Top with cheese and sprinkle crushed potato chips or French fried onions around edge. Bake at 325 degrees until cheese melts and casserole is bubbly.   May substitute other cream soup for cream of mushroom, if you want to.

CABBAGE WITH SOUR CREAM AND BACON

Fry ½ pound of bacon until crisp, set aside. Drain most of the grease from the pan. add 1 medium head cabbage, sliced, 2 sliced potatoes, 2 sliced carrots, sprinkle with 2 T. flour, pour 1 ½ cups boiling water; 3 T. vinegar, over vegetable mixture, salt and pepper to taste. Stir well, cover and cook slowly until vegetables are almost tender, place in casserole and top with ½ pint sour cream and the bacon, crumbled. Bake at 325 degrees F. for 20 minutes.

.

CHEESE FROSTED CAULIFLOWER

Trim whole head of cauliflower, remove center of core, but leave whole, steam until almost done, carefully place in oven-proof serving dish. Sprinkle 1 cup shredded cheddar cheese over entire head, bake, covered without touching, for 5 minutes, or long enough for the cheese to melt but not run, serve. May also mix ½ cup mayonnaise with 2 T. prepared mustard, spread over steamed head, sprinkle with the cheese and bake at 375 degrees F. until cheese is bubbly. Serve.

FRIED GREEN TOMATOES
Although this is commonly thought of as a Southern dish, the first recipe for it apparently appeared in 1870 in New York City. Basically, you slice three large green tomatoes into one quarter inch thick slices and pat them dry.
Prepare three plates: one containing a half a cup of plain flour; another with two hand beaten eggs and a half a cup of buttermilk, and a third with a quarter cup of flour and a half a cup of corn meal.
Dip each slice in the plate of flour, then the beaten egg/buttermilk, then the cornmeal/flour mix. Make sure both sides of each slice are well covered.
Meanwhile, have a few slices of bacon frying. When done, remove the bacon and drain the grease into a bowl.
Sparingly use the bacon grease to fry the coated tomatoes until they are a golden crispy color on both sides. Serve hot. You can, of course, use oil, spray or butter, instead of bacon grease.

GLAZED CARROTS OR SWEET POTATOES

Steam or boil 7 or 8 carrots, or 2 or 3 sweet potatoes, sliced, until almost tender. Drain. Combine 1 T. sugar, 1 t. cornstarch, 1/4 t. salt, 1/4 t. ground ginger (optional) 1/4 cup orange juice in a small pan. Bring to a boil, stirring constantly, until thickened. Toss with vegetables and serve.

May use brown sugar instead of white sugar, for a different flavor. Increase to 3 T., omit ginger, use 1/4 cup water or cooking liquid instead of orange juice. After cooking sauce, add 1 T. butter or margarine.

I like rice and also, quinoa. Quinoa may be used in place of rice in almost any recipe. Here are a bunch of Rice Recipes.

MEXICAN OR SPANISH RICE
1 c plain white rice, uncooked
1/4 c diced tomatoes
1 tsp onion powder
1 T. margarine
2 cups chicken broth
1/8 tsp minced green pepper
2 T. oil or melted fat
In a 2 qt pan over med heat, heat oil and margarine together to melt and blend. Add rice, stir and saute until tan, about 3 min. Add onion powder (garlic powder if you added it too; or 1/2 c minced fresh onion). Cook and stir another 5 min. Add broth, bring to a boil without stirring over med heat. When it boils, lower heat to low, gently stir in tomatoes and green peppers. Cover and simmer until liquid is absorbed, 15-18 min. Remove from heat, fluff with a fork, then put lid back on and steam off heat fo0r 5 min before serving.

MEXICAN RICE, (everything to taste)
1 head garlic chopped onion
bouillon powder, herbs, spices, tomato paste
salt & pepper, cumin
chili powder
1 T. oil, green onions, chopped
juice of 2-3 limes, cut up tomatoes
chopped fresh parsley

Wash rice, put in a pot with required water. Add remaining ingredients. Cover rice, bring to boil, then lower heat and cook until rice is done, about 30-40 min.

MEXICALI RICE (easy)
1 c rice
2 c water
1 T. butter
1 – 2 onions
2-4 large cloves garlic
1 small can tomato paste
1 meat flavored bouillon cube
seasoned salt, chili pepper, etc
Put all ingredients in pan, bring to a boil. Lower heat, simmer until rice is done (20 min.). Stir in more water if needed.

May substitute Quinoa for rice in any of these recipes.   Same measurements.

RICE PILAF (8 servings)
2 cups rice
2/3 stick margarine
4 cups liquid (chicken broth; beef broth)
3/4 cup chopped celery
3/4 cup chopped carrots
3/4 cup chopped green onions
1 cup slivered almonds
salt and pepper to taste
Brown rice lightly with butter in a skillet. Place in casserole with boiling broth. Cover and bake for 1/2 hour at 375 deg. Take from oven and add vegetables and nuts, stirring and mixing well with fork. Return to oven for 1/2 hour.

BROWNED RICE 6-8 servings
1 cup rice
1/4 cup shortening
1/4 c each - chopped onion, meat, celery
½ tsp salt
other vegetables 3 1/2 cups water
Heat shortening in a skillet. add rice. Cook, stirring constantly, about 10 minutes or
until lightly browned. Add vegetables and continue cooking 2-3 minutes. Add

salt and water. Simmer over low heat 20 to 25 min. or until rice is tender and excess liquid has evaporated.

RICE WITH PEAS
1 cup rice
3 cups hot water
3 cups cooked new peas
2 tablespoons   butter
4 teaspoons flour
1/3 cup milk
Wash the rice thoroughly, drain, add the hot water and let boil gently until the water is evaporated and the rice looks dry; then cover, and set on the edge of the
stove to steam for 15 minutes. Rub the butter and the flour together in a small saucepan, add the milk, and stir over the fire until smooth. Add the cooked rice, and mix with a fork; then add the cooked new peas, mix lightly, put into the oven in a covered dish until hot through, and serve.

RICE MILK
4 cups hot/warm water
1 cup cooked rice (I've used white or brown)
1 tsp vanilla
Place all ingredients in a blender and blend until smooth. Let the milk set for about 30 minutes, then without shaking pour the milk into another container (I use an old honey jar) leaving most of the sediment in the first container. This makes about 4 - 4 1/2 cups. Notes: When I have used cold water and the rice was taken out of the refrigerator, it just doesn't come out that well. I don't know why but its best to use warm water and warm rice (you can nuke it if its leftovers but freshly made is best) I have even let it set longer than 30 minutes (overnight) without it making a difference.

RICE MILK, COMPLICATED
Rinse 2 cups of rice (to clean it). Pour 4 cups of boiling water over rice and let

it soak for 1-2 hours. Blend 1 cup of soaked rice with 2 1/2 cups of water (can be cold water). Blend rice to a slurry, not a completely smooth liquid. Pour into a pot & repeat with the rest of the rice. Bring to a boil & then reduce to low heat simmer for 20 minutes. Line colander with nylon tricot or a few layers of cheesecloth. Pour rice mixture into colander with a bowl under colander. Another 1 cup of water (more or less) can be poured over the rice. Press with the back of a large spoon twist nylon & squeeze out as much liquid as possible. This milk is very plain and can be flavored with oil, vanilla, salt, etc.

FANCY RICE MILK
Rice milk is a good substitute for milk in coffee drinks.
2/3 c. hot rice 3 c. hot water
1/3 c. cashews 1 tsp. vanilla
1/4 tsp. salt 2 tbsp. honey
Blend all ingredients, chill and serve. Servings: 4.

HORCHATA
This is a Mexican rice water or rice milk. It is a dessert.
1 cup rice, washed, 2 quarts water
1 cinnamon stick, Sugar to taste
Mix together all ingredients; let stand 3 hours. Simmer for 1/2 hour. Puree in a blender and strain through a cloth. Taste for sweetness and add sugar if necessary.
Chill and serve over ice.

RICE MILK, PLAIN
A good way to make rice milk is to use fresh rice that is still hot.
1 c rice, (short grain is best)   4 c hot water (cold water & cold rice won't work)
1 tsp vanilla
Put all in blender, puree for about 5 minutes (until smooth) let sit for 30 minutes or longer, then without shaking pour into container being careful not to let the
sediments at the bottom pour into the new container. Alternatively, if you are in a hurry strain through cheesecloth. To complicate things and get a smoother milk, re-cook the rice with part of the water until it's very soft. Add salt and sweeteners, soaked, blanched almonds or nuts and flavorings. Then run it through a blender, food processor, or juicer.

RICE, WHITE
2 cups water one-half teaspoon salt

1 cup of rice
Simmer gently covered (do not stir) 15-20 minutes.

RICE, CINNAMON
1 C Long Grain Converted Rice
1/4 C Raisins
1 Tsp. Cinnamon
Dash of Salt
2 1/2 C Water
1/2 Tbs. Sugar -- to taste
Milk & Butter to taste
Heat water to boiling. Add rice mixture and lower heat. Cook until rice is
tender.
Add butter and milk. Serve. This may be prepared ahead of time by combining
all ingredients except the margarine and milk and storing in a bag.

RICE MIX, CHICKEN FLAVORED
4 C Long Grain Rice
1 Tsp. Salt
2 Tsp. Dried Parsley flakes
4 Tbs. Chicken Bouillon -- instant
2 Tsp. Dried Tarragon
1/4 Tsp. White Pepper
Combine all dry ingredients in a large bowl. Stir until evenly distributed. Store
in a cool, dry place and use within 6 to 8 months. Makes about 4 cups of mix.
Use 1 cup of mix to 2 cups of water to cook.

RICE MIX, DILL LEMON
4 C Long Grain Rice
4 Tsp. Dill Weed Or Dill Seed
8 Tsp. Chicken Bouillon – dried
5 Tsp. Lemon Peel -- grated, dried
1 Tsp. Salt
Combine all ingredients in a large bowl and blend well. Put 1-1/2 cups of mix
into 3 pint airtight containers and label. Store in a cool, dry place and use
within 6 to 8
months. Makes about 4-1/2 cups of mix. 1 cup mix - 2 cups water, cook.

CHEESE & RICE
4 1/2 Oz Dehydrated Cheddar Cheese

3 3/4 Oz Instant Rice
2 Tbsp Margarine, Salt -- to taste
3 C Water
Bring water to a boil and add rice and salt. Simmer until rice is tender. Stir in cheese and margarine. Cover the pot and let stand a couple of minutes to rehydrate the cheese. Makes about 4 cups.

RICE WITH LENTILS
1/2 c dried lentils
2-3 T. oil
¼ to ½ tsp salt
 1 1/2 c water
3/4 c rice
Wash dried lentils & soak them for 2 hours. Drain. Bring water, salt, and oil to boil in saucepan. Add rice and soaked lentils. Cover saucepan tightly and reduce heat to low. Cook for 20 minutes.

SPANISH RICE
1 1/4 cups water
1/2 – 3/4 cups cooked tomatoes &
3/4 cups juice
1 T. oil, chili powder to taste
salt & pepper to taste
chopped onions
Cook rice in water. When almost soft, add other ingredients and heat through.

RICE & PASTA
2-3 tsp curry powder
20 strands spaghetti, broken into 1/2 inch strands
2 T. butter
3/4 c rice, washed
1 med onion, chopped
2 cups water, 1 chicken bouillon cube
Melt butter and sauté all ingredients except water and cube in a med. sized sauce pot for 5 min over medium heat. Add 2 cups water, cube, stir, cover and cook on low heat until done, about 10 min. Serves 2-3.

FRIED RICE
3 c cooked rice
3 eggs

2 T. oil
1/3 c green onions, chopped
Heat oil in a pot and add the rice. Stir until rice is well coated. Add onions and stir. Form a well in the center of the rice and crack the 3 eggs in the well. Wait until the eggs are partially set and toss until they are finished cooking. 4 servings.   Or scrape rice to one side of pan, pour beaten eggs in cleared area, cook until set, turn and cut into small pieces with spatula.   Stir into rest of rice and add soy sauce to taste.

INDIAN FRIED RICE
1 c cooked rice
2 T. oil
1 onion, chopped
1/2 tsp cumin seeds
1/2 tsp turmeric powder
salt & cayenne pepper
coriander leaves
lemon juice
Heat oil in a pot. Add cumin seed & turmeric to hot oil. Sprinkle cayenne and salt on cooked rice. Add onions to the oil and fry for a few min so the onions are soft. Add the rice, to the oil and stir until the rice is coated, yellow and hot. Garnish with coriander leaves and sprinkle lemon juice on top if desired. Also good with yogurt. Makes 1 cup rice.

CURRIED FRIED RICE
3 c cooked rice
1 small cabbage, chopped
1 onion, fine chopped
4-5 fine chopped carrots
2-3 eggs
2 chopped green peppers
1-2 T curry powder
4 T oil
1 bouillon cube
Heat oil in skillet, stir fry vegetables, adding onions and carrots first. Cook until tender but not mushy. Add curry and other seasonings, mixing well. Add rice and fry until hot and mixed with vegetables. Eggs can either be scrambled

separately and added to rice or fried and eaten with rice.

MUTHYA
1 c cooked rice
1 small piece of ginger, minced
1/2 c wheat flour
½ tsp salt
1/2 c bean flour
1/2 tsp turmeric
1 onion, chopped
1 T. oil
hot pepper, chopped & seeded (to taste)
1 T. milk or yogurt
Mix rice, flours, vegetables and spices together. Add oil and milk. Add more milk if needed to make a manageable but not sticky dough. Form into sausage like shapes (about the size of a D battery) with your hands. You should get 8-10 muthyas. Place a metal colander in a pot with boiling water (to steam them) and place muthyas in colander. Cover and steam until hard, about 30 min. Add more water if levels get too low. These are good plain or dipped in sauce, such as garlic butter.

VEGETARIAN JAMBALAYA
3 c cooked rice
2 large tomatoes, peeled & chopped
1 med onion, diced
1/2 tsp paprika
2 1/2 c mushrooms (optional)
2 TB parsley
2 TB butter
oregano to taste
2 med green peppers, chopped
sweet basil to taste
1 stalk celery, chopped (optional)
thyme to taste
1/2 c melted butter
Saute onion and mushrooms, if available in butter until onion is transparent. Combine all vegetables with the rice. Add seasonings and butter and mix well. Place in a 1 quart pan and bake covered until desired consistency.

RICE CAKES
2 c cooked rice
1/4 tsp salt
1/2 c flour
1/2 tsp baking powder
2 T sugar
1 beaten egg
Combine all dry ingredients, mix well. Add egg and stir with fork until all grains
are coated. Shape into cakes about 2 inches in diameter and 1/4 inch thick.
Coat sides with extra flour, place in hot oil and sauté on both sides until light
brown. Serve plain or with jelly and butter.

CURRIED RICE
2 med onions , chopped
2 c water
1 large apple, chopped
1/4 tsp salt, opt
2 1/2 TB curry powder or to taste
1 c raw rice
1/2 tsp cayenne or to taste
peanuts, raisins
1 tsp cumin or to taste butter or oil
Simmer apple & onions in butter or oil. Add curry, cayenne, and cumin to taste.
Simmer until brown. Add remaining ingredients. Bring to boil, cover, lower
heat and cook until rice is done, about 20 min. Serve with yogurt.

RIZ CREOLE
oil
1 tomato, sliced
1 onion, sliced
salt, pepper to taste
1 small can tomato paste
2 c uncooked rice
1 can mushrooms, drained
3 portions of Vach Qui Rit (small soft cheese rounds "The Laughing Cow" in
USA)
1 can peas, drained
1 TB butter

4 c water

Heat a thin film of oil in pot with a tight lid. Saute onions; add 2 tsp tomato paste and mushrooms and cook 2 min. Add peas, tomato, salt and pepper. Cover and simmer 3-4 min. Pour 4 c water into pot, salt and bring it to a boil. Add rice. Once rice boils again, add cheese and butter. Stir. Cover tightly and cook over low heat 15 min until water is absorbed.

RICE PILAF

1/4 – 1/2 c butter or oil

1 3/4 to 2 c chicken broth, made with bouillon okay

2 c　rice

2 1/4 c tomato juice (or paste + water)

pinch sugar

Saute rice in butter or oil until golden. Mix with other ingredients in an oven safe casserole. Cover and bake about 45 min at 375. Fluff and let sit covered 5 min before serving.

CHICKEN – RICE PILAF (good with leftover chicken)

1 T. butter

1 can whole tomatoes (800 ml)

3 T. chopped onion

1 1/2 c cooked diced chicken　　`1q

1 T. chopped parsley

1 bay leaf

1 c rice

1/2 tsp tarragon

salt, pepper

　1/2 c peas

Saute onion in butter. Add rice and brown for 3 min. Add salt, pepper, tomatoes, chicken, spices and bouillon. Bring to boil and lower heat. Let simmer covered for about 10 min; 5 min before rice is done, add peas & parsley. Stir with a fork.

PAELLA

1/4 c olive oil

10 slices chorizo or any hard, spicy sausage

3 cloves garlic

2 c　rice

1 chicken, cooked, cut in chunks

4 c hot chicken bouillon

1 can drained peas
saffron (1/4 to 2 tsp)
10 raw shrimp
20 clams, washed, in shells
Heat oil & garlic in a deep large casserole. Remove garlic and add rice. Cook until lightly browned. Add bouillon and saffron. Add sausage. Place chicken on top of mixture, cover and bake at 350 for about 30 min to heat through. Remove from oven, stir in peas. Place shrimp and clams on top. Cover, return to oven and steam another 10 min or until seafood is done and all clams have opened. If clams are unavailable, add more chicken and shrimp.

CHINESE RESTAURANT WHITE RICE
1 c rice
2 c water
1 Tbsp oil
1 Tbsp lemon juice
1 splash white vinegar (or rice vinegar)
Put it all in a pot, and bring to a boil. Stir once, reduce heat to a simmer, and cover. Simmer until all the water is absorbed, about 20 minutes. Remove from heat and let rest 5 minutes. Fluff with fork, and serve.

CHICKEN-FLAVORED RICE MIX
4 c uncooked long grain rice
1 tsp salt
2 tsp dried parsley flakes
4 Tbsp instant chicken bouillon
2 tsp dried tarragon
1/4 tsp white pepper
Combine all ingredients in a large bowl. Stir until evenly distributed.
Put about 1 1/3 cups into three 1-pint containers, and label as Chicken-Flavored Rice Mix. Store in a cool, dry place, and use within 6 to 8 months.
Makes about 4 cups of mix.

CHICKEN-FLAVORED RICE: Using Mix above
Mix 1 1/3 cups chicken-flavored rice mix with 2 cups cold water and 1 tablespoon butter or margarine in a medium saucepan. Bring water to a boil over high heat. Cover and reduce the heat, and cook for 15 to 25 minutes, until liquid is absorbed.

Makes 4 to 6 servings.

THAI RICE
I c rice
2 c liquid (water, broth, etc.)
1 Tbsp fat (oil, butter, etc.)
1/4 c chopped onion
1 Tbsp chili powder
1 Tbsp cilantro
1 tsp ginger
1/8 tsp turmeric
2 Tbsp lime juice
1/4 c roasted peanuts
Put everything EXCEPT the lime juice and peanuts in a pot. Bring to a boil.
Stir once, reduce heat to simmer, and cover. Let simmer until water is absorbed,
about 20 minutes. Remove from heat, and let sit 5 minutes. Stir in lime juice
and roasted peanuts, and serve.

YELLOW RICE - SPANISH STYLE
1 c rice
2 c liquid (water, broth, etc.)
1 Tbsp fat (oil, butter, etc.)
1 packet Goya brand "sazon con cilantro y achiote"
(Optional):
1 (15 oz) can green peas
1 c meat or poultry pieces, cut up, cubed, or just throw the meat in the pot
whole
Put it all in a pot; bring to boil. Stir once, reduce heat to simmer, and cover.
Cook until all the water is absorbed, about 20 minutes. Remove from heat, and
let sit 5 minutes. Fluff with fork and serve.

CURRY RICE
1 c rice
2 c liquid (water, broth, etc.)
1 Tbsp fat (oil, butter, etc.) 1 c chopped carrots
1 chopped onion 2 cloves garlic, minced
1 tsp curry powder 1/8 tsp pepper
1 Tbsp lemon juice (Optional) 1 lb shrimp, chicken cubes, etc.
Put it all in a pot; bring to boil. Stir once, reduce heat to simmer, cover. Simmer
until water is absorbed, about 20 minutes. Let sit 5 minutes. Fluff with fork and

serve.

CURRIED RICE WITH CHICK PEAS
1 c rice
2 c liquid (water, broth, etc.)
1 Tbsp fat (oil, butter, etc.)
1 tsp cilantro
1/2 tsp cardamom
1/2 tsp turmeric
1/2 tsp hot pepper sauce dash salt
1/8 tsp cinnamon
1 c chopped carrots
1 (15 oz) can chick peas, rinsed and drained
1 c peas
2 Tbsp mint OR parsley
Put everything EXCEPT the chick peas and mint in a pot. Bring to a boil. Stir
once, reduce heat, let simmer about 20 minutes, until the water is absorbed.
Remove from heat, and let rest 5 minutes. Stir in chick peas, sprinkle mint on
top, and serve.

SOY SAUCED RICE
1 c rice
2 Tbsp cooking oil
garlic powder onion powder
(optional) bouillon 3 Tbsp soy sauce with half teaspoon vinegar (in place of
lemon juice) salt to taste
(optional) parsley flakes
NOTE: You can boil bouillon with the rice, but omit salt as package suggested.
Cook rice according to package, except omit butter. You can adjust saltiness
later. In a non-stick skillet (preferably), heat cooking oil. Add cooked rice,
garlic, onion powder, and the soy sauce-vinegar mixture, and keep stirring. The
amount of soy sauce can be adjusted to suit how dark you want your rice to be.
Cook for 5 minutes, and add parsley flakes (if desired).
Serve this with any meat, beans, and veggies on the side.

PANTRY RISOTTO No heavy cream needed.

1 c rice
3 2/3 c chicken broth
1 Tbsp fat (or non-stick spray)
1/2 tsp white pepper
1 1/2 c fresh spinach
1/2 c peas
1 tsp dill
1/2 c grated Parmesan cheese
1 tsp grated lemon peel

In a medium saucepan, bring broth and pepper to simmer. In the large saucepan, either use cooking spray or butter to grease the bottom. Put in the dry, uncooked rice. Cook and stir it for 1 minute. Stir in 2/3 cup of the broth - cook and stir until the broth is absorbed. Do the remaining broth, 1/2 cup at a time, waiting till one batch of broth is absorbed before adding the next. With the last 1/2 cup of broth, stir in the spinach, peas, and dill. Cook, stirring gently, until all the liquid is absorbed, and the rice is tender but firm to the bite. (Total time for adding broth is about 40 minutes.)
Remove saucepan from heat. Stir in cheese and lemon peel.

SPICY PEANUT BUTTER RICE
1 c rice
2 1/2 c liquid (chicken broth preferred)
1 Tbsp fat (oil, butter, etc.)
1 onion, sliced
1/2 c raisins
 3 Tbsp peanut butter
1 Tbsp honey
1 tsp curry powder
1/4 tsp salt
1/4 tsp ginger
1/4 tsp cinnamon

Sauté onion. Put all ingredients in a saucepan. Stir it so the sticky ingredients are sort of blended in. Bring to boil. Stir once, reduce heat, cover, and simmer about 20 minutes, until the rice is done. Remove from heat, let rest 5 minutes. Fluff with fork and serve.

BAKED RICE
1 can cream of mushroom soup*

1 can consommé*
1 c white rice
Mix, pour into greased casserole, bake at 350° F for one hour to one hour fifteen minutes. *Really good with ham or stuffed green peppers.*Cream of mushroom soup can be changed to any cream of and/or the substitute for creamed soups.   *You can use a bouillon cube and boiling water for the consommé.

CHILI RICE - A ONE-DISH MEAL (2 VERSIONS)
1 c converted rice
1 can Vienna sausages (or 1/2 can Spam, or ham(opt)
1 can corn kernels
1 c canned/cooked kidney beans
1/2 tsp garlic powder
1/2 tsp onion powder
1/2 tsp chili powder
1/4 tsp ground cumin
1 c cut-up canned tomatoes
2 Tbsp cooking oil
VERSION 1:
Cook rice according to package directions. (Note: If using any canned veggies, you can use the liquid from these veggies to add to the water needed to cook the rice. This not only helps you save water, but also uses the nutrients found in those liquids.)
In a non-stick pan, heat the cooking oil, and sort of brown the meat on all sides. Add the tomatoes, and let simmer for 5 minutes. Add the rest of the ingredients, including the cooked rice, and keep simmering and stirring for another 5 minutes. Serve.
VERSION 2: (Much simpler and more into fuel-conservation!)
In a non-stick pan, heat oil and brown meat on all sides. Add tomatoes, and simmer for 5 minutes. Add un-cooked Uncle Ben's rice, and necessary amount of liquid to cook it. Add everything else, and cook rice in this mixture.
NOTE: You have to cook this dish following the directions on rice package, as far as covering the pan, so rice will cook properly.

20 MINUTE SUPPER
This recipe was made in desperation... nothing interesting in the fridge to make after being out all day, but my kids love it!

Bring four cups of water and 2 packages dried onion soup mix to boil. Add four cups instant rice, and set aside to do its thing. In a frying pan, brown 1/2 lb hamburger (or more if you have it). I also shred a couple of carrots into this to get veggies into the family. Add burger to rice and stir... very filling!
*Can have a green veggie with it, and maybe homemade pudding, because a meal with dessert always seems better.
*Very cheap if you don't put the meat in, and use dried soup.
*Can be made with real rice - if I have time, I put the rice/soup mix in my rice cooker or Dutch Oven.

DIRTY RICE
1 pound smoked bacon diced
1 tub of chicken liver, cleaned
2 large onions
1 red pepper
1 green pepper
6 ribs of celery diced
2-3 Tbls. chopped garlic
3 C. uncooked rice
6-7 cups broth, we use chicken
Cacheris Cajun seasoning

In a 6 quart iron dutch oven cook and brown your bacon, remove to a bowl. Add the veggies to the bacon drippings and cook till just tender. Add the chicken livers and cook until no longer pink inside, mash while cooking, mash to an almost pureed consistancy add Tony Cacheries seasoning to your taste. Add the bacon back to the veggie and meat mixture.
Add rice to meat and veggies, add 6 1/2 cups of broth and stir well.. Bring to a nice simmer and cook for 20 - 30 minutes, check to make sure it isn't too dry, till rice is tender. Check every so often to see if the pan needs more broth, add as needed. Once rice is tender taste and add seasoning as needed. Cover pan and let rest for about 15 minutes.

HASHBROWN CASSEROLE - Copycat
Ingredients
2 lbs frozen hash browns
1/2 cup margarine or butter, melted

1 (10 1/4 ounce) can cream of chicken soup
1 pint sour cream
1/2 cup onion, peeled and chopped
2 cups cheddar cheese, grated
½ teaspoon salt
¼ teaspoon pepper
Directions
1 Preheat oven to 350°F and spray an 11 x 14 baking dish with cooking spray.
2 Mix the above ingredients together, place in prepared pan and bake for 45 minutes or until brown on top.

VEGETARIAN STEW

Make a rich stock by roasting a few vegetables in the oven until well browned.   A good selection would include onions, potatoes, carrots, turnips, sweet potatoes, celery and peppers.   After they are well browned, cover with water and season to taste.   Rosemary, Marjoram, Thyme and a touch of cayenne are all good. Simmer a while to get all the flavor possible out of the vegetables and loose from the pan and strain.   Caramelize one sliced large onion in olive oil while the vegetables roast.   Toss diced assorted vegetables with ½ cup of flour to coat them.   Add more chopped onion and minced garlic to the caramelized onion: add the diced vegetables and cook, stirring, to cook the flour.   Add to the strained broth, adjust the seasonings.   Cook until thick and tender.   A good assortment of diced vegetables is limited only to what you have on hand.   Roasting a few at the start will make a rich tasting broth.

SOUTHERN CORNBREAD DRESSING (A Side Dish)

One large pan of white cornbread, crumbled up fine (you can use yellow cornbread, not quite the same)
1 cup of diced celery, brought to a boil and drained
1 cup diced onion, brought to a boil and drained
4 hard boiled eggs, peeled and sliced
Diced cooked giblets and neck meat (usually turkey)
Melt ½ cup of butter and add to list of ingredients in a large mixing bowl. Add 4 beaten raw eggs and enough broth to make a soupy mess.   Add 2 T coarse ground black pepper and 1 t salt.   Pour into well greased baking dish and bake at 350 degrees F. until puffed up a bit in the middle.

POTATO GNOCCHI   (Great use for leftover mashed potatoes)
Mix:

1 cup flour, 2 cups mashed potatoes and 4 T. butter. Knead until smooth. Divide into 4 equal pieces. Roll each piece out like a pencil, rolling dough back and forth with your hands. Slice into ½ inch pieces. Drop in boiling liquid until pieces rise to the top, stirring once in a while to keep from sticking to bottom of the pan. Let cook a couple of minutes after they have risen, drain. May be served with Alfredo sauce, marinara sauce, or just buttered and sprinkled with garlic.

LEFSE (more mashed potatoes) Similar to flour tortillas
4 cups mashed potatoes, using butter and heavy cream to mash. Mix in 2 scant cups flour and 1 T. sugar. Knead well until it is fairly smooth. Roll out like a log rolling back and forth with your hands. Divide into 14 equal pieces. Roll each out on floured board until very thin. Cook on preheated griddle in oven at 450 to 500 degrees F. When it bubbles, turn and bake on the other side. Watch carefully. Remove and lay between dish towels to cool. Store in a plastic bag when cool. Reheat and serve with melted butter.

CREAM SOUPS & GRAVY

Creamed soups are usually thickened with roux or pureed vegetables or a combination of both. I usually have a container of roux handy to thicken soup, gravy, stew or to add body to any broth.

ROUX

Melt 1 cup plan or butter flavor shortening or clarified butter. Add 1 cup white flour, stirring to blend. Cook slowly over low heat for at least 5 minutes Do not allow to brown for plain roux.

If you wish to make a browned gravy or sauce, allow the flour to brown to the desired color. This adds flavor, but lessens the flours' ability to thicken, so you must use more roux to reach the desired thickness. A dark brown roux is essential to thicken gumbo and adds to the distinctive flavor. Try it in a plain stew for a flavor treat.

CREAMY CHICKEN SOUP MIX

1 cup nonfat dry milk powder

1 T. dried onion flakes

2 T. cornstarch

2 T. chicken boullion powder

1/4 t. pepper, white, if you don't want to see the specks

1/2 t. poultry seasoning

When ready to use, add 2 1/2 cups cold water, stir constantly over medium heat until soup reaches a boil. Optional additions: May add one or any combination of chopped celery, cubed cooked chicken, cubed cooked potatoes, sliced mushrooms, chopped broccoli or grated cheese.

BROCCOLI SOUP (May use Cauliflower it place of Broccoli) A BASIC MIX

Remove florets, set aside. Peel the tougher thick stems, dice, chop the remaining tender stems. Add 1/4 to 1/2 cup chopped onion cover vegetables with water, simmer gently until tender. Fast boiling ruins the flavor and makes bad odors in the kitchen. Mash or puree the simmered vegetables, adding plenty of the cooking water to make a thin soup. Return to saucepan add reserved florets, bring to simmer. Add roux, a small spoonful at a time, blend thoroughly into mixture until it reaches the desired thickness, salt and pepper to taste, garlic optional. Stir in 1/2 to 1 cup evaporated milk or half' n half, heat but do not boil. Serve.

May add shredded cheese with the milk, stirring until melted and blended.

May substitute almost any vegetable for the broccoli, almost all make good cream soup

POTATO SOUP

Use peeled, diced potato in place of broccoli in the above recipe. Mash coarsely if you want chunky soup, puree if you want smooth soup. Serve hot with a pat of butter melting on top, or chilled, with a dollop of sour cream garnish.

CLAM CHOWDER

Make chunky potato soup, adding chopped celery to the potatoes and onions. Add chopped or minced clams and their juices. Add 1/4 to 1/2 cup crisp fried, diced bacon just before serving.

CORN CHOWDER
Make as for clam chowder, except add creamed or whole kernel corn in place of clams.

MUSHROOM SOUP OR GRAVY

Start as for broccoli soup, using mushrooms, sliced or diced. May use chicken broth or beef stock in place of water to simmer mushrooms. Reserve part of the mushrooms before blending, or do not blend at all. Add roux, simmer until thickened to desired consistency. Add milk or wine (white with chicken broth base), (red with beef broth base), heat and serve. Add more roux to make an excellent mushroom gravy.

BEEF OR TURKEY GRAVY

Pour juices from roasting pan into saucepan, skim fat or use ice cubes to remove as much fat as possible. Sir in roux; a spoonful at a time until gravy starts to thicken, over medium heat. If your gravy is a bit lumpy, use a whisk or mixer, it'll smooth out. If pan juices are not as browned as you wish, use a brown roux. You may prefer the flavor.

CREAMY PAN GRAVY

After frying meats, loosen drippings left in skillet with a fork. have about 2 T. each, hot fat and flour per cup of liquid used, depending on how thick you like your gravy. Cook the flour in the fat for a few minutes; but not browning, if you desire a white cream gravy. Brown flour until it reaches desired color; stirring constantly with a fork, remove from heat. Add evaporated milk or half -n- half stirring quickly while pouring, but keeping back from the steam so you don't burn yourself. Return to heat, still stirring, thin to desired consistency with hot water; season to taste. Gravy will start thickening as it cools, so make it a bit thinner than what you want it to be when served. Add coarse ground black pepper for COUNTRY GRAVY.

QUICK GRAVY

If you want gravy, but have no pan drippings, make a broth with bouillon cubes or soup base. Heat to simmer; add roux, a spoonful at a time to thicken.

To chicken gravy, add a dash of curry powder or poultry seasoning and turmeric. To beef gravy, add a dash of chili powder or spice of your choice and thin with red wine.

LO-CAL GRAVY

Remove all fat from roasting pan juices or use fat free broth. Heat to simmering. For each cup of liquid, (may add water to make desired amount,) use 1 T. cornstarch or arrowroot mixed with 1/4 cup cold water to form smooth paste. Pour into hot liquid stirring constantly to prevent lumps, season to taste. Does not reheat as well as roux-based gravies. May use more cornstarch if thicker gravy is desired, or add a bit of water, if gravy is too thick.

SPECIAL K LOAF (Fake meat loaf)
2 cups cottage cheese
4 eggs
1/2 cup onion, chopped
1 Tbsp. Wheat germ
7 1/2 oz. Special K cereal (I sometimes use more..LOL)
1/2 cup margarine (1 cube)
1 Tbsp. Poultry seasoning
Mix all ingredients and turn into a greased pan. Bake for one hour at 350

HOMEMADE VEGAN BURGERS
1 pint homemade / 16 ounces home canned kidney or pinto beans, drained, and well rinsed
1-2 C. rolled oats
1/2 C. all-purpose whole wheat flour (use grain of choice in comparable amount)
1 egg, beaten

1/2 C. fresh mushrooms, finely chopped
1/2 C. onions or leeks, finely chopped
1-2 carrot(s), shredded
1/2 C. red bell pepper, chopped
3 clove garlic, pressed or minced
1 tbsp. soy sauce, or Worcestershire sauce
1/2 tsp. salt
Spices and herbs to taste.
** You can use dehydrated veggies that have been rehydrated from food storage

Instructions: Throw all ingredients (start with only one cup of oatmeal) in food processor or blender. Pulse until coarsely chopped. Add more oatmeal as needed, until patties hold together well. If your patties want to fall apart, add a tad more liquid to moisten until they hold shape. Chill mixture for about an hour, Use a 1/4 cup ice cream scoop to portion then shape into patties. Broil patties 4-6 inches from heat about 10-15 minutes, until browned and heated throughout.
OR
Heat a bit of olive oil and cook patties over med-high heat 6-7 minutes a side, until crisp outside and cooked through.
These freeze well for later use.

TOFU
    Soak 2 and a half cups dried soybeans overnight
.then you drain off soaking water and thoroughly wash three times in clean water stirring briskly   that stirring and rinsing helps get the beany taste out
then put 7 cups water on them
it also helps heat up your beans if you use hot water
then you blend up your beans with hot water
but first ready your strainer, inside the strainer lay unbleached muslin or nylon curtain material for a straining cloth--about 1 yard. Depending on container size
then if you have a 1 quart   blender-but about 1 1/2 soaked beans...add 2 cups of boiling water. Put the blender lid on, cover that with a towel and keep children and pets away
run on low for 3 to 4 minutes and then on high for 5 more
then 1/4 cup cider vinegar or lemon juice in it, always stir in the same direction and pour in the mixture very slowly, it curdles quickly
now pour it in to something to set up, get firm and get its shape
the Japanese pour the curd into large wooden frames with wire bottoms into

which they sort of press it and that helps drain out the extra whey.   Only you can use cheesecloth on a frame...

to store your tofu, cut into squares like an inch on each side and keep the squares in cool water in your refrigerator until you get them used up

change the water daily

BREAD AND BUTTER PICKLES

Mix 6 quarts sliced cucumbers, 6 sliced medium onions and 2/3 cup pickling salt (NOT Iodized Salt), and let stand for 3 hours. Rinse and drain.

Make syrup of 6 cups sugar, 6 cups vinegar, 1 t. turmeric, 1 t. mustard seed, 3 T. pickling spice, 1 T. celery seed and ¼ t. cayenne, bring to a boil, add cucumbers and return to boil. Have jars ready, put mixture in the jars, leaving headroom and seal.   Makes 7 or 8 pints.

MUSTARD   PICKLES

Cut 3 heads of cauliflower into florets, cut 6 sweet red peppers into 1 inch squares, cut 4 cups green tomatoes into chunks and clean 3 pounds pickling onions OR cut 4 large onions into chunks.   May use other vegetables as you like or have on hand.

Let stand overnight in enough water to cover the vegetables, with 1 cup salt dissolved in it. Do not use iodized salt. Rinse and drain well. Cover with water and 1/2 cup vinegar and bring to a good boil. Simmer until vegetables are tender. Drain, rinse and drain. Combine 3/4 cup flour, 1 cup sugar, heaping tablespoon of tumeric, 4 ounces prepared mustard, add enough vinegar to form a smooth paste. Put 3½ quarts vinegar in kettle and heat, place some of the hot vinegar into

the flour mixture and stir well. Add to the hot vinegar; stirring constantly.   Add 4 cups sugar and   2 good shakes of ground red pepper. Heat slowly to prevent scorching, stirring   often until boiling.   Place vegetables in prepared jars, place knife in jar as vinegar mixture is poured to prevent jar cracking. Place lids on and seal.

DILL PICKLES

In each jar, place one head of dill or 1 t dried dill weed, 1 or 2 cloves garlic and I dried red pepper (optional, but good). wash fresh cucumbers and pack in jars. Mix I quart cider vinegar, 2 quarts water and I scant cup plain or pickling salt, not iodized. Bring to boil, pour over cucumbers, place lids on jars and tighten. Not necessary to seal, takes about 6 weeks to be pickles. Store all pickles in cool, dark place.

GREEN TOMATO SWEET PICKLES

Slice 8 quarts green tomatoes and 2 onions, sprinkle with 1 cup salt, let stand overnight. Strain, add 2 quarts water and I quart vinegar, boil 15 minutes and strain. Add 2 quarts fresh vinegar, 3 pounds sugar and 2 T. each, cloves (whole) allspice, ginger, mustard and cinnamon. Boil 5 minutes, pour into jars and seal.

DILLED ZUCCHINI

In large bowl, place 16 cups thin sliced zucchini, 2 cups thinly sliced celery, 2 large onions, chopped, and 1/3 cup plain salt, not iodized. Let stand 3 hours with layer of crushed ice over the top and covered. Drain well. Combine 2 cups sugar. 2 T. dill seed and 2 cups vinegar in a kettle, heat, stirring constantly, to boiling, stir in vegetables. Return to a full rolling boil,, stirring as needed. Ladle into hot sterilized jars, add 1 or 2 garlic cloves to each jar, push down into contents. Place lids on jars and seal. About 12 pints. May also add 1 diced rep pepper to each jar, before sealing.

HIGDOM

If you like sauerkraut, you'll probably like higdom.

For the brine: 4 cups of cider vinegar; 1 and 1/2 cups sugar; 1 teaspoon peppercorns; three very finely chopped garlic cloves; 1 teaspoon whole allspice; and 1/2 teaspoon red pepper flakes.

Bring to a boil, simmer for 10 minutes, let cool and store in the fridge overnight.

For the vegetables: 10 cups finely chopped cabbage; 5 pounds finely chopped green tomatoes, with most of the seeds rinsed out; 2 large onions, finely chopped; 2 large red peppers, finely chopped; three fourths of a cup of pickling salt.

Put all of these ingredients in a bowl, stir well, cover and put in the fridge overnight. (If you don't have enough cabbage or enough green tomatoes, then simply put in more of the other. I have had higdom made with 80 percent green tomatoes and other times with mostly green cabbage.)

The next day, rinse the bowl of vegetables well, squeeze hard to remove excess water and put in a large pan. Strain the brine and add it to the vegetables.

Bring to a boil and simmer for about 15 minutes. As the vegetables cook, there will be juice released but that should begin to cook off and the mixture thicken. If not, let it cook a bit longer. Keep stirring so nothing burns.

When the mixture is ready, ladle into pint jars, leave half an inch of head space and process for 15 minutes in a boiling water bath

CAJUN-STYLE PICKLED GREEN BEANS & CARROTS

For one quart jar of pickled veggies, start with a total of 1-1/2 pounds green beans and carrots. I prefer very thin organic baby carrots for this, purchased with their greens still attached so I know they're fresh & sweet.

You can use more of one or the other -- green beans of carrots -- if you'd like, or just do all carrots or all beans.

Wash them, and trim them to fit the jar. I like to use a pair of kitchen scissors to trim the stem end off the green beans.

Be sure the carrots and/or beans aren't sticking above the shoulder of the jar. You need space for other things, like garlic, spices and brine, and you don't want the veggies to touch the sealing lid either.

Pack the jar as full as you possibly can.

The veggies will shrink a tad bit during processing.

Make a brine by adding together in a sauce pan:

1 cup cider vinegar

1/2 cup water
1 teaspoon white sugar
1 teaspoon pickling or kosher salt
Heat to boiling, stirring to dissolve the sugar and salt, then immediately remove pan from heat once the sugar and salt are no longer visible. Set brine aside to cool.
Add directly to the jar:
1 bay leaf
1 or 2 cloves of garlic
6 black peppercorns
1/2 teaspoon celery seeds
1/2 teaspoon yellow mustard seeds
1/4 teaspoon cayenne pepper
1/4 teaspoon dried thyme
1 dried chili pepper, if you like it
Note: it helps to use a chopstick to tuck the bay leaf, garlic and chili pepper - if using - along the side of the jar.
~~~~~
Pour brine over the vegetables.
Wipe the rim of the jar if needed, and place a sealing lid atop the jar. Next, screw a ring onto the jar finger-tight and process in a boiling water bath for 10 minutes. Once properly sealed, the pickles will keep for one year on the shelf. You can also skip the processing step and store the pickled veggies in your refrigerator, but they won't have the same flavor since the processing adds to the way the veggies soak up the brine.   Sometimes I precook the carrots a little bit so they are almost tender so they don't get rubbery in the vinegar.

VEGETABLE PICKLES

I seldom have enough fresh cucumbers to use as pickles, so I substitute small zucchini in the same recipes. Full length green or yellow snap beans, packed in the jar look very nice and taste wonderful, dilled.   Experiment with what you have on hand.

Use recipe for dill pickles, for vinegar, water salt, garlic, dill and red pepper. Almost any fresh vegetable makes good pickles. String beans, small onions, celery, snap peas, cauliflower, carrots, green or red peppers, even florets of broccoli although they tend to lose color. Slices of turnip may be pickled, but recommend not adding to other vegetables as may change flavor of whole jar. Carrots and cauliflower should be blanched before placing in jar. Continue as for Dill Pickles.

PICKLED EGGS
- 12 hard-boiled eggs, peeled
- 1 large empty sterilized glass jar
- 4 cups vinegar
- 1 teaspoon salt
- 2 medium onions, chopped
- 1/3 cup sugar
- 1 tablespoon pickling spices   Optional: Add 1 cup beet juice for pink pickled eggs

Directions:
1 Put the peeled hardboiled eggs in the large jar.
2 Boil the remaining ingredients together for 5 minutes.
3 Pour over the eggs in the jar.
4 Cover; leave on counter overnight.
5 Keeps in refrigerator for weeks, in theory.
6 In reality, if you love pickled eggs, these will disappear.

STEPS IN CANNING

Various products require different handling, but basically the principles are very similar, no matter what the product is.

<u>Clean containers</u> - Wash cans or jars, check for nicks in jar rims.

<u>Pack</u> - Pack cold & preheat in containers - pack cold, add boiling syrup or brine, or preheat in syrup or brine and pack hot.

<u>Seal</u> - Tin cans, seal tightly. Glass jars, wipe rim, place lid on and screw ring on

firmly tight.

Process - Check charts and recipes. Never guess or estimate, unless you have a photographic memory, check every time.

Remove from Canner and Cool - If using pressure canner, allow pressure to return to zero. Slowly open petcock or remove weight. Open lid carefully, tipping the edge away from you up first, so the steam doesn't burn you. Tin cans may be cooled in cold water. Jars must be placed out of drafts, on towels or several thicknesses of paper to cool.

If using boiling water bath, remove from heat source, open lid away from you to allow steam to escape without burning you. Continue as above.

After cooling, check for sealing, label and store in cool dry place. Actually, it is best to wait about a week after canning, to store your containers. This usually gives plenty of time for any that are not sealed properly to be noticed. It's not very pleasant to notice these a couple of months later in your storage area.

The main thing to always remember, KEEP EVERYTHING CLEAN. This can not be stressed enough. Illness from home-prepared foods is either lack of cleanliness or not following the time and pressure schedules correctly. If you can follow directions, you can successfully can or cure foods at home. Then you are sure of the care that has been taken in your food's preparation.

Fruit is handled the same as vegetables. Choose at the peak of ripeness, canning will not improve over or under ripe fruit. Always remove any bruised or damaged spots. Prepare as you would to serve fresh. Wash thoroughly, peel if required. Peaches and tomatoes may be dipped in scalding water, then into cold water to allow skins to slip off in your hand. This speeds up the peeling process, too. Most fruits taste better if the pit or seeds are removed from large-seeded varieties.   Core and peel apples and pears, leave as halves or slice, as you prefer.   Pack fruit loosely into jars, cover to within ½ inch of the top of the jar with syrup or juice.   Thawed apple juice concentrate works well, mixed half 'n half with water as a syrup, if you wish to can without using sugar or honey.   For berries, crush and strain ripe berries for juice to cover the ripe berries you are canning.   Following is a table of syrups.

Sugar	Water	Syrup		Use for:
2 cups	4 qts.	Very thin	Very sweet fruit
6 cups	4 qts.	Thin	Medium sweet fruit
16 cups	4 qts.	Thick	Sour fruit

Fruit may be canned, unsweetened or in unsweetened fruit juice, but you should always add at least 1 teaspoonful of sugar, honey or fructose to a pint of fruit if you are using water, or the fruit will taste flat when opened. It doesn't. hurt the fruit any, just the flavor.   More sweetener may be added after opening the fruit.

First, everything <u>must</u> be clean.   The food, the jars, the workspace and your hands.   There must be no contamination from dirt.

Second, pack your jars in the same manner as for pressure canning.   If the food is thick,(chili, spaghetti sauce, shell beans) it is advised that the food be boiling when packed in the jars and placed in the canner of boiling water.   If the food is packed cold (room temperature) the water in the canner kettle should also be cold.   If the food is starchy (corn, creamed corn, mature peas) it should be packed hot, also.

The <u>Boiling Water Bath</u> method of canning is recommended for fruits, pickles and tomatoes, only.   There is more danger of food poisoning with this method of canning than there is with the pressure canner.   Of course there is always danger if the directions for time, temperature and pressure are not followed.   Get creative on the recipes, but not on the rest.   IF, however, your life depends on your preservation of food and you do NOT have a pressure canner, the old time method of Boiling Water Bath canning is presented here.

BOILING WATER BATH CANNING

First, everything MUST be clean. The food, the jars, the workspace and your hands. There must be no contamination from dirt.

Second, pack your jars in the same manner as for pressure canning. If the food is thick, (chili, spaghetti sauce, shell beans) it is advised that the food be boiling when packed in the jars and placed in the canner of boiling water. If the food is packed cold (room temperature) the water in the canner kettle should also be the same temperature. If you are canning starchy food (corn, creamed corn, mature peas) it should be packed hot, also.

Third, the water should just cover to the lids of the jars. Do not start timing until the water surrounding the jars has come to a complete rolling boil. Keep the lid on the canner at all times, only raising an edge to check the water level in the canner. Have another large kettle of water boiling to add to the canner if the water level drops below the edge of the jar lids. Never add cold water. Never set the jars directly on the bottom of the canner kettle, either. If you are using a regular canner, it should have either a wire rack or a trivet to place on the bottom to set the jars on. If not, place a towel or other heavy cloth on the bottom before placing jars and water in the canner. There must be space for several inches of headroom above the tallest jar in the canner and all the jars should be the same size if possible. This allows for rapid boiling without spilling over onto the stove. Time the kettle for the largest sized jar used in the batch of food you are preparing and the food requiring the longest time to process.

Fourth, if in doubt about how long something takes, add an hour, at least.

PINTS   QUARTS

<u>VEGETABLES</u>	2 1/2 hours	3 hours(except Beans, Corn & Peas)
<u>MEATS</u> & <u>Beans, Corn</u> & <u>Peas</u>	3½ hours	4 hours
<u>FISH</u>	5 hours	not

recommended

If the canner stops boiling for some reason, add the time onto the remaining time to boil. If it stops boiling for more than a few minutes, start the timing over.

At the end of the processing time, remove jars from canner and place on newspaper or towels on a flat surface away from drafts. Leave room around the jars for cooling but do not attempt to speed cooling by opening a door or using a fan. Allow jars to cool at their own rate. Rapid cooling may cause jars to break.

This is not a recommended method of food preservation. A pressure canner is much safer. Always boil food 10 to 15 minutes before tasting, after opening the jar. If there are any off-odors or if the food appears odd, discard safely. If it may cause harm to humans, it will also harm animals.

The foods that may be canned are limited only by the imagination. Experiment on recipes that you like. Some seasonings tend to change flavor during canning, so I usually limit the amount of spice added and season to taste after opening the jar for use. Milk products usually don't can well and gravies should be thickened after opening so the starch doesn't slow the amount of heat reaching the center of the jar during processing. Macaroni, rice and potatoes usually lose their shape and become a layer of starch in the bottom of the jar, so may be added after opening the jar.

DEFINITIONS OF CANNING TERMS

Cold Dip - Plunging blanched or scalded product into cold water.

Pre-heat - To bring a product to the boiling point or close to it, before packing them. With some products, pre-heating means wholly or partially cooking them.

Hot Fill or Hot Pack - Packing pre-heated products while still hot.

Process/Sterilize - Process, sterilize, cook and boil are used almost inter-changeably. They all refer to cooking a product until it will "keep." Process is a more accurate term in canning, because it means to cook long enough to kill or render inactive the germs of spoilage while retaining. as much as possible the food qualities of the product.

Steam - This term is often used in place of the word "blanch," it is also used in the same sense as "process".

DETECTING SPOILAGE

All canned food, whether home or commercially canned, should be carefully examined when opened. Discard the product if the ends of the can is bulged. In glass jars, be suspicious of the product if the seal is broken. Discard, if it contains gas bubbles or if the liquid squirts out when container is opened. Discard if contents are particularly soft, mushy, slimy or moldy in appearance. Discard if contents has a peculiar or unusual smell. Do not taste canned products until after they have passed the appearance and odor tests. Taste only a small portion. If the taste reveals any queer, sour or musty off-flavor, under no circumstances should the food be used. When heating vegetables for serving, note the odor. An odor so slight as to be unnoticed in a cold product may be quite plainly noticed when heated. When food has to be discarded for any of these reasons, discard in such a manner that animals will not eat it. It's as detrimental to them as it would be to you. You should never be too busy to check every can or jar of food used. Don't take any chance on "slightly-off" food. Destroy it safely.

　Fermentation - Any bulging can or jar with loose seal is usually due to the production of gas from fermentation. Fermentation comes from undercook mg or from the introduction of air from a leak or improper seal.

　Flat Sour - With flat sour, there are no outward appearances to suggest spoilage, but it smells and tastes sour. More thorough processing and speed in working, from harvest to process mg, so as to avoid holding the vegetables at lukewarm temperatures is the preventive. Corn, peas, beans, greens and asparagus are the usual vegetables with a tendency for flat sour. The old saying, "Two hours from garden to can" is still appropriate. Don't pack the containers too tightly, don't let them stand too long after being packed. Bring to boiling as soon as possible, don't try to can too much at a time.

Botulinus - Botulinus spores are found in the soil. Thoroughly wash all products before canning. Be careful not to under-process. This is the main reason for using a pressure canner. Foods can be canned using the water-bath method, but it is not recommended.

Do not pack items too tightly in the jars or cans, get the heat to the center of the container.

Molds - Must have air, grow well in acids. They are easily controlled, for they are killed by short exposure to boiling, or even less than boiling, temperatures. Usually found in fruits, jellies and tomatoes.

Yeasts - Need similar growing conditions as molds, although will not grow in acid conditions. Feed upon the sugars and form gas, causing fermentation and bulging cans and jar lids. Also easily killed by boiling.

Bacteria - There are many types and varieties, growing best in protein food, such as beans, meat and corn. Bacteria spore are almost everywhere and are the main cause of spoilage in home canned foods that have been handled improperly.

Storing - Canned goods should be stored in a cool, dry place. Glass jars should also be in the dark, as light fades the color of the food. This does not hurt the food, but is not appealing to the eye. Spoilage is greater if the storage temperature is over 80 degrees F. Increase your cooking time in processing if this is a problem.

CANNING TIME TABLE FOR MEAT, CHICKEN & FISH

PROOUCT	POUNDS PRESSURE	#2 Cans	Minutes Processed #3 Cans
Pint Jars	Quart Jars		

Roast Meat	10	65	 90	. ..75	90
Meat Rolls	10	65	 90	 75	90
Steaks	10	65	 90	 75	90
Stew	10	65	 90	 75	90
Hamburger	10	65	 90	 75	90
Fried Brains, Jellied Pigs					
Feet	10	80	 90	... 80	90
Meat Loaf, Hash	10	75	 90	 75	90
Corned Meat	10	65	 90	 75	90
Soup Stock	10	20	 25	 20	25
Boiled Tongue	10	75	 90	 75	90
Pork Chops	10	75	 85	 75	85
Pork Tenderloin	10	70	 80	... 70	80
Sausage	10	70	 80	 70	80
Spare Ribs	10	70	 80	 70	80
Scrapple	10	90	 110	... 90	110
Fried Chicken	10	55	 75	 65	75
Chicken Fricasee, Gumbo	10	55	 75	 65	75
Roast Fowl	10	70	 80	 70	80
Duck	10	85	 95	... 85	95
Rabbit or Squirrel	10	55	 75	 55	75
Potted Meats	10	65	 90	--- 75	90
Fish - Plain	10	70	.... *	....	80
Fish - Fried	10	50	.	... *	60	*
Crab Meat	5	80	....*	90	*
Clams	10	60	....*	70	*
Oysters 50	* 10	42	.... *		
Frog Legs 80	* 10	80	.... *		
Lobster ... 90	* 10	90	.... *		
Shrimp Wet Pack 35	* 10	30	.... *		
Dry Pack 75	* 10	70	.. .. *		

* Not recommended to use this size container for this food

Game animals should be handled the same as Beef, Pork or Chicken. If in doubt, use the longer processing time listed on the chart.

CANNING TIME TABLE FOR VEGETABLES & FRUIT

PROOUCT	POUNDS PRESSURE	Minutes Processed			
		#2 Cans	#3 Cans	Pint Jars	Quart Jars
Asparagus	10	20 25	25	30	
Beans, Shell	10	65 75	65	75	
Beans, String	10	25 30	20	25	
Beets	10	30 35	30	35	
Carrots, Parsnips, Turnips	10	25 30	25	30	
Corn, Cream-style	10	105	*		95
Corn, Whole Kernel	10	60 65			
Hominy	10	60 80	60	70	
Mushrooms	10	30 35	30	40	
Okra	10	25 40	25	40	
Peas, Green	10	30 35	40	45	
Peas, Black-eyed	10	35 40	35	40	
Peppers, Pimento	Boiling Water	30 40	30	40	
Pork & Beans	15	90 ..105	85	105	
Potatoes, Sweet	10	80	.10575	100	
Potatoes, White	10	35	40	35	40
Pumpkin, Strained	10	75 90		75	90
Rhubarb	Boiling Water.... 10	10	10	10	
Sauerkraut	Boiling Water....	15	25	30	
Vegetable Soup	10	40 45		40	45
Spinach	10	65 75		70	90
Swiss Chard	10	50 55		55	60
Squash, Winter	10	75 90		70	90
Succotash	10	75 90		85	95

Tomatoes, Whole Solid Pack

Boiling Water 45 60

35 45

Tomatoes in Juice

Boiling Water 10 10

10 10

Tomato Juice Boiling Water 10 10

10 10

Tomato Paste Boiling Water 50 .... 60 50

60

Apples, Figs, Grapes Boiling Water 15 20

15 20

Apricots, Guavas, Pineapple Boiling Water 25 .... 30 25

30

Berries, Cherries Boiling Water 15 20

10 15

Fruit Juices Boiling Water 5 5

5 5

Gooseberries, Peaches,
 Pears, Plums, Prunes...

Boiling Water 20 30

20 25

PICKLED 3-BEAN SALAD

1 1/2 c cut and blanched (frozen thawed) green, wax, or a combination of both beans

1 1/2 c cooked kidney beans (or 1 can, rinsed well)

1 c canned, drained garbanzo beans OR navy beans

1/2 c thinly sliced sweet pepper (1/2 a pepper)

1/2 c thin celery slices

1/2 c thin onion slices (1 medium onion)

1/2 c white vinegar

1/4 c lemon juice

3/4 c sugar

1 1/2 c water

1/4 c oil

1/2 tsp salt

Wash, snap, blanch string beans if using fresh. Cool immediately. Rinse and drain other beans. Prepare other vegetables.

Combine vinegar, lemon juice, sugar and water. Boil in non-reactive pot. Remove from heat as soon as they boil. Add oil and salt to vinegar mixture, mix well. Add vegetables and beans, bring to a simmer. Move to refrigerator and marinate 12-14 hours. Reheat entire mixture to a boil, then fill clean hot jars to 1/2 inch from the top with solids, and add hot liquid up to 1/2 inch from the top. Cover with sterilized lids, and process 10 minutes in a boiling water bath. Makes 5 - 6 half-pints.

CANNED COLESLAW
1 head shredded cabbage
1/2 c chopped onions
2 cups sugar
2 tsp salt
1 tsp celery seed
1/2 scant cup vinegar
optional: shredded green peppers

Mix, let sit 4 hours. Pack into jars, to 1/2 inch of the top. Process in boiling water bath 7 minutes - DO NOT OVER COOK!!

This makes a sweet-sour pickle, served like slaw. You can drain and add some oil before serving if you want.

CANNING SOFT CHEESE
Home canned "soft cheese" has better cooking properties than store bought bottled cheese meant for snack food. It contains no preservatives and is more economical than commercial products for cooking purposes. These instructions yield a product that is similar to "Cheese Whiz", yet better tasting for a recipe of macaroni and cheese. This simple to do recipe for home canned cheese will keep for 2 years plus.

Ingredients:

* 1 (5 oz.) can evaporated milk
* 1 T. vinegar
* ½ tsp. salt
* 1 lb. Velveeta cheese or any processed cheese
* ½ tsp. dry mustard

Melt milk and cheese in double boiler. Add rest of ingredients and mix well. Fill pint jars about 3/4 full and seal. Place in Boiling Water bath for 10 minutes.

CANNING CHEDDAR CHEESE

Cut up cubes of cheese, sitting a wide-mouthed pint jar in a pan of hot water, on the stove.

As the cubes of cheese melt add more until the jar is full to within half an inch of the top.

Then I put a hot, previously boiled lid on the jar, screwed down the ring firmly tight and added the cheese to a batch of jars in the boiling water bath canner to process. Pints 40 min.

To take the cheeses out of the jar, dip the jar in a pan of boiling water for a few minutes, then take a knife and go around the jar, gently prying the cheese out. Store it in a plastic zip lock bag.

CANNING PICKLED EGGS:

Lots of folks pickle eggs, but don't can them.

After placing your eggs in wide mouth jars, adding your brine and spices, place in boiling bath canner for 10 min. (basically like pickles) I do mine in dill pickle style, also the pickled garlic cloves.   One bunch dill, one T. red pepper flakes or a couple of   dried red peppers, a t. of plain or pickling salt and apple cider vinegar per pint.. For pretty eggs, use the juice from pickled beets and add more vinegar.

MILK   (This is iffy and be very careful with it)

The milk is   like evaporated milk in a can. In fact, you can substitute your home canned milk for the evaporated in a can stuff. It is a bit more condensed, and it does separate,   just shake the jars every now and then.

I would check on them every couple of months and shake, If you have a jar come unsealed and it isn't found for a   while, it will be *nasty* when found . So, keep an eye on them.

Canning fluid milk can be done safely I believe though again there are no USDA guidelines for doing so. It would have to be pressure canned, 10 lbs for at least ten minutes, to be safe. Fluid milk is a low-acid food so boiling water bath will not do. The end product is definitely going to have a cooked flavor and probably a slight tan color and be perhaps a bit thicker in consistency. But it will be fluid milk that you can cook with.

CANNED BUTTER

It must be made clear that the procedure for canning butter discussed below is not approved by the USDA or any state cooperative extension service that I know of. There are no USDA approved methods for canning dairy products that I've been able to find. Nevertheless, it has been used by many people and there have been no problems reported, IF you correctly follow the directions. I've used it myself, but you do so at your own risk.

If you have an Asian market or a health food store you may find a product called "ghee" which is basically clarified butter. It's been in use in India for centuries. You can make your own ghee if you like.

To make it you must start with unsalted sweet cream butter. It's important to not use the salted kind because the finished product will be excessively salty if you do. I use 1 pound salted butter to 4 pounds unsalted butter when making Ghee. It takes roughly three and a half sticks of ordinary unsalted butter to fill a pint jar after clarifying and a bit more than one and a half sticks for a half-pint jar. Without refrigeration, I recommend processing your butter in the half-pints to have less exposed to the air at one time. Since you're melting it, you obviously would not want to use whipped butter as it will just about melt away to nothing. Nor do I recommend the near or almost butter products to be found. This procedure can be used with unsalted, solid (not whipped) margarine, but you should add about 10-20% more to achieve equivalent finished volume. Naturally, reduced fat "spreads" will not work well here either.

Place the butter in a heavy bottomed pan over low heat and melt it. Continue heating it until all of the water has been driven off and the butter solids begin to fry. At this point you can take it off the heat if you want a paler, more subtle flavored product or you can continue to gently brown the butter solids until they've taken on a golden-brown color. This will impart a nice color to the finished product and a pronounced flavor. You must use a low heat so as not to burn the butter when the moisture content drops. Margarine should not be browned, just make sure the water content has been boiled off. If the butter gets hot enough to smoke, it's ruined and you should toss it, wash the pan and start over. Burned fat is oxidized fat and oxidized fats are bad news for long term health.

Once the moisture content of the butter has been driven off and it's at the color you want, remove from the heat and strain through a clean coffee filter into dry, hot, sterilized canning jars. When full to a half-inch from the top screw on a hot sterilized canning lid and ring. Boiling water bath the jars for ten minutes which eliminates the mold risk. It's not required, but I prefer to use it. In a properly sealed glass canning jar in a cool, dark place the ghee should remain quite usable for many years. There should be a noticeable amount of vacuum in the jar from after the contents cool. I still water bath process the filled jars for 10 minutes, just to be sure.   I seldom actually strain through a filter, I carefully skim the surface and dip out as much as possible and then use the rest in cooking.

TURNIP KRAUT
4 to 5 pounds Turnips, shredded
2 teaspoons pickling or canning salt, not iodized, per pound of turnips
2 tablespoons pickling or canning salt, not iodized, for brine
1 quart water

   Toss the washed, peeled and shredded turnips with the first measure of salt. Pack into clean sterilized jars, loosely place the lids on and do not seal. Place jars in an enamel or plastic pan in a cool, preferably dark place and allow to ferment for 10 days.

   After fermenting, make brine of 2 tablespoons salt dissolved in a quart of water. Fill jars to cover kraut, just below the lip of the jar. Process 11 minutes in hot water bath. One pound of shredded turnips makes 1 pint of kraut.

CANNING BREADS AND CAKES

Bread or cake may be canned with very satisfactory results in tapered wide-mouth jars. These may be used straight from the jar, or removed from the jar, wrapped in foil and heated in the oven, before serving. Fancy nut or fruit breads make a lovely personalized gift for special occasions or holidays. Fruitcake or plum pudding, in a sparkling jar with a colorful ribbon tied on, is a treat. Unexpected guests pose no problem, just open a jar or two, slice rounds and arrange on a plate.

I use a lot of the ½ pint size jars to make individual servings. They are very handy for lunches and the contents are always fresh.   Whenever cake is being made, spoon a couple of spoons of batter into a jar and bake at the same time. Seal and label.   Soon you have a good selection to choose from.

HOW TO CAN BACON

If you have a large quantity of bacon, or just want to take some camping with you, without worrying about spoilage, consider canning it.   Use tapered wide-mouth jars, pint size.   Cut a large sheet of parchment paper, twice the size of the amount of bacon.   About a pound of sliced bacon fills 1 pint jar. Lay the bacon on the center of the parchment paper,   Fold the top and bottom to meet, over the bacon, Fold the bacon almost in half, and slide into the pint jar, being careful not to tear the paper.   Wipe the rim of the jar, vinegar works well to wipe jar rims for greasy foods, place the lid on and tighten the band.   Process at 10 pounds pressure for 90 minutes.

A WORD ABOUT CANNING JARS   (Well, maybe more than one)

I know it is not recommended to use any jars but the ones on store shelves sold expressly for canning.   For myself, I use any jar that a small, medium or wide-mouth jar lid fits correctly.   I use mayonnaise jars, mustard jars, any jars I can find, including certain types of instant coffee or tea, jars. In all my years of canning, I have only had two jars break while canning.   Both jars were store-bought standard canning jars.   As long as a canning lid will fit snug and firm and the jar is definitely not plastic, it should be safe to use.   You must keep drafts from hitting hot jars, also stray splashes of water. Use a lot of common sense, when canning and you should never have a problem. Always check rims of jars for nicks or cracks, discard, if any are found.   Check bands to make sure none are bent, dented or very rusty.   A spot or two of rust won't hurt, but try to keep bands clean and dry to prevent rust.   Discard, rather than try to repair.

HAMBURGER SAUCE TO CAN

Brown 10 pounds of hamburger, add 8 large onions, chopped, 4 cups chopped celery and cook until limp.   Drain as much fat as possible from meat, add 1 gallon chopped tomatoes and 1 gallon tomato sauce.   Bring to a boil. Ladle into hot, clean jars, wipe rim clean and place lids on firmly.   Place in pressure canner and process, pints 75 minutes, quarts, 90 minutes, at 10 pounds pressure.

Variations: May add chopped green peppers, chopped pimentos, sliced mushrooms, chopped parsley and/or minced garlic to sauce.   Do not season until using, as some spices lose or change flavor during processing and storage.

USES: Hamburger sauce can be the base for many different dishes.   I use it for spaghetti sauce, pizza topping, chili, lasagna, sloppy joes, soup base, hamburger pie and many other things.   Just add the appropriate seasonings when you open the jar.

SPAGHETTI SAUCE, add 1 t. oregano, 1/2 t. Italian seasoning and 1 bay leaf per pint of sauce.   May add mushrooms and 1 clove minced garlic, also.

SPANISH RICE, heat 1 pint sauce, add 1/2 cup chopped green peppers, 1 8-ounce can tomato sauce, 1 cup uncooked rice, 1/2 cup chopped sausage, bring to boil, turn heat down to simmer, cover, stirring once, until liquid is absorbed and rice is tender.   May add 1/2 cup chopped ham, 1/2 cup cleaned shrimp and 1/2 cup sliced scallops, last 3 minutes of cooking.   Do not overcook after adding seafood.

CHILI, add 1 pint sauce to 4 cups cooked red or kidney beans, may use 2 cans drained beans, add I clove minced garlic, 1 T. chili powder, or to taste, 1 chopped green chili pepper, 1 t. cumin, simmer for 1 hour or longer. Mix 1 T. masa harina or white cornmeal in 1/4 cup cold water, Stir into chili, return to a boil, stirring constantly. Taste, adjust seasoning. Mash leftovers and use as refried beans to fill burritoes.

HAMBURGER PATTIES

Form 5 pounds of hamburger into a roll, just a bit larger in diameter than a wide mouth jar lid. Place in freezer just long enough to firm up to make slicing easier. Remove from freezer and slice in 1/2 inch thick slices. Press edges to make a firm patty. Broil or fry until almost cooked through. Keep warm in covered pan until there are enough to fill jars for one canner full. Slide patties into tapered pint or pint and a half wide mouthed jars. Pour hot broth to within ½ inch of top of jar, wipe rim, place lids on firmly and process at 10 pounds pressure, pints, 75 minutes, pint and a halfs, 90 minutes. May drain and grill, to serve, or heat in juices and serve. If you prefer a drier texture patty, have the cooked patties very hot when packing into jars and wipe the rims and screw on the lids for dry packing and process.

HAMBURGER

Brown 5 pounds of hamburger, add 5 cups chopped onion, (optional,) and 2 1/2 cups sliced mushrooms, (optional). Salt and pepper to taste, continue cooking until onions and mushrooms are tender. Ladle into pint or half-pint jars, wipe rim, place lids on and tighten. Process at 10 pounds pressure for 75 minutes.

TO USE:

Use as browned hamburger in any recipe. One pint is equal to 1 pound browned burger. Or make hamburger gravy by adding to cream gravy. SOS anyone?

SAUSAGE PATTIES or LINKS

Proceed as for hamburger patties, but slice a little thinner, unless you like thick sausage. After packing in jars, pour hot water or broth over and proceed with instructions.   To use, drain and fry or grill until lightly browned, serve.

HOT DOGS

Cover hot dogs with water, simmer at least 5 minutes, pack loosely into wide mouthed jars, proceed as for hamburger patties. Be sure hot dogs have expanded as much as they are going to, before loosely packing in the jars.

TAMALES

Cover 1 soup bone, 1 pound lean meat, 1 pound pork or chicken, 1 quartered onion, 3 cloves crushed garlic and 3 T. salt with water in a kettle, cook until meat is tender. Remove any meat from bone and discard bone. Grind the meats, 2 cloves garlic and an onion. Add 4 T. chili powder, 1 t. salt, ½ cup melted lard or shortening, 2 cups of the broth the meat cooked in, ¼ t cayenne and 2 T. flour. Cook until thick, stirring often. Prepare the meal mixture.

4 ½ cups cornmeal (white, but yellow is okay), I T. salt, ½ cup melted lard

or shortening, 2 t. chili powder, 4½ cups of the broth the meat cooked in, and 2 cups water. Mix together until smooth, bring to boil, stirring constantly, until of a consistency to spread, but still hold it's shape. Cut parchment paper (cooking parchment) into 3 x 6 inch strips and scald it. Have pieces damp but not wet, to work with. Spread meal mixture ¼ inch thick on parchment, allow space at each end and one side to fold over. Down the center of the meal, spread about 2 t. of the meat mixture, roll up, fold ends to cover and lap side to paper to seal together. Pack in sterilized wide-mouth quart jars. To help pack the last tamale in center of jar, place it between 2 knives and slip in the center of pack. Add I T. tomato juice or water to each jar, put on lids and seal. Process in pressure canner 90 minutes at 10 pounds pressure.

To serve, gently remove from jar, using reverse of packing the jar. Place tamales in baking dish, top with tomato sauce, a sprinkle each of chili powder, garlic and chopped onion. Bake until heated through, gently remove parchment paper to retain shape of tamale, serve.

These may be made using corn husks, also, but sometimes it's difficult to find nice corn husks. They do add a lovely flavor though.

Any lean meat may be used in this recipe. Stewing hens may be used in place of all the meats called for. Discard skin, bones and most of the fat, do not add extra melted fat.

MEATBALLS OR MINI-MEATLOAVES

Combine 6 pounds lean ground meat, 1½ cups dry bread crumbs OR 1 stovetop type stuffing mix, 1½ cups water, 6 eggs and 4½ t. garlic salt or salt. Mix well. Shape into small balls, I use a teaspoon and dip about the same amount each time, roll slightly to shape and place almost touching on a cookie sheet with sides to hold grease during cooking. Bake a pan at a time, pour off drippings and keep meatballs warm in covered container. Only bake them about half-done. While meatballs are cooking, prepare sauces. This recipe for meatballs is enough for one recipe of each of the following sauces. Have sterilized jars and pressure canner ready. After sauces are ready, pack jars with meatballs, pour sauce over, wipe jar rim, put lids on and process pints 75 minutes, 10 pounds pressure. If canning mini-meatloaves, make thin brown gravy to cover. Same time and pressure.

ITALIAN SAUCE

Fry 4 slices chopped bacon until crisp, Dump all but 2 T. of the grease, add 1 large onion, chopped, cook till golden. Add I minced garlic clove, and 1 can (1 lb. 12 oz.) pear tomatoes and liquid. Break up tomatoes or chop, 1 t. each, basil, oregano, sugar, 1/2 t. salt, 1 bay leaf and 1½ cups beef broth. 2 T. cornstarch dissolved in 1/2 cup broth, simmer 20 minutes. Sauce for one-third meatball recipe.

CURRY SAUCE

Heat 1/4 cup butter or margarine, add 1 large onion, chopped, saute until limp, add I mashed garlic clove and 2 T. curry powder. Add 4 T. flour, 1 T. cornstarch, 2 t. sugar, ½ t. salt and dash of cayenne, cook and stir until bubbly. Add gradually, 2 cups chicken broth, cook until thickened. After opening jar and reheating curry, add ½ cup cream, stir to blend. Serve with rice. Sauce for one-third meatball recipe.

SWEET AND SOUR SAUCE

Drain juice from 2 (13 ounce each) cans pineapple chunks, reserve pineapple. Combine juice with 1 ¼ cups chicken broth (may make with bouillon cubes), 1/2 cup packed brown sugar, ½ cup vinegar, 1 T. each - soy sauce and catsup and 4 T. cornstarch. Cook over medium heat, stirring, until thick. Add 1 cup chopped onion, ½ cup chopped green pepper and pineapple chunks. Cook until onion and pepper are almost tender. Sauce for one-third of meatball recipe.

TERIYAKI SAUCE OR MARINADE

One cup soy sauce, 1 to 1 ½ cups brown sugar, 2 T. fresh grated ginger, 3 cloves garlic, minced.   Combine ingredients and use as sauce or marinade.   If canning with meatballs, dilute to taste with broth.

HOT SMOKEY CATSUP
5 lb ripe tomatoes, coarsely chopped (or 3 - 28 oz. cans crushed tomatoes)
1 large onion, finely chopped
1 large poblano chili finely chopped
2 jalapeno chilies coarsely chopped
2 dried or canned chipotle chilies
1/2 cup cider vinegar
1 cup (packed) brown sugar
1 tsp celery seed
1 1/2 tsp mustard seed
1/4 tsp cayenne
1 tsp black pepper
1 1/2 tsp salt
May add a drop or two of liquid smoke for a smokier flavor
Combine all ingredients in a large non reactive pot and bring to a boil over medium heat. Reduce heat and simmer 1 1/2 hours, stirring occasionally until vegetables are soft and sauce is reduced by 1/4. (I like it chunky, so stop here.) Puree in food processor. Strain through a sieve into a clean pot (I skipped this direction since I liked the consistency it was at that point).
Bring to a boil over medium low heat and simmer (partially covered to prevent splatters) for 1 hour or until quite thick and dark brownish red. Process in pint jars in boiling water bath for 10 minutes.

PICCALILLI
1 quart chopped cabbage
1 quart chopped green tomatoes
2 chopped sweet red peppers
2 chopped sweet green peppers
2 large onions chopped
¼ cup pickling salt
1-1/2 cups cider vinegar
1-1/2 cups water
2 cups firmly packed brown sugar
1 t. dry mustard
1 t. turmeric

1 t. celery seed

Mix together the cabbage, tomatoes, peppers, onions and the salt. Let stand overnight. Drain and press to remove as much liquid as possible. Boil vinegar, water, sugar, and spices for 5 minutes. Add the vegetables and bring back to a boil. Pour into jars, leaving 1/2" headspace put on cap, and screw band firmly tight Process in Boiling water bath 5 minutes.

DIXIE RELISH
1 pint chopped sweet red peppers
1 pint chopped green peppers
1 quart chopped cabbage
1 pint chopped onions
2 chopped hot peppers
5 tablespoons salt
4 tablespoons mustard seed
2 tablespoons celery seed
1/2 cup sugar
1 quart vinegar
Mix vegetables together, and cover with salt. Let stand overnight. Drain; add spices, sugar, and vinegar. Pack into sterilized jars leaving 1/2" head space. Add lid and ring; process 5 minutes in boiling water bath.

JAMS, JELLIES & BUTTERS

This is a basic fruit butter recipe and other fruits and spices may be substituted. Pears, peaches and cherries can all make good fruit butters.

OLD-FASHIONED APPLE BUTTER
2 gallons apple cider
2 gallons peeled, cored and chopped, apples
2 cups brown sugar
4 cups granulated sugar
2 T cinnamon
2 t. allspice
Dash of salt
1 T vanilla
Cook cider down to 1 gallon, add apples. Bring to boil and reduce heat. Cook 5 hours, stirring often. Add sugars and spices, cook for 1 hour more, stirring very often to prevent sticking. Add vanilla and stir in well. Pour into sterilized pint jars and seal. Recommended to water bath 10 minutes after putting lids on. Makes 9 - 10 pints. I like to add a dash of cayenne to mine.

GREEN TOMATO JAM

The yield   is about six half-pints of a marmalade-style preserve:

 5 pounds of green tomatoes, diced into small pieces (some people prefer to rinse off the seeds, I do not); 6 cups of sugar; the juice and zest of one large lemon and two large oranges; and a teaspoon of butter. (You make zest by grating off the outside of the lemon and oranges, stopping when you reach the white pith underneath the outside color.)

Mix all the ingredients except the butter together and put in the fridge overnight.

The next day, bring the concoction to a boil and then, stirring frequently, let it simmer for about two hours, or until it reaches a thickness that suits you. Stir in the butter about half way through and at the end spoon off any scum that may have formed. Fill half pint jars, leaving a quarter inch of head space. Use the boiling water canning method, process for 10 minutes.

ROSE PETAL JAM

2 cups rose petals (finely chopped, remove the white part,   bottom of the petal, and discard it.)

2 cups boiling water

2 3/4 cups sugar

3 tablespoons honey

1 tablespoon lemon juice

Cover the rose petals with boiling water, simmer for 10 minutes. Strain and reserve both water and petals. Add sugar and the honey to the water. Simmer for 30 minutes. add lemon and finely chopped petals and simmer 30 minutes. Pour into hot jars.   Water bath 10 minutes.

SPRUCE TIP JELLY

3 cup spruce tip juice

4 cups sugar

1 package pectin

Day One: Prepare the Spruce Tip Juice

1. Rinse 3-4 cups of spruce tips in cold water. Drain and then lightly chop them.

2. Place the spruce tips in a small saucepan with 3 1/2 cups cold water. Bring to a boil and then immediately remove them from the heat.

3. Transfer the tips and liquid to a heatproof bowl, cover tightly, and let steep overnight.

Day Two: Make Your Jelly

1. Sterilize 5 half-pint jars.
2. Collect the spruce tip juice by straining the liquid through a jelly bag, or several layers of cheesecloth. (If you use a jelly bag or cheesecloth, be sure to dunk it in scalding water first — not just to cleanse it, but to hydrate it so a dry cloth doesn't soak up the juice.)
3. Measure 3 cups of spruce tip juice into a 6- or 8-quart saucepot.
4. Measure the sugar into a separate bowl.
5. Stir the entire packet of pectin into the saucepot. (I had heard some great things about MCP pectin. Also, it dissolved nicely, without lumps. If you use a different brand of pectin, be sure to follow the recipe directions in that box. I'd use the proportions given for mint jelly.)
6. Bring the mixture to a full rolling boil, on high heat, stirring constantly.
7. Quickly stir in the sugar. Return the mixture to a rolling boil and boil for exactly 2 minutes, stirring constantly. Remove from heat and skim foam.
8. Ladle or pour the hot jelly into the sterilized jars, leaving 1/4-inch head space. Wipe the rims with a clean, damp cloth and secure the lids. Process in a water-bath canner, using the correct time for your altitude: 5 minutes for 0-1,000 feet above sea level, plus 1 minute for every additional 1,000 feet. Yields about 5 half-pint jars. (If you want more than this, plan to make multiple small batches. As with most jelly recipes, doubling the batch MAY NOT WORK SO WELL.)   I prefer it with a few mint leaves steeped with the tips for a minty flavor.

TOMATO MARMALADE
12 cups peeled, chopped tomatoes (keeping juice)
2 thinly sliced and quartered lemons
2 thinly sliced and quartered oranges
10 cups sugar
2 T whole cloves
6 cinnamon sticks, broken
1 cup chopped walnuts, optional
If you don't want the tomato seeds, sieve the tomatoes.   Place tomatoes and juice in large kettle.   Add sugar and stir until dissolved.   Add orange and lemon slices.   Tie cloves and cinnamon sticks in cheesecloth bag and put in kettle.   Boil rapidly, stirring often.   Cook until clear and thick, about 1 hour. Remove spices, stir in chopped walnuts.   Pour into sterilized jars and seal, water bath for 10 minutes.

OLD FASHIONED JAMS AND JELLIES
   Usually use equal amounts of fruit and sugar.   For jam, don't remove the seeds in berries or leave the fruit in small pieces or grind and add sugar and

cook until it reaches the jell stage on a candy thermometer or sheets off a cool plate when dropped on it and tipped. If berries have too many seeds for your taste, only put part of them through a sieve to remove most of the seeds but retain the pulp. For jelly, mash fruit and drain through a jelly bag without squeezing to make a very clear jelly. If you don't mind some pulp in the jelly, go ahead and squeeze the bag to get all the pulp through, also. This makes more of a spread than a jelly, but it is very good. If your fruit doesn't want to jell easily, add some unripe apples or lemon juice to the fruit. Unripe apples are rich in pectin. Barely ripe fruit jells easier than fully ripe fruit. Some unripe berries add pectin to the jell mixture. Stir the mixture often while cooking so it doesn't stick or scorch. You can use honey to make jams and jellies but it takes a bit longer and more prone to burning if not careful. The finished product may be darker, too. Use your imagination and combine different fruits and berries. Write down what you do, so you can repeat it if you like it or vow to never do it again, if you don't. When the product reaches the jell stage, ladle into hot jars, leaving ½ inch headroom and water bath process 10 minutes. I know folks used to use wax to seal the jars but there can be a lot of spoilage that way and why allow good food to spoil? The wax tends to pull away from the jars as temperatures fluctuate and rodents and insects can chew into it. That just doesn't appeal to me, nor the mold that can work its way under the wax.

For different flavors in your jams or jellies, add extracts or flavorings just before adding the jelly to the jar and stir in quickly. Extracts and flavorings can lose most of their flavor if boiled in open kettle too long.
I like to add almond extract to chokecherry jelly for a maraschino cherry flavored jelly.
Another favorite is pineapple mint or cinnamon pear. Brandy extract is good in peach jam or jelly. Adding some nutmeg makes a spiced brandy peach jam. Apple jelly takes other flavors very well and you can experiment to your hearts' content. Apple cinnamon with a dash of nutmeg is a great apple pie flavored jelly.

A very old version of making jams and jellies is to spread the fruit/sugar mixture thin on trays and stir often, in the sun, until thick.

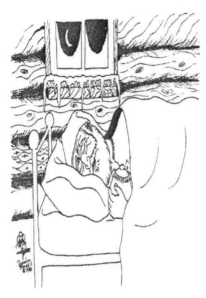

Sourdough, Breads, Cakes, Pies and Candy

...and how to make them

USE OF HONEY IN BAKING AND COOKING
For baking cakes and cookies, reduce liquid by 1/2 cup for each cup of honey used to replace sugar. Unless buttermilk or sour milk are used, add about 1/5 teaspoon soda to neutralize acidity in one cup of honey.

For freezing fruit, use 1 part mild flavored honey to 4 or 5 parts fruit. In canning fruits, use recipe for thin syrup, replacing one cup sugar with one cup honey.

Candied Fruit from Canned Fruit
May use home-canned or store-bought canned fruit. Fruit should not be overripe or soft. Drain 16 oz. can or jar of fruit. and measure the syrup. Add enough water to make 1+ c. liquid and place in pan with 1 c. sugar. Heat, stirring constantly, until the sugar dissolves. Bring to boil, then pour over fruit. Use a plate to weight the fruit down, it must stay under the syrup. Let stand 24 hours. Drain the syrup, add ½ c. sugar, heat and stir until sugar dissolves, bring to boil and pour over fruit, again, weight the fruit down and let stand 24 hours. Repeat this process 2 more times using 1/4 c. sugar each time. Check the syrup for consistency. It should be thick.

Maraschino Cherries
41/2 pounds Royal Anne Cherries (not too ripe)
2 Tbs. salt
1 qt. water

1 t. alum

4 ½ cups sugar

1 oz. red food coloring

1 oz. Almond extract

Juice of one lemon
Pit cherries carefully and soak overnight in brine of the water, salt and alum. The next day wash the cherries until the salt taste is gone. Boil 4½ c. sugar, 3 c. water, 1 oz. red food color, Add cherries, remove from heat, add 1

oz. almond extract & juice of 1 lemon. Heat, pack in small jars and seal.

BAKING TIPS

Baking everything for the whole week at one time is a timesaver and almost everything can be baked at the same time by watching the oven a little more closely. Of course, a delicate cake or pastry needs it's own space and temperature, but almost everything else can be baked at 350 to 375 degrees by watching the progress and switching from one shelf to another half way through cooking. This saves on clean-up and conserves fuel. In the Winter in Interior Alaska, there is never any worry about freezer space to store items baked ahead. The entire outdoors, against any outside wall on the inside and even at floor level in some places can serve as a freezer.

Don't bother sifting flour, just don't pack it down. Dip measure into the flour and level it off with a knife blade, or spoon it gently. If you wish to weigh it, 1/4 cup of flour equals 1 ounce, 4 cups of flour equals 1 pound.

Homemade Baking Powder Recipe
Royal Baking Powder was a single-acting product made years ago. Here's a recipe for single-acting baking powder you could use in old recipes calling for Royal brand.
- 2 tablespoons cream of tartar
- 1 tablespoon baking soda

1 tablespoon cornstarch

Combine ingredients and store tightly covered. For double-acting baking powder, use 1/4 teaspoon of baking soda and 1/2 teaspoon of cream of tartar for each teaspoon needed.

Warm your flour before baking bread. A pan of flour can be warmed in the oven as it heats. Be careful not to brown it. Or microwave it, 2 1/2 pounds of flour for almost 1 minute at high power.

SOURDOUGH & BREAD, FROM SCRATCH

My father's oldest brother came to Alaska during the Gold Rush at Nome. He and a few others didn't like the crowded conditions on the beaches and the bickering over claim lines, so crossed on the winter ice to Siberia. They spent the Summer mining and dodging the Russians and came home quite happy with themselves. He said that to carry the sourdough starter from place to place and prevent freezing, they would mix the starter with flour to a stiff ball of dough, put it in a well-floured pouch around their neck and go. The dough has a distinctive aroma and anyone wearing a pouch of starter was bound to share that smell. This was his explanation for the name Sourdough. It sounds as good as any other tale.

The best way to get started with sourdough is to get a "start" from a friend. But an easy starter is simply to mix 1 cup flour, 1 cup warm water and 1 teaspoon yeast together. Let set 24 hours in a warm spot in the house. It should develops a pleasantly sour odor, similar to buttermilk. Always use a pot large enough for expansion. Sometimes sourdough will go to great lengths to run over the sides of it's container.

The night before using, add equal amounts of flour and water to the pot, quantity depending on type of recipe or amount of people to feed. Never use metal utensils to keep sourdough in, as it tends to have a corrosive action on metal. Also, do not cover your sourdough pot tightly or you may have an extremely messy explosion.

Sourdough can be used for just about anything, even, in a pinch, as log chinking. It is practically indestructible when dried, as you will discover   if the pancake batter bowl is allowed to dry without rinsing.

Bread making does not have to be a difficult task.   From the extremely simple Pita or Pocket bread that only takes   1 hour from start to finish with 45 minutes of that being spent letting the dough rest, to   finicky salt-rising bread that requires practice and no drafts, you should be able to find ones that suits your styles of cooking and tastes.   If you get absolutely discouraged with the dough, or want a quick sample, pinch off small pieces, flatten them out and deep fry until puffy and golden brown.   Almost any dough will raise and taste great, fried.   Or you can use a recipe especially for frying, Indian Fry Bread. It's delicious.

SOURDOUGH PANCAKES
Night before, add 2 ½ cups flour, 2 cups warm water to the Starter.   Leave in a warm place overnight, loosely covered.
In the morning leave 1 cup of Starter in the container and add to the remaining Starter:
1 egg
2 T. cooking oil or melted grease
¼ cup milk
Beat well and add 1 tsp salt, 1 tsp. soda and 2 T. sugar, blend
gently.   To assure soda dissolves,   save   a few drops of the milk to add to the soda before adding it to the mixture to assure it dissolves well.   Cook on hot griddle.   For waffles, add 2 T. more oil to batter before using.

SOURDOUGH BREAD

Night before, add 2½ cups flour, 2 cups warm water to Starter.   Next day.

Save 1 cup for Starter.   Dissolve 1 package yeast in 2 cups liquid, (potato water, water, milk, whatever) add ¼ cup margarine, oil or shortening, ¼ cup honey or sugar.   Add sourdough and 2 cups flour, stir until well mixed. Beat 50 strokes to develop gluten.   Blend 2 T. sugar, 2 t. salt, 2 t. soda until no lumps, sprinkle over top of dough and stir in gently.   Cover, let rise ½ hour.   Stir down and add 4 cups flour, turn out and knead well.   Shape, place in greased pans, pans should be half full, let rise until double.   Bake at 400 degree oven for 20 minutes, turn down to 325 degrees, bake until it starts to pull away from the pans.   Turn out on racks to cool.   Butter loaves if you like a soft crust, brush with water if you like crusty loaves, as soon as loaves are placed on rack.

SOURDOUGH BREAD, LONG SPONGE METHOD

Put 1 cup Starter in a large bowl, add 4 cups flour, 2 cups liquid and mix well. Cover and let stand 14 to 36 hours.   When ready, add ¼ cup oil, ¼ cup honey or sugar, 2 t. salt and mix well.   Add 2 cups flour, turn out and knead well. Do not add yeast or soda.   Form loaves, place in greased pan, let rise until double.   Bake at 400 degrees F. for 20 minutes, turn oven down to 325 degrees F. and bake until loaves start to pull away from pan.   Turn out on racks, brush with butter or water, cool.

PINCH-OFFS (Biscuits)

Night before, mix ½ cup Starter 1 cup milk and 1 cup flour, cover and let sit.   Next day, turn out on   1 cup flour, mix   1 T. sugar, ½ t. salt, 1 t. baking powder, ½ t. soda with ½ cup flour, sprinkle over dough, mix well. knead lightly,   Roll out ½ inch thick and cut.   Dip tops in grease, place in greased pan, let rise ½ hour.   Bake at 375 degrees for 30 to 35 minutes.

MUFFINS

Mix in order, do not beat vigorously

2 cups flour

½ cup oil
½ cup milk
1 egg
1 cup berries, raisins, nuts (optional)
3/4 t soda
3/4 cup starter

Drop into muffin tins, filling half full, bake at 375 degrees for 30 to 35 minutes.

These bake slowly, be sure they are done.

SOURDOUGH CORNBREAD

1½ cups cornmeal

1 3/4 cups milk

Add and beat:

2 eggs

3 T. sugar

1 cup starter

Add, stir until blended:

½ t. salt

¾ t. soda

Pour into greased 10 inch skillet, bake at 450 degrees for 30 minutes.

SOURDOUGH DOUGHNUTS

Mix together, set aside:

2 cups flour

½ cup sugar

½ t. baking powder

¼ t. soda ½ t. salt

1/2 t. cinnamon or nutmeg

Beat together, then add dry ingredients:

1 egg

½ cup starter

¼ cup milk

2 T. oil

Turn out and knead lightly, roll out to 3/8 inch thickness. Cut with doughnut cutter or omit spice and cut for maples bars or other pastries. Place on lightly greased baking sheet, cover, lest rises 30 to 40 minutes. Carefully lift with spatula and drop into hot deep fat (370 degrees), fry to golden brown, drain, eat plain, roll in sugar or frost. Makes about 1½ dozen.

OATMEAL COOKIES

Mix:

1½ cups brown sugar

1 cup shortening

Add and mix well:

2 cups thick starter

3 cups rolled oats

1 t. cinnamon

½ t. cloves

½ t. allspice

1 t. soda

1½ cups flour

Chill, roll out, cut and bakes at 375 degrees for 12 to 15 minutes. Cool on rack. May be put together with Lingonberry or Blueberry jelly for a sandwich cookies

CHOCOLATE CAKE

Cream together 1 cup sugar

½ cup shortening Beat in

2 eggs

Add and beat 2 minutes

1 cup thick starter

1 cup milk

1 t. vanilla

1¼ t. cinnamon
3　1 oz. squares semi-sweet chocolate, melted
Mix together, sprinkle on batter, fold in gently

1½ t. soda　and 1/2 t. salt

Add:
2 cups flour

Fold into batter until smooth.　Pour into 9 x 13 pan and bake at 350 degrees until toothpick comes out clean, about 40 minutes.

SPICE CAKE

Omit chocolate, add ½ t. cloves, 1 t. cinnamon, ½ t. nutmeg.　May add raisins and/or nuts.

SOURDOUGH APPLESAUCE CAKE

Mix:
1 cup starter
¼ cup dry milk
1 cup flour
1 cup applesauce

Let sit in warm place while creaming together:-
½ cup white sugar

½ cup brown sugar

½ cup butter or margarine

Combine creamed mixture with sourdough mixture, add:

1 egg

Beat 100 strokes, add:

½ t. salt

1 t. cinnamon

½ t. nutmeg

½ t. allspice

½ t. cloves

2 t. soda   Bake in 9 x 9 pan, 30 to 35 minutes, 350 degrees, test for doneness.

SOURDOUGH FRUIT CAKE

1½ cup raisins

1½ cup currants

3 cups (or more) mixed candied fruit

1 cup hard cider, sherry, brandy, whatever. Cream until fluffy, then beat in eggs:

1 cup sugar

          (substitute 1½ cups honey for both sugars)

 1 cup brown sugar

1½ t. cinnamon

1 t. nutmeg

½ t. allspice

2 eggs

Stir in 1 cup starter.   Combine with fruit mixtures, add 1 cup nuts, add:

4 cups flour, mixed with

1 t. soda

1 t. salt

Mix thoroughly.   Pour into 2 S x 5 x 3 loaf pans lined with greased paper. Bake in 275 degree oven, with pan of hot water on lower rack, about 2½ hours. Cool, remove paper, spoon 2 or 3 T. additional liquor over each cooled loaf.

Wrap in foil or plastic.   Age at least I month before serving.   Additional basting with brandy is traditional.   Should be aged 3 months.

CINNAMON STICKY ROLLS.

Follow Sourdough Bread recipe until time to place in pans. Roll dough out about ½ inch thick. Cover with thin layer of brown sugar and cinnamon, roll up, sealing edges to hold while slicing. Cut to fit bread pans at this point, if you want Cinnamon bread. Generously butter bottom of baking pan, sprinkle brown sugar and cinnamon on butter, trickle a fine line of corn syrup over mixture in pan. Not too much, just well distributed over the bottom of the pan. Slice rolled dough in 1 inch thick slices, lay carefully in pan, lightly mash rolls with your hand, so all are touching and flattened slightly. Allow to rise until almost double. Bake in 375 degree oven, watching carefully, as soon as top begins browning, remove from oven. Let sit for 5 minutes, invert on platter. Butter top and cover with plastic wrap while still hot. These are best served warm.

SALT RISING BREAD   (1914)

Yeast:

1 pint very warm water

1 t. salt

1 heaping tablespoon white corn meal

11 heaping tablespoons flour

Beat all but 1 T. flour until smooth, then sprinkle remaining flour on top. Cover and let stand 5 hours in warm place. Drain clear water off and beat mixture thoroughly. Set aside for another hour, mixture should be light and frothy. Now it's ready to use.

Place about 10 cups flour on board, makes well in center, place 1 heaping Tablespoon lard

½ teaspoon salt 1 pint warm milk in well, add yeast mixture, starting from outside edges, slowly work flour into middle, making stiff dough, knead until smooth.   Place in greased pans and let rise until double.   Bake at 375 degrees about 45 minutes or until starts to pull away from pan: Turn out on rack, brush with water, cool.   Makes 4 loaves.

BURNT SUGAR SYRUP

In heavy cast iron skillet, slowly melt and brown 2 cups white sugar. Stir at first, to prevent scorching.   Watch closely as it browns, as soon as it reaches a lovely caramel brown, remove from heat, pour 1 cup boiling water into skillet.   Wear a mitt or use a long handled cup to pour from as there will be a lot of scorching steam.   Return to heat, carefully stir until sugar once again melts into the hot water.   Remove from heat, serve over pancakes, waffles or french toast. A very flavorful syrup, may be used in desserts or over ice cream, also.   Great on baked custard.

Do not allow to scorch or overbrown, as it will not be sweet and will taste bitter.

WHIPPED BUTTER

Bring 1 pound of real butter to room temperature.   Place in large mixing bowl, start mixer and slowly turn to high speed.   Slowly add 1 cup good quality vegetable oil,   I like a good quality olive oil,   whipping until well combined.   Slowly add 1 cup ice water.   Continue whipping for several minutes.   If you desire added color, add 2 or 3 drops yellow and I drop red food coloring, while whipping.   Place in containers and refrigerate or freeze. Due to the added water, this is not suitable to fry with and may not work well in some recipes.

ANTLER BUTTER

Cut fresh shed antlers into pieces small enough to fit into kettle.   Cover with water and boil 2 days and I night.   Set aside to cool.   There should be about 2 inches of white "butter" on top of the water.   Skim this off and mix with a little salt to taste.   May add food coloring, if desired.

BREAD TIP

    To check rising bread, poke your finger into the dough.   If the hole
rapidly closes in, the dough needs to rise a bit longer.   If the hole stays, the
dough is ready to shape.   If the dough collapses, punch it down and shape into
loaves, watch more carefully this time.   After the shaped dough has risen,
lightly press with your finger, if the slight dent stays, the dough is ready to bake.
If the dent rounds out rapidly, allow more time to rise.

When you are upset or angry, make bread.   Taking frustrations and anger out
on a lump of dough makes lovely loaves of bread and gives you time to
recover.

    BREAD

Dissolve 2 packages yeast in 1/2 cup warm water, add to 5 cups warm water.
Add 1/2 cup sugar (optional), 2 T. salt (also optional) and 1/2 cup cooking oil
or melted shortening (yes, optional).   Beat in 5 cups flour.   Beat a minimum
of 50 strokes. Add 8 more cups of flour, a little at a time, kneading after
mixture becomes too stiff to stir.   Dough should just hold it's shape and not

be sticky. Grease bowl, place dough in bowl, turn to grease top, cover with a towel and let rise in a warm place until double in bulk.   Poke your finger in dough, to test, the indentation should hold it's shape.   If the dough is still rising, the hole will fill in quickly.   Punch dough down and knead well to remove all the large air bubbles.   I do all the kneading right in the bowl I mix the dough in.   It saves a lot of clean-up.   Shape bread into loaves, biscuits, cinnamon rolls or whatever you want.   Place in well oiled pans.   Let rise again until almost double in size,   Bake at 375 degrees until loaves sound hollow when thumped, or starts to pull away from the pan.   Remove from pans .and brush with butter or water.   Butter makes a tender crust, water makes a crusty crust.

May substitute 2 cups rye flour for 2 cups of the white flour, for a delicate rye flavor.   Also use the sugar or honey. Add 3 T. caraway seeds.

For French bread, omit the sugar and oil.   When time to shape, shape in 2 long loaves and place on cookie sheet that has been sprinkled generously with corn meal.   With sharp knife, gash tops every 2½ inches, diagonally, 1/4 inch deep.   Beat 1 egg white until foamy, add 1 T. water.   Brush over tops and sides of loaves.   Place tall glasses around loaves and cover with damp cloth.   The glasses should keep the cloth from touching the loaves.   When bread has doubled. bake at 375 degrees, brushing again with egg white after 20 minutes.

For a rich sweet dough, add 1 cup of sugar, beat in 6 eggs when adding the flour and salt, add 1 more cup of flour during the initial beating.   May need to add more flour during kneading.   Dough should be quite soft.   Use to make pastries.

ENGLISH MUFFINS (Do not require an oven)

In large bowl, mix 2 cups flour, 2 T. sugar or honey, 2 t. salt and   1 T. or envelope dry yeast.   Set aside.   In pan, heat   1 3/4 cups milk, 1/4 cup water, and   1 T. butter or margarine until very warm (120 to 130 degrees). Add gradually to flour mixture and beat at least 150 strokes.   Add 1 egg and   1 cup flour.   Beat as fast as you can another 150 strokes. Add enough flour to make a soft dough.   Knead until smooth and elastic, adding more flour if dough is sticky.   Cover with plastic wrap and let rise in warm place until double, about 1 hour.   Punch down.   Cover and let rise again about 45 minutes, punch down.   Roll out to ½ inch thick.   Cut with 3 1/4 inch round cutter or clean tuna can with both ends removed.   Sprinkle cookie sheets lightly with cornmeal, place muffins about   1 inch apart and sprinkle with additional corn-meal.   Cover lightly and let rise until double.   Heat lightly greased griddle or heavy skillet.   With wide spatula, carefully remove muffins to griddle. Do not puncture or compress or muffins will collapse. Cook   over very low heat 8 to 10 minutes on each side or until light brown.   Muffins should sound hollow when tapped.   Cool on racks.   Makes about 24.

Add 1/4 to ½ cup wheat germ to flour mix. Add 2 cups   Rye or Whole Wheat flour for 2 cups of the white flour in the flour mix.   Add   1 cup oatmeal or cornmeal for 1 cup flour in flour mix.

PUMPERNICKLE BREAD

   Preheat oven to 350 degrees F.   Dissolve 1 pkg. of yeast in 1/4 cup lukewarm water, set aside.
   Combine:
1 1/2 cups cold water
3/4 cup cornmeal

Stir until smooth, place over heat and add:

1 1/2 cups boiling water.

Cook 2 minutes or until it forms much, stirring constantly.   Add:

1 tablespoon sugar

2 tablespoons butter

Let stand until lukewarm. Add:

2 cups mashed potatoes and the yeast mixture

6 cups Rye flour

2 cups wheat flour

Knead until smooth stiff dough forms, using either flour or cornmeal on kneading surface.   Cover and set in a warm place until double in bulk.   Shape into 3 or 4 loaves and let rise to top of pans.   Bake 1 hour or longer, until done.   Loaves should sound hollow when thumped.   This   is an old recipe, from the 1930's.   Add 2 T dry cocoa to dry ingredients if you want black bread.

PILOT BREAD   (Sort of, no leavening)

Mix 5 cups flour,   1 T. sugar,   1 T. salt with as little water as possible to make a stiff dough.   Knead and pull quickly, until smooth.   Roll out as thin as soda crackers, score and bake in 12 by 12 inch sheets at 350 degrees until just lightly browned, 10 or 12 minutes.   Keeps almost indefinitely if kept dry and wrapped airtight.

INDIAN FRY BREAD

Combine 4 cups flour, 4 t. baking powder, 2 t. salt and ¼ cup butter or margarine.   Add enough hot water to make a stiff dough.   Knead until rubbery.   Let rest 15 minutes then roll paper thin.   Cut into 3 inch squares and deep fry until puffy and browned.   Eat while hot, with honey or jam.

HOBO BREAD

Soak overnight in large bowl, 2 cups raisins, 4 t. soda and 2½ cups boiling water. In morning, add 1 cup white sugar, 1 cup brown sugar, 4 T. oil or melted butter, 4 cups flour ½ t. salt and spices (optional) 1 t. cinnamon, ½ t. nutmeg, 1/4 t cloves. Mix well. Divide between 3 well-greased 1 pound size coffee cans. Bake 1 hour at 350 degrees. Let cool in can before removing.

BEER BREAD

In bowl, mix 3 cups self-rising flour, 1/4 t salt and 1 12 ounce can of beer (your choice). Put into greased loaf pan, turn, to grease top, and bake at 400 degrees for 40 minutes. Cool for 10 minutes, turn out on rack. Allow to cool 20 to 30 minutes before slicing and slice thick. Best fresh.

SKILLET EGG BREAD

Heat oven to 425 degrees. Stir together, 2 cups cornmeal, 2 t. salt, 1 t. baking soda. Beat in 2 eggs and 2 cups buttermilk until dry ingredients are moistened. Heat ½ cup butter or margarine in skillet until hot. Stir butter quickly into batter, pour batter into skillet and bake about 25 minutes.

POPOVERS

Place muffin pan in oven and preheat oven to 450 degrees. Mix 1 cup flour, ½ t. salt, 2 eggs, 1 cup milk and 2 t. oil until smooth. Fill muffin cups about ½ full of batter, bake at 450 degrees 20 minutes, 350 degrees, about 20 minutes more.

BAGELS

Boil 1 medium potato in 1 ½ cups water until well done. Mash or blend until you have a soupy looking mess. You should have 2 cups of this mixture, if not, add water to make 2 cups. While mixture is still warm, place in a large bowl, add 2 T. or 2 packets dry yeast and 1 t. honey, sugar or molasses. When yeast has dissolved, beat in 1 egg. Add about 5 cups flour, ½ cup at a time, beating until smooth after each addition. Knead as much of the remaining flour in as it will take, when it becomes to stiff to beat any more. Knead dough 5 to 10 minutes.

Let rise in oiled bowl until doubled, punch down, knead briefly, let rise again until double. Turn dough out and knead, divide into 16 pieces. Roll each piece into a rope, with the palms of your hands, each rope about 6 inches long and tapered at the ends. Form doughnut shape and seal overlapped ends together. Let rest, not touching each other, while a large kettle of water is brought to a boil. Drop bagels carefully into the boiling water, after bagel comes to the surface, allow to boil 1 or 2 minutes, turn over and allow to boil 2 or 3 minutes more. Remove from water with slotted spoon and allow to drain on cake racks which have been covered by paper towel. Place bagels on lightly oiled cookie sheet dusted with cornmeal and bake at 400 degrees for about 40 minutes or until golden brown.

Variations: May add 1 cup wheat germ in place of 1 cup of flour, add with egg.

May use ½ whole wheat flour in place of ½ the flour.

May use 1 cup rye flour in place of 1 cup flour.

May add 1 cup sauteed finely chopped onions after the egg.

May add ½ cup raisins, with the flour. May also add ½ cup chopped nuts. May add I t. cinnamon, ½ t. nutmeg with the egg. Good with the raisins and nuts. I like to split them, spread lightly with butter and toast on a hot griddle, spread with cream cheese and enjoy.

KIPPELS (SWEDISH FLOAT DOUGH) Kids like to fix this one

Dissolve 1 ½ T dry yeast in ½ cup warm water, add 3 T. sugar. Mix ½ cup butter or margarine, 4 ½ cups flour, 1 t. salt and 3 T. sugar. Beat 4 egg yolks, add 1 cup milk, 2 t. vanilla and ½ t. lemon juice, add yeast and stir. Add flour mixture, mix but to not knead. Place in large zip closed type plastic bag, large enough to allow dough to double in size. Close securely, drop into large container of tepid water. When bag comes to the surface, remove and open. Drop a heaping tablespoon of dough into mixture of 2 cups sugar, 3 T. cinnamon and 1 cup very finely ground nuts. Roll dough in this mixture to cover well. Twist into a U shape and place on lightly greased cookie sheet. Let rise until double and bake at 350 degrees F. about 25 minutes until done.

SISKY

Add 13 ounce can evaporated milk to 1 t. salt, 3 T. sugar and ½ cup soft butter or margarine. Heat to melt butter, but barely, when lukewarm, add 1 T. yeast, let sit 5 minutes. Add 2 cups flour and mix well, let stand in warm place about 1 hour or until light and spongy. Add 3 egg yolks, 1 t. vanilla and 2 more cups of flour, mix thoroughly. Let rise until double. Knead lightly, roll out on lightly floured surface to ½ inch thickness, Cut with doughnut cutter or shapes you prefer, and let rise 1 hour. Deep fat fry with raised side down first. Roll in sugar after draining. May be frosted.

POTATO DOUGHNUTS

Boil 3 large peeled potatoes, mash well and while still hot add 1 large T. butter and 2 cups sugar, beat well.   Add 2 cups milk, 3 beaten eggs, 4 heaping t. baking powder, pinch of salt and 1 t. nutmeg, mix well, roll out to ½ inch thick, cut with doughnut cutter or into bars.   Carefully put into deep hot fat and turn at once.   Cook until done, drain, roll in sugar or frost.

SODA CRACKERS (Saltines)

Mix 4 cups flour, ½ t. baking soda and 1 t. salt.   Add 1 cup shortening or margarine.   Add 3/4 cup sour milk, makes stiff dough.   Knead thoroughly for 10 minutes.   Roll out 1/4 inch or less, thick.   Cut into squares, punch holes with fork, place on greased cookie sheet.   Bake at 400 degrees until lightly browned.   May sprinkle lightly with salt before baking, for saltines.

CORN CRACKERS

2 cups flour, 2 cups corn meal, 1 t. salt, ½ t. cream of tartar, 1/4 t. soda, ½ cup minus 1 T. oil, 1 cup of water.   Continue as for soda crackers.
Bake at 275 degrees for 30 minutes.

May add sesame seeds to dough, or sprinkle over dough and roll into it.

May use half whole wheat flour in either recipe, in place of half of the white flour.

HONEY GRAHAM CRACKERS

Mix together:

¾ cup butter

½ cup honey

1 t. vanilla

Sift together and add to the above ingredients:

3 cups graham or whole wheat flour

½ cup wheat germ

½ t. baking powder

Cover and chill several hours or overnight. Divide dough in half and place each half on a small greased cookie sheet. Roll out dough with a flour covered rolling pin until dough covers each sheet in a thin layer, about ¼ to 1/8 inch thick. Try to be uniform for the whole sheet and as even as possible on the edges. Cut into squares and prick each square at least 3 times with a fork. Bake at 325 degrees F. about 30 minutes. May add 1 t. cinnamon to the dry ingredients before combining with the rest.

SIMPLE FLOUR TORTILLAS
3 cups Flour
2 tsp. Baking Powder
1 tsp. Salt
4-6 Tbsp. Vegetable Shortening
1 ¼ cup Warm Water

- Mix the dry ingredients in a large bowl.
- Add Vegetable Shortening by using a fork to cut in the shortening (or just use clean hands).
- Next add a little Warm Water at a time. Do this until your dough is soft, but not sticky.
- Knead dough for a couple of minutes.
- Divide the dough into 12 small balls and let them "rest" for 10-15 minutes.
- Heat up your skillet to a medium-high heat.
- Dust each ball of dough with a little flour before you roll them out. Using a rolling pin, roll the dough until it is fairly thin. If you do not have a rolling pin, you can use a glass or even your hands to shape the dough into a thin, round tortilla.
- Lay the tortilla onto the hot skillet. Watch carefully as it only takes a few

seconds to cook. Flip the tortilla to the other side. You know the tortilla is done when you see many brown spots. Place the tortillas onto a plate and cover with a clean dish towel until ready to serve.

Note: due to the shortening in the tortilla dough, it is not usually necessary to use oil for "frying" the tortilla. If you notice any sticking, use a small amount of cooking spray or oil.

Yields: 12 tortillas

MORE IDEAS FOR USING FLOUR TORTILLAS

A simple complete protein meal is that of a tortilla with beans. The bean burrito is a classic example as well as a bean and cheese quesadilla. Both of these examples can be adapted to fit your families tastes and what ingredients that you have on hand.

Thin crust pizza can also be made using tortillas! Use two tortillas with cheese placed between the layers to make the crust, top with sauce and toppings of choice. These can be backed or put into a large cast iron skillet for the stove top. It is best to cover with a lid as the steam will help to cook the pizza. Besides being a meal, the tortilla can become a dessert too!

- Try making apple enchiladas (canned apples, powdered sugar, tortillas, cinnamon…etc.).
- My grandmother used to give me buttered bread sprinkled with sugar and cinnamon. Why not do the same with a tortilla.

Don't have graham crackers? Make a new version of S'mores using a tortilla.

FLOUR TORTILLAS (Flavored and colored if you add the mashed veggies)

Mix together until fine grained, 3 cups flour, 1 t. salt and 5 T. shortening. Gradually add about 1 cup lukewarm water, may use ½ cup mashed beets or spinach or carrots or tomatoes and ½ cup water, may need a bit more water, stirring until dough clears bowl. Turn out on floured surface and knead 5 minutes. Divide into 12 balls, let stand 15 minutes. Roll each ball to a nine inch circle. Put on hot, ungreased griddle or skillet about 2 minutes per side, or until flecked with brown. May roll half of dough at a time in very thin sheets, cut around a plate to make perfect circles. This wastes a lot of dough and is time consuming. Use for burritoes, enchiladas, fajitas or just an unleavened bread.

PITA BREAD (Pocket Bread) No salt, sugar or fats

Dissolve 1 T. or 1 pkg. yeast in 1¼ cups warm water.   Add 2 cups flour, beat at least 50 strokes, add 1½ to 2 cups more flour, knead in the bowl. Divide dough into 12 pieces, roll out to 1/4 inch thick.   Let rest 45 minutes.   Heat oven to 500 degrees, turn dough over and place on ungreased cookie sheet. Bake 5 minutes on bottom rack of oven, directly over heat.

NOODLES

Beat 1 egg, add 2 T. water, beat to blend.   Add 1 cup flour, mixing well. Add enough additional four to make a fairly stiff dough.   Knead on floured surface until smooth.   Roll out to about the thickness of a dime.   Allow to set until slightly dry or sprinkle liberally with flour.   Loosely roll up and slice in ¼, ½ or 1 inch wide noodles, whichever you want.   Shake out coils and allow to dry if you want.   They may be dropped immediately into boiling liquid and cooked until tender.   Use as any noodles.

Variations:

GREEN NOODLES

Add ¼ to ½ cup pureed spinach to egg.   Proceed as above.

RED NOODLES

Add 1/4 to ½ cup pureed beets to egg.   Proceed as above. May use whole wheat flour for noodles.

ORANGE NOODLES

Add 1/4 to 1/2 cup pureed carrots, squash or sweet potatoes to egg. Proceed as above

May add more water, up to ½ cup.   Add enough flour to make stiff dough. Cut noodles very wide for Lasagne.   May add without precooking to Lasagne, increase liquids or watch closely while baking.   Add liquid as needed.

RAVIOLI

Prepare noodle dough as above.   Roll out and cut in half.   On one half place teaspoonfuls of filling, spaced 1 inch apart.   Moisten spaces between filling with water.   Place other half of dough over filling.   Lightly press down along the moistened strips.   Cut down moistened strips to separate the little pillows of filling.   Press edges of any that look like they might leak.

FILLING: Mix chopped, cooked spinach with riccota cheese and 1 egg, lightly season with oregano.   Or use browned hamburger, onion and cheese. Experiment, use fruit and make a sweet sauce to serve over after cooking, or deep fry instead of boiling.

Cook ravioli in boiling water, drain, serve in tomato sauce or spaghetti sauce. Cheese sauce is very good, also.

BAKING MIX

In a very large bowl, combine 10 cups flour (8 cups if using half whole wheat) 1 ¼ cup nonfat dry milk powder, ½ cup sugar, 1/3 cup baking powder, 2 tsp. salt (optional), and 2 cups vegetable shortening.   Cut shortening into dry ingredients until mixture resembles fine crumbs.   Store in cool dry place in an airtight container.   Use as you would store bought biscuit mix.

RECIPES USING BAKING MIX

PANCAKES

2 cups mix,   1 egg, 2 cups water, mix but not too well, fry on lightly greased griddle.

BISCUITS OR DUMPLINGS

2 cups mix, 2/3 cup milk or water.   Mix for a soft dough.   For biscuits, drop into greased pan for drop biscuits by heaping tablespoons full.   Pat or roll out to ½ inch thick and cut, dip in grease to lightly coat tops, place in greased pan for rolled biscuits.   Bake biscuits at 400 degrees 10 to 15 minutes.

For dumplings, drop by tablespoonfuls onto boiling liquid, (stew, soups or thickened fruit or berries) cover tightly, boil gently 15 to 20 minutes, without removing lid.

BISCUIT VARIATIONS

Add any one or two of the following to the biscuit recipe.   ½ cup shredded cheese, ½ cup crumbled crisp bacon or cracklings, ½ cup sautéed onions, ½ cup wheat germ, ½ cup chopped nuts, ½ cup raisins, ½ cup berries.   Proceed with recipe.

PIZZA CRUST

Use biscuit recipe, pat dough onto greased pizza pan, top with favorite toppings. Bake at 425 degrees, 20 to 25 minutes.

WAFFLES

2 cups mix, 1 egg, 2 cups water, 2 T. oil.   Mix lightly.   Follow directions for waffle iron.

EASY SOURDOUGH PANCAKES

Easy Sourdough pancakes can be made with baking mix. To 1 cup baking mix, add ½ cup sourdough starter, 1 t. baking soda and sufficient water to make batter as thick or as thin as you like it. Fry on lightly greased griddle or skillet. To test for doneness, lightly press with finger in center of turned pancake. If pancake springs back, it is done.

CHOCOLATE CAKE

Mix 4 rounded tablespoons of cocoa with the sugar before adding to the above ingredients. Add a dash of cinnamon to bring out the chocolate flavor. ¼ t. soda

SPICE CAKE

Add 2 t. cinnamon, I t. nutmeg, ½ t. allspice, 1/4 t. cloves to above recipe.

APPLESAUCE CAKE

Add ½ cup applesauce to the spice cake, add ½ cup chopped nuts and ½ cup raisins, if desired.

OVEN-FRY MIX

1 cup mix, 2 t. season salt, ½ t. paprika, ½ t. pepper, 1 t. dried herbs or. poultry seasoning. (May use Italian seasoning, cumin, chili, rosemary, thyme) Combine ingredients in plastic or. paper. bag. Shake to coat 3 pounds poultry pieces or. chops, or. 2½ pounds fish fillets. More mix will stick to meat if meat has been rinsed with water.. Generously grease baking pan. Place meat in pan so pieces don't touch. Bake uncovered in 400 degree oven, turn once during baking. Poultry about 50 minutes, chops about 60 minutes and fish about 20 minutes.

CHEESE BISCUITS

Ingredients

2 cups baking mix

2/3 cup milk

1/2 cup shredded cheddar cheese (extra sharp?)

1/4 cup butter

1/4-1/2 teaspoon garlic powder

Directions

Preheat oven to 450*.

Combine mix, milk and cheese with a wooden spoon until soft dough forms.

Beat vigorously 30 seconds.

Drop dough by heaping tablespoonfuls onto an ungreased cookie sheet.

Bake 8-10 minutes until golden brown.

Combine butter and garlic powder; brush over warm biscuits before removing from cookie sheet.

Serve warm.

Makes 10 large biscuits.

VEGETABLE PIE

In 10 inch pie pan, combine 2 cups blanched, chopped vegetables, your. choice, 1 cup shredded Cheddar. cheese, ½ cup chopped onion and ½ cup chopped green pepper. (optional) may use soaked dried onion and peppers.   Beat or blend 1½ cups milk, 3 eggs, 1/4 cup mix, 1/2 t. salt and ¼ t. pepper. until smooth.   Pour. over vegetable mixture, bake until set and browned, about 40 to 50 minutes at 400 degrees.   Let set 5 minutes before serving.   Broccoli and cauliflower. are good in this recipe.

LEMON CUSTARD PIE

Butter a 9 inch pie pan. Combine 4 eggs, 3/4 cup sugar, 1 1/2 cups milk, 2 T. oil, 1/2 cup mix, 1/2 cup lemon juice and 3 T. grated lemon rind (zest), beat at high speed for 3 minutes or blend at low speed, 3 minutes. Pour into greased pan, let stand for 5 minutes, bake 40 - 45 minutes at 350 degrees, serve cool or cold.

COCONUT PIE

Butter a 9 inch pie pan. Combine 4 eggs, 2 cups milk 3/4 cup sugar, 1/2 cup mix, 1/4 cup butter or margarine and 1 1/2 t. vanilla. Beat at high speed for 3 minutes or blend at low speed 3 minutes. Pour into pan, let stand for 5 minutes. Sprinkle with 1 cup flaked or shredded coconut. Bake at 350 degrees for 40 minutes. Serve cool or cold.

FRUITCAKE BARS

Mix 2 cups mix, 2 T. brown sugar and 1/4 cup firm margarine or butter thoroughly. Press mixture with floured hands into an ungreased jelly roll pan. Bake 10 minutes at 350 degrees. Sprinkle 1 cup coconut over baked layer, mix 2 cups chopped candied fruit, 1 cup chopped dates and 1 cup chopped nuts, sprinkle over coconut layer. Carefully pour 1 (14 ounce) can sweetened condensed milk over top of whole works. Return to oven and bake 25 to 30 minutes more. Cool completely, cut into bars.

FUDGE OATMEAL BARS

Grease jelly roll pan. Mix 2 cups packed brown sugar, 3/4 cup soft margarine, 2 eggs, 2 t. vanilla, 2 1/2 cups mix and 3 cups quick-cooking oats. Press 2/3 of mixture into greased pan. In saucepan, heat 1 package (12 oz.) semisweet chocolate chips, 1 cup sweetened condensed milk, 2 T. margarine or butter, and a dash each of salt and cinnamon, stirring constantly until smooth. Add 1 cup chopped nuts and 2 t. vanilla. Spread over mixture in pan, drop tablespoons of remaining mixture on top. Bake about 30 minutes at 350 degrees. Cool, cut into bars.

BUTTERSCOTCH BUBBLE LOAF

Use any recipe for 1 loaf bread dough, after bread has risen once, punch down and shape into small balls as for small biscuits. Dip each ball into dry non-instant Butterscotch Pudding Mix. Place in Bundt pan that has been sprayed with non-stick cooking spray. Alternate layers of dough balls and sprinkles of chopped pecans or walnuts. Combine 1/2 cup brown sugar and 1/2 cup butter or margarine, heat until butter is melted and a syrup is formed. Microwave about 1 1/2 minutes. Pour syrup over dough in pan. Cover loosely and let rise until double in size. Uncover and bake at 350 degrees F. for 30 to 35 minutes. Cover with foil the last 15 minutes of baking. Immediately after removing from oven, loosen sides from the pan by running a kitchen knife around the inside of the pan, invert onto a serving plate.

BREADSTICKS

Use any bread recipe for 1 loaf. Divide into 8 equal pieces, after the first rising. Roll each piece between your palms to form a long roll. Melt 1/4 cup of butter in a 9" x 13" baking pan, roll each dough piece in the melted butter to coat well.

Sprinkle coarse garlic salt and grated parmesan cheese on top, loosely cover and allow to rise until double is size. Remove cover and bake at 350 degrees, F. for 15 to 20 minutes.

May use rock salt for salt sticks, omit garlic and cheese.

BAKED SANDWICH

Use any recipe for 1 loaf of bread. After dough has risen once, roll or pat out into a 12" x 16" rectangle. Carefully place on a cookie sheet. Leaving a 4 inch wide strip uncut down the middle, cut 2" wide strips down each side. Pour 1/3 cup Light cheese dressing or mayonnaise with garlic and cheese mixed in, down the uncut center. Top with layers of thin sliced lunch meat, like 1/2 pound of pastrami, and 8 slices of cheese, Swiss is good. If using the pastrami - Swiss cheese combination, top with 2 cups of sauerkraut. Begin braid by folding top and bottom up over filling. Start at the top or edge farthest from you and fold strips of cut dough over to the center so they overlap, left, then right, then right over left until finished. Brush braid with 1 beaten egg white and sprinkle with 2 T. Caraway seeds for this sandwich, may use sesame seeds for other sandwich fillings.

I like to brown a 1/2 pound of burger, mix some chopped onion, celery and green pepper with it and spread down the middle of the dough. Top with some sliced cheese for a cheeseburger sandwich, braid as above. Spoon BBQ sauce on burger before braiding, for BBQ sandwich. Use chopped cooked chicken, onion and cheese for a treat. Any meat combo is usually great. Cheese helps hold the filling together after slicing.

ZUCCHINI BREAD
Preheat oven to 325 degrees

Beat12 eggs until light and fluffy, then add 9 cups sugar, 8 teaspoons vanilla, 4 cups oil, 8 cups grated zucchini blending together well. Then add 1 teaspoon cayenne, 1 teaspoon cloves, 1 teaspoon allspice, 8 teaspoons cinnamon, 4 cups chopped nuts and 4 cups raisins. Nuts and raisins optional. Add 12 cups flour, 4 teaspoons baking powder, 2 teaspoons salt, 4 teaspoons baking soda and stir well. Loaves remove from pans easier if you line the pans with tinfoil or waxed paper before adding dough. Bake for one hour or until tests done. Makes 10 large loaves.

ORANGE PINEAPPLE CARROT CAKE (No Sugar)

Beat 3 eggs until light, add 6 T. vegetable oil, 1 t. vanilla and 1 t. pineapple extract (optional but best if used). Add ½ t. allspice, 1½ t. cinnamon, 1/2 t. salt, 3/4 t. baking powder and 3/4 t. baking soda. Add 2 cups flour and 3/4 cup orange concentrate, mixing well.   Stir in 3/4 cup very well drained crushed pineapple, 1 1/2 cups grated raw carrots and 32 chopped dates.   Bake in 9 inch square pan at 350 degrees about 35 minutes.

RAISIN APPLESAUCE CAKE (No Sugar)

Cook 2½ cups dark seedless raisins in 2 cups water until raisins are soft.   Drain well. (Water may be used to cook apples in to slightly sweeten). Beat 2 eggs until light, add 3/4 cup vegetable oil and 1 cup plus 3 T. unsweetened applesauce.   Beat until well blended.   Add 2 t. vanilla, 1/4 t cloves, ½ t. allspice, ½ t. nutmeg, 2 t. cinnamon, I t. baking soda and 2 cups flour.   Mix well.   Add the drained raisins.   Bake in 9 x 13 pan at 325 degrees for about 40 to 45 minutes.   Serve slightly warm.

WHIPPED TOPPING #1 (Fake Whipped Cream)

Soften 1 t. gelatin with 2 t. cold water, then add 3 T. boiling water, stirring until gelatin is completely dissolved.   Cool until tepid.   Place ½ cup ice water and ½ cup nonfat dry milk in chilled bowl.   Beat at high speed until stiff peaks form.   Add 3 T. sugar or artificial sweetener to taste, still beating, then add 3 T. vegetable oil and gelatin mixture. Place in freezer about 15 minutes, then place in refrigerator until ready to use.   Stir before using.

WHIPPED TOPPING # 2

Combine ½ cup ice water, 2 T. lemon juice and I t. vanilla in chilled bowl. Sprinkle ½ cup dry non-fat milk over, beat at high speed until stiff, add sugar or artificial sweetener to taste.   Serve.

LEMON PUDDING CAKE..

Blend 1 ½ cups sugar, 1 ½ T. butter, 3 well beaten egg yolks and 3 T. flour. Mix until smooth, add 1 ½ cups milk, grated rind (zest) and juice of 3 lemons, fold in 3 stiffly beaten egg whites. Pour into large pie pan or square baking pan. Bake at 350 Degrees F about 45 minutes. Sponge cake on top, lemon custard on bottom, when done. Serve warm or cool. May pour into unbaked pie shell, then bake, for something different.

VERY STRAWBERRY CAKE

Mix 1 package white cake mix, 2/3 cup oil, ½ 10 ounce package thawed strawberries, 1 - 3 ounce package strawberry jello, ½ cup water, 4 eggs and 1 t. vanilla. Beat until smooth. Bake at 350 degrees until done, 25 to 35 minutes. Cool. Top with whipped cream with other ½ package thawed strawberries added, add more sugar, to taste.

CHOCOLATE SAUERKRAUT CAKE

If kraut is salty, rinse and drain well. Combine 1 1/4 cups sugar, 2/3 cup shortening, add 3 well-beaten eggs. Mix ½ cup cocoa, 2 1/4 cups flour, 1 t. baking soda, 1 t. baking powder together, add, alternating with 1 cup water to egg mixture. Stir in 1/4 cups chopped sauerkraut and 1 t. vanilla, add a dash of cinnamon. Bake at 350 for about 30 to 35 minutes. Cool and frost.

FROSTING FOR SAUERKRAUT CAKE

Combine 1 cup milk and 2 T. cornstarch, cook, stirring constantly, until thick, cool. Cream 1/4 cup shortening and 1 1/4 cup sugar, add cooled mixture and 1 t. vanilla. Don't worry if it looks strange, it'll be okay. Beat until smooth and spread on cake.

CARROT CAKE

2 cups flour
2 cups sugar
1 t. cinnamon
1 t. nutmeg
2 t. soda
1 t. salt
   Add:
3/4 cup oil
3 eggs
   Mix until fairly smooth and add:
3 cups coarse ground or grated carrots
½ cup coconut
Mix well, bake at 350 degrees in tube pan for I hour 15 minutes.

PINEAPPLE CARROT CAKE

Mix:
2 cups sugar
1 cup oil
3 eggs
Add:

3 cups flour

2 t. soda

1 t. salt

2 t. cinnamon

1 small can crushed pineapple,1 cup coconut, 1 cup chopped nuts, 2 cups grated carrots, pour into 9 x 13 pan, bake at 350 degrees F 50 to 60 minutes. Topping: Boil together for 5 minutes, 1 cup sugar, ½ cup buttermilk, 1 T. lt. corn syrup, 4 t. soda, 1 t. vanilla   Pour boiling hot over hot cake.

CHOCOLATE PUDDING CAKE

   3/4 cup sugar
1 1/4 cup flour
2 T. cocoa
2 t. baking powder
1 t. salt

Add:

2 T. oil

1 T. vanilla

1 cup milk

　　Mix well, pour into 9 x 9 pan, then mix:

1 3/4 cup brown sugar

1/4 cup cocoa

1½ cup hot water

　　Pour over cake batter and bake at 350 degrees for 40 to 45 minutes.

Serve warm.

FRUIT COCKTAIL CAKE

1 1/2 cups sugar

2 eggs

2 cups flour

1　#303 can fruit cocktail and juice

2 t. soda

1 t. vanilla

pinch of salt

　　Mix well, pour into 9 x 13 pan and sprinkle with:

1/2 cup brown sugar　and ½ cup chopped nuts.　Bake at 350 degrees for 50 minutes, watch closely the last 10 minutes.　5 minutes before done, boil ¼ lb. butter,

3/4 cup sugar and ½ cup　milk for 5 minutes, add 1/2 cup coconut, pour over cake.

MAYONNAISE CAKE

Small Cake	Medium Cake	Large Cake
3/4 cup sugar	1 cup sugar	1 1/2 cups sugar
1 ¼ cups flour	2　cups flour	3 cups flour
3 T. cocoa	4　T. cocoa	6 T. cocoa
1 ½ t. soda	2　t. soda	3 t. soda
1/2 t. baking powder	1 t. baking powder	1 ½ t. baking

powder

| dash salt | I t. salt | 1 ½ t. salt |
| dash cinnamon | 1/4 t. cinnamon | 1/2 t. cinnamon |

Mix thoroughly, add:

3/4 cup mayonnaise	1 cup mayonnaise	1 1/2 cups mayonnaise
scant 1 cup water	1 ½ cup water	1 3/4 cup water
1 t. vanilla	1 1/4 t. vanilla	1 ½ t. vanilla

Mix well, bake at 350   degrees:

| 9 x 9 deep dish, 40 minutes | 10 x 10 deep dish, 50 minutes | 9 x 13 deep dish, 60 minutes |

I usually split the mayonnaise cake when cool and fill with chocolate pudding.   Then add chocolate to whipped cream to top the cake with.   Makes a very moist, rich chocolate dessert.

CHOCOLATE PUDDING

5 level T. cornstarch

4 T. cocoa

1 cup sugar

After mixing the above ingredients well, add:
4 cups milk   (may use half and half for richer pudding)
1 t. vanilla
3 T. butter or margarine
Bring to boil, stirring constantly, boil 2 or 3 minutes, remove from heat. Cool with plastic wrap on pudding to prevent skin from forming.   May use to fill chocolate cake, then add whipped cream to the container and the amount

of pudding sticking to the sides should be enough to flavor the whipped cream.

NO-BAKE FRUITCAKE   (No sugar)

Steam 1 cup chopped dates and 1 cup raisins for 10 minutes.   Combine with 1½ cups crushed, packed Wheaties or corn flakes, 1 cup candied fruit, ¾ cup orange juice concentrate, 1 cup toasted wheat germ, 1 cup chopped nuts and ¼ cup honey. Pack firmly into waxed paper lined ring mold. Place weight on top and refrigerate for 1 or 2 days. Unmold and slice.

May use ½ cup white corn syrup in place of honey, increase crushed flakes to 2 cups. May add ½ t. brandy extract for flavor.

CRAZY CAKE

Mix in 9 x 9 pan:

1 1/2 cups flour

1 cup sugar

1 t. soda

1/2 t. salt

3 rounded T. cocoa

   Add:

6 T. oil

1 T. vinegar

1 t. vanilla

1 cup cold water

   Mix thoroughly with fork, bake at 350 degrees, 30 minutes

ICING WITHOUT SUGAR

   1 pkg. sugarless whipped topping mix,   1 pkg. instant sugarless pudding mix, small size, any flavor, 1½ cups cold milk.

   Beat with mixer at high speed until it holds stiff peaks. Keep cake refrigerated after frosting with this icing. Freezes well. This is an easy icing to make, using mixes with sugar, too.

EASY CHOCOLATE MARSHMALLOW ICING

In top of double boiler, combine 1 square unsweetened chocolate, 6 large marshmallows, 4 T. milk and ¼ t salt. Steam until melted. Add 3 T. butter and cool, stirring until a smooth paste is formed. Gradually work in 2 cups powdered sugar until smooth and thick enough to spread. Add more sugar if thicker icing is desired.

CARAMEL FROSTING

Melt ¼ cup butter or margarine, add 3/4 cup brown sugar and ¼ cup canned milk or half and half. Heat, stirring, until sugar dissolves. Cool slightly and beat in 2½ cups powdered sugar and 1 t. vanilla.

BUTTER FROSTING

Cream ½ cup butter, work in 2 cups powdered sugar. Add 1½ t. vanilla, 2 T. light cream or canned milk. Add 2 more cups of powdered sugar, a little at a time. Add more cream, a few drops at a time, until of spreading consistency.

May use other flavorings in place of the vanilla.

May mix 2 T. cocoa with some of the powdered sugar, for chocolate cream.

WHITE CREME FROSTING (Like Twinkie Filling)

Cream ½ cup good quality shortening (Crisco), work in 2 cups powdered sugar. Add 1 t. vanilla and 2 T. boiling water. Whip at high speed, adding up to 2 cups more powdered sugar. May add more hot water, a drop at a time, until light and fluffy.

PIE PROBLEMS & SOLUTIONS

BOIL - OUT - - A normal condition during last 10 minutes of baking
Reduce by decreasing temperature after boiling begins.

PUFFED CRUST -- Water vapor cannot escape through crust during baking
Cut vent holes in top crust to permit steam to escape during baking.

WATERY FILLINGS -- Pie not baked long enough to fully cook fruit and allow starch to mix with juices. Bake 5 to 10 minutes longer. Filling should simmer 10 minutes.
BURNED EDGES, PALE CENTER -- Oven temperature too high. Uneven heat in the oven.
Lower temperature in oven. Rotate pie during baking cycle, if burned on one side only. Center pie in oven with respect to the heating elements.

OVER-BROWNED OR DARK TOP CRUST -- In oven too long. Pie too close to heating element. Oven too hot. Reduce baking time. Center pie in oven using middle rack position. If baking several pies at the same time, rotate the pies to different racks and positions.

RAW BOTTOM, BAKED TOP -- Oven heat too high, bottom element too low. Check oven temperature with a reliable thermometer. Pie tin warped or bent, not on a flat surface. Baking sheet warped or has carbon deposit. Check pans and baking sheets. Pies placed too close together, preventing good heat circulation. Pie placed too high in the oven. Bake fewer pies and allow proper spacing for good heat circulation.

PIE CRUST
1 cup shortening or   3/4 cup butter or lard
2 cups flour, dash of salt, mix together with fork, but not too well. Add cold water, a little at a time, until mixture balls up. Do not mix well. Makes 2 9" crusts
or 1 two crust pie.

CHOCOLATE FUDGE PIE
Prepare 9" pie shell, then mix:
1/4 cup butter or margarine
3/4 cup brown sugar
3 eggs
12 oz. semi-sweet chocolate, melted
1/2 t. rum extract

1/4 cup flour
1/2 cup chopped walnuts
Pour in unbaked pie shell, sprinkle 1/2 cup chopped walnuts over top.   Bake at 375 degrees for 25 minutes.   Extremely rich.

COTTAGE CHEESE PIE #1

2 cups cottage cheese

2 eggs separated, for denser filling, don't separate, just add

7/8 cup sugar

1 T. butter

2 T. milk

2 T. flour

½ t. vanilla

1 unbaked pie crust

Cinnamon or nutmeg

Mash cottage cheese with a fork, add egg yolks or eggs and beat some more. Stir in sugar, butter, milk, flour and vanilla.   Fold in stiffly beaten egg whites if you are separating the eggs.   Pour into pie crust.   Sprinkle top with either cinnamon or nutmeg, whichever you like best.   Bake at 350 degrees F for 45 minutes until browned and only slightly jiggly in middle.

COTTAGE CHEESE PIE #2
Lightly beat:
3 eggs
Add:
3 cups cottage cheese
Dash of salt
½ t. cinnamon
½ cup chopped blanched almonds
1 cup raisins
Mix well and pour into 1 unbaked pie shell.   Sprinkle top with some cinnamon and sugar.   Bake at 350 degrees F. until lightly browned and done.

MOCK PECAN PIE
Ingredients:
Pastry for a 9-inch pie
1 cup cooked pinto beans, rinsed
1 cup light brown sugar
1 cup white sugar
1/3 cup margarine
4 eggs, well beaten
2 teaspoons vanilla
Directions:

- (1) Puree beans in blender until smooth, or mash the beans really well.
- (2) Mix beans and other ingredients well.
- (3) Pour into an unbaked pie crust.
- (4) Bake at 375 degrees until center is set. Tastes just like pecan pie ...really!

ANOTHER MOCK PECAN PIE
Ingredients

- 1 cup white sugar
- 2/3 cup packed brown sugar
- 3 eggs
- 1/3 cup butter
- 1 cup pinto beans, cooked and mashed
- 1/3 cup chopped pecans
- 1 recipe pastry for a 9 inch single crust pie

Directions
Preheat oven to 350 degrees F (175 degrees C).
Cream together butter, sugars and eggs (slightly beaten). Add beans and nuts, mix well and pour into unbaked pie shell.
Bake at 350 degrees F (175 degrees C) for 35 to 40 minutes.

PINTO BEAN PIE
This pinto bean pie recipe is made with coconut and nuts.
Ingredients:

- 1 cup cooked pinto beans, mashed with a little of the cooking liquid
- 1 1/3 cups coconut (small can)

- 1 cup chopped pecans
- 4 eggs
- 3 cups granulated sugar
- 1 tbsp vanilla
- 2 sticks melted butter or margarine
- 3 unbaked 9" pie shells

Preparation:

Mix all ingredients together and pour into pie shells. Bake for 1 hour in a 300° oven. Makes three 9-inch pies.

PINTO BEAN PIE (MOCK PUMPKIN PIE)

Preheat the oven to 425 degrees F.

Puree in a blender 2 cups cooked, unseasoned pinto beans with about 1/4-1/2 cup of liquid (water or apple juice) until the beans are very smooth. Scrape this into a bowl.

Add and mix in the following ingredients in this order:

3 eggs,

1 13 oz can of evaporated milk

1 cup sugar

3/4 teaspoon salt

1 teaspoon cinnamon

1 teaspoon ginger

1/4 teaspoon clove

1/4 teaspoon nutmeg

Pour into a 9-inch unbaked pie shell. Bake at 425 for 15 minutes, then reduce the heat to 350 and continue baking for another 45 minutes or until a knife comes clean from the center.

PINTO BEAN PIE (also mock pumpkin pie)

Ingredients:

1 1/2 cups of unseasoned cooked pinto beans (can use a one 15oz. can if you prefer)

1 cup of light brown sugar

2 eggs

1/2 cup (1 stick) of butter at room temperature

1 teaspoon vanilla

1 teaspoon cinnamon

1/4 teaspoon nutmeg

1/4 teaspoon allspice

1/4 teaspoon clove
A pinch of salt
1 unbaked 9-inch pie shell
Method:
Preheat the oven to 350 degrees.
In a blender, cream the sugar, butter and eggs.
Add the beans, and blend until it's thick and smooth.
Add the spices and vanilla.
Pour pie filling into an unbaked pie shell, and bake for one hour or until an inserted knife comes out clean.

APPLE PIE CRUST WITH A DIFFERENCE

Make a batch of cinnamon rolls to the point that they are rolled and ready to cut. Cut the rolls very thin and place in a greased pie pan. Flatten very thin so they are about the thickness of pie crust and allow to rise a bit, then partly bake until done but not browned. Fill with your favorite pie filling and add a crumb topping and bake until done and the crust is browned.

ANOTHER GOOD UNUSUAL CRUST

Use a recipe for the cookies of your choice and pat the dough out fairly thin in the pie pan. Make sure to cover the bottom and sides very well. Bake and use as crust for cream pies. A good one is to layer softened cream cheese over the baked crust and then fill with cooked pudding, top with whipped cream.

VINEGAR PIE (Old Fashioned Pie)

Prepare crust for 2 crust pie, line 9" " pan with 1 crust. Combine 1 cup brown sugar, 2 cups water and 1 cup cider vinegar, heat to boiling. Add 2 T. butter or margarine, stirring until melted. Mix ½ cup flour with small quantity of cold water until smooth. Add slowly to boiling liquid, stirring constantly, until thickened. Pour filling into crust-lined pan. Cut other crust into lattice strips and arrange on top of filling. Bake at 400 degrees for 10 minutes, reduce heat to 350 degrees and bake about 25 minutes longer. Serve cold.

CANNED FRUIT COBBLER

Melt 1/2 cup butter or margarine in 8 x 10 pan. Blend 1 cup flour, 1 cup sugar, 1 T. baking powder and dash of salt, gently stir in 3/4 cup milk. Pour batter over melted butter, DO NOT MIX. Pour 1 quart fruit (peaches, apricots, berries, whatever you have on hand) over batter. Sprinkle 1 t. vanilla over fruit, spread 1/2 cup suqar over entire top of cobbler Bake at 350 degrees for one hour or until browned.   Serve warm, with or without whipped cream.

APPLESCOTCH PIE

Peel and slice 6 or 8 apples.   Heat 3/4 cup dark brown sugar, 1 cup water and 2 t. vinegar, add apples and simmer until tender.   Remove apples from syrup to pastry lined deep dish pie pan.   Mix 3/4 cup dark brown sugar 4 T. flour and dash of salt, add slowly to syrup.   Cook until thickened. Remove from stove and add 2 T. butter and 1 t. vanilla, pour over apples. Top with crisscross pastry or crumb topping.   Bake at 375 degrees for about 45 minutes.   May omit top crust and top with meringue after baking, then return to oven to brown meringue.

BERRY PIE   (No Sugar)

Place 4 to 6 cups clean berries in saucepan.   Add ½ to 1 full can thawed apple juice concentrate, depending on tartness of berries.   Combine 6 T. cornstarch with 1 cup water, add to berries, add enough water to almost cover berries.   Bring to boil, stirring constantly, boil 2 minutes, remove from heat, pour into baked pie shell, cover with plastic wrap until cool.   Top with whipped cream.   Instead of covering with plastic, may use meringue and brown.   Sweeten with fructose or artificial sweetener, if sugar is a problem.

Variations: May use same amount of sliced fruit, peaches, apples, cherries in place of berries for sugarless pie.

May use a layer of sugarless custard or vanilla pudding in bottom layer of pie, especially if you are short of fruit.   This makes a very lovely pie and delicious.

May spread a layer of softened cream cheese in bottom of pie shell. Heavenly.

PUMPKIN PIE

Prepare 2 unbaked pie shells, (9 inch).   Combine 4 eggs, 3 cups strained pumpkin or 1 29 ounce can pumpkin, blend in 1 ½ cups sugar (white or brown) ½ t. salt, 2 ½ t. cinnamon, 2 t. ginger, 1 ¼ t. nutmeg and ¼ t. cloves (optional).   Add 2 cans, 13 ounce size, evaporated milk or 3 ½ cups half 'n half.   Mix well.   Divide into 2 pie shells, bake at 425 degrees F for 15 minutes, reduce heat to 350 degrees F and bake an additional 45 minutes.   May add 1 t. vanilla with milk.

May substitute equal amount of carrots, winter squash or sweet potato, mashed smooth or whipped in blender until smooth, for the pumpkin.   Most people can't tell the difference as long as it's the right color.

PUMPKIN CHIFFON PIE

Combine 1 ½ cups strained or canned pumpkin, 2/3 cup evaporated milk, ½ t. salt,   1 t. ginger,   1 t. cinnamon, 1 ½ t. nutmeg and 1/2 cup sugar in double boiler. Heat, add to 3 slightly beaten egg yolks, return to double boiler and cook, stirring constantly, until thick.   Dissolve 1 T. or package plain gelatin in ¼ cup cold water, add to pumpkin, blend thoroughly, cool until almost set. Beat 3 egg whites until stiff, add ½ cup sugar.   Fold into pumpkin mixture and pour into baked, cool pie shell.   Chill and garnish with whipped cream. Flavor whipped cream with 3 T. molasses.

May substitute artificial sweetener for sugar.

RHUBARB CUSTARD PIE

Prepare pie crust.   Combine 2 well-beaten eggs, 2 T. melted butter or margarine and 3/½ cups sliced or diced rhubarb.   Mix and add 1 1/2 cups sugar, 1/2 t. cinnamon, ½ t. salt and 7 T. flour, blend well.   Pour into pastry shell, moisten edges and add top crust, trim, leaving ½ inch beyond edge of dish.   Fold under edges, pinch up and flute between fingers and thumb.   Bake at 350 degrees F for 50 to 60 minutes.

SUPER CHOCOLATE ICE CREAM PIE

CRUST: In saucepan, stir together   1 cup light corn syrup,   1 cup sugar, ¼ cup margarine and   1 cup chocolate chips or baking chocolate over low heat. Stirring constantly, bring to boil.   Remove from heat, stir in 5 cups crispy cereal, stirring well. Press mixture into lightly buttered pie pans - 3 9-inch or 2 10-inch deep dish pans.   If you wish a thinner crust, use less mixture and either make more pies or press into buttered pan and cut for candy.

FILLING: Soften your favorite chocolate flavored ice cream enough to spoon into crusts.   Fill pies evenly, mound slightly. Place in freezer.

TOPPING: Mix   1 package instant chocolate fudge pudding mix with 1 pint whipping cream and   1 cup milk.   Whip until thick and holds soft peaks.   Spread on top of pies, forming swirls and peaks.   Return to freezer until shortly before serving.   Remove pie from freezer a ½ hour before serving, place in refrigerator, dip knife in hot water to cut smooth slices. Sprinkle shaved chocolate curls on top of whipped cream before serving, if you like.   May have chocolate fudge sauce on the side for those who want even more chocolate.

Variations: Use butterscotch or peanut butter chips instead of chocolate in the crust.   Use ice cream of your choice for filling.   Maple nut, almond mocha, what the heck, vanilla, all are good.   Flavor the whipped cream with liqueur for a different treat.

CHOCOLATE OATMEAL PIE

Beat 2 eggs until thick and lemon colored, add   1 cup sugar, ¼ t. salt, 1 cup light corn syrup, 2 T. melted butter or margarine and   1 t. vanilla, beat until smooth.   Stir in ½ cup each, coconut, quick-cooking oatmeal (not cooked) and semi-sweet chocolate chips.   Pour into prepared unbaked 9-inch pastry in pie pan.   Bake at 350 degrees for 50 to 55 minutes.   Pie will be very dark. Cool completely before serving.   Serve with whipped cream.

RED-HOT APPLE PIE

Prepare crust for double crust pie.   Peel, core and slice apples.   Arrange a layer of apple slices in crust, sprinkle ¼   cup red-hot cinnamon candies over alternate layers of candy and apples until crust is filled.   Moisten edge of bottom crust, place top crust over after cutting design or just slashing to allow steam to escape during cooking.   Lightly pinch edges into a raised edge all around the pie.   Flute edge, pinching between left and right thumb and forefinger The raised edges help prevent juices from escaping onto the oven floor.   Bake at 350 degrees until bubbling and browned.   Use   1 to   1½ cups red-hots to a pie, depending on taste.

RHUBARB STRAWBERRY PIE

Prepare double crust, line pan with bottom crust.   Wash, trim and slice rhubarb.   Layer sliced rhubarb with 1 to 1 ½ cups strawberry preserves or jam in the prepared crust.   Proceed as above.

Variations.   Use apples in place of rhubarb.   If using apples, may use pineapple, orange or mint jam or jelly although strawberry is very good, too.

May use any fruit and jam combination for a distinctive pie. Peaches with apricot jam is lovely.

PLUM PUDDING

Combine 2 cups cooked ground meat, 1 cup sugar, 1 cup raisins, 1 cup chopped suet, 1 cup currants, 1 cup bread or cracker crumbs, 1/2 cup chopped candied orange peel, 1½ cup candied cherries, 1/2 cup candied pineapple and 1 1/2 cup candied fruit, 1 cup chopped apples, 3 eggs, 1/2 cup milk. Add 1 t. allspice, 1t. cinnamon, 1 t. soda and 2 cups flour. Pack in clean wide mouth pint jars to within 2 inches of top. Put lids on firmly, process in Pressure canner 60 minutes at 10 pounds pressure.

POP TARTS (Sort Of)

3/4 C . shortening

3/4 C sugar

3 eggs

3 3/4 C flour

3 Tbsp baking powder

1/2 C preserves

1 egg yolk, beaten with 2 tbsp. light cream

Cream shortening and sugar. beat in one egg at a time. Sift together flour and baking powder, stir into shortening mix to make a soft dough. Chill for 1 hour.

Turn dough onto a floured surface and roll out 12 rectangles each 8 x 12". Spread about a Tbsp of preserves over 1/2 of each rectangle staying well within
the edges. Fold dough over the preserves and trim the edges or crimp to close.

Place tarts on a greased cookie sheet and brush w/the egg yolk cream mix. Bake
in a 350 degree F. oven for 20 minutes.

PIE TIP

An average pie requires ¾ cup sugar or equivalent for a 9" pie. Unless your fruit or berries are extremely sweet or extremely tart, this is sufficient quantity of sweetener. If using granulated fructose, decrease by ¼ to 1/3 cup per 1 cup sugar called for in the recipe. Do the same if using honey for sweetener.

If using honey, also decrease the liquid by ¼ cup per 1 cup of honey or add 1 T. flour as extra thickener.   It mostly depends on your personal taste.

APPLE PIE   (No sugar)

Prepare crust for 2 crust pie, set aside.   In saucepan, combine 6 oz. can thawed apple juice concentrate, 2 T. cornstarch or arrowroot, 5 large apples, peeled and sliced,   1T. margarine,   1 t. cinnamon, 1/4 t   nutmeg and a dash of salt.   Cook until just thickened, pour into unbaked pie shell. Brush edges of crust with water, put on top crust, cut vent holes.   Brush top crust with milk, bake at 375 degrees for 40 minutes or until nicely browned.   Serve warm with sharp cheddar cheese or cold.

TOPPING FOR FRUIT PIES

Instead of a top crust, you may like this topper.   Combine 2/3 cup wheat flakes or corn flakes, ½ cup chopped nuts, 2 T. brown sugar and 2 T. melted margarine.   Mix thoroughly and sprinkle over pie.   Bake for 10 minutes to toast lightly.   May use quick rolled oats in place of the flakes, if desired. This is good as a topping for a precooked crust, thicken berries or fruit, pour into crust, add topping and bake additional time to toast.   Serve with whipped cream or ice cream.

CHEESECAKE

Mix ½ cup butter with   1 cup flour until crumbly.   Add lemon juice, a few drops at a time, until mixture almost holds together.   Pat into the bottom of a spring form pan and seal the edge where it joins the bottom. Bake at 450 degrees, until lightly browned.   Cool.

Soften 4 8-ounce packages cream cheese,   beat until fluffy.   Add 2 cups sugar or i½ cups granulated fructose, 4 T. lemon juice, 2 t. vanilla and a dash of salt.   Mix well.   Add 8 eggs, beating after each one.   Pour filling into baked crust, bake at 300 degrees for an hour.   It should still be slightly sunk in the middle.   Turn oven off and let return to room temperature with cake still in the oven.   Refrigerate and chill several hours before serving.

For richer cheesecake,   increase eggs to 12 and add   1 pint sour cream. Blend thoroughly, bake as above.

May top with cherries, strawberries, blueberries or whatever your heart desires.

PETITE CHEESECAKES

Line 24 cupcake pans with 24 paper liners.   Place a vanilla wafer in the bottom of each.

In bowl, beat 2 8-ounce pkgs. cream cheese, 3/4 cup sugar, 2 eggs,   1 T. lemon juice and 1 t. vanilla until light and creamy.   Fill cups 2/3   full with cream cheese mixture. Bake at 325 degrees about 30 minutes or until set.

CUSTARD

Combine 3 slightly beaten eggs, 1/4 cup sugar, 1/4 t   salt and 2 cups milk. Mix well, add 1 t. vanilla, bake in 1 quart casserole dish or 6 custard cups. Place shallow pan of water under custard while baking.   Double recipe and pour into unbaked pie shell, bake, also.   Bake at 325 degrees until knife inserted off-center comes out clean.

BREAD PUDDING

Use recipe for custard.   Butter 5 slices day-old bread, cut into cubes. Place bread in baking dish, add ½ cup raisins, pour custard over bread, let sit 30 minutes, sprinkle with nutmeg or cinnamon.   Bake as for custard.

RICE PUDDING

Use recipe for custard.   Add 3 or 4 cups cooked leftover rice and ½ cup of raisins.   Bake as for custard.   Sprinkle with cinnamon or nutmeg before baking.

CARAMEL CUSTARD

Melt 12 caramels in ¼ cup milk in top of double boiler, stirring occasionally. Place in bottom of baking dish or bottoms of custard cups, pour custard, using recipe above. over and bake.

STIRRED CUSTARD

Combine ingredients as for custard, except vanilla.   Cook in double boiler stirring constantly, until custard coats metal spoon.   Remove from heat. Place pan in cold water and stir a minute or two.   Add vanilla.   Chill.

NO-WEEP MERINGUE

Cook, stirring constantly, 1 T. cornstarch, 6 T. sugar and ½ cup of water, until smooth and thick.   Cool.   Add 3 egg whites, beat at high speed until mixture stands in satiny peaks; . Spread on pie or other dessert and bake at 350 degrees for 20 minutes or until nicely browned.

If using on Baked Alaska, bake at 500 degrees about 3 minutes, serve.

SOFT ICE CREAM - Copycat

2 envelopes unflavored gelatin

1/2 cup cold water

4 cups whole milk

2 cups sugar

2 teaspoons vanilla extract

1/2 teaspoon salt

3 cups cream

Soak unflavored gelatin in cold water. Heat milk, but do not boil.

Remove from heat, and add gelatin, sugar, vanilla extract

and salt. Cool and add cold cream. Chill 5 to 6 hours.

Pour into a 4 to 6 quart ice cream freezer can. Process as

per manufacturer's instructions.

COOKIES - ARTIFICIAL SWEETENER

Combine   1 1/4 cup water,   1/3 cup oil or butter, 2 cups raisins, 2 t.
cinnamon and ½ t. nutmeg and boil 3 minutes, cool.   Dissolve ½ t. salt, 1 t.
soda and 2 t. liquid artificial sweetener in 2 T. water and add 2 beaten eggs.
Stir in the cooled mixture, add 2 cups flour and 1 t. baking powder, add ½ cup
chopped nuts, mix well.   Drop by teaspoonfuls on lightly greased cookie sheet
or bake as bar cookies, at 375 degrees 10 to 20 minutes.

NORWEGIAN LACE COOKIES

   Grind 2/3 cup almonds.   Melt ½ cup butter in skillet, add dash of salt, ½
cup sugar and 1 T. flour, stir over heat until sugar melts.   Add ground almonds
and 2 T. milk and blend.   Drop from teaspoon onto greased cookie sheet,
leaving plenty of space as they spread.   Bake at 350 degrees for 6 to 8 minutes.

SUGAR COOKIES

Cream ½ cup butter or margarine, ½ cup oil, ½ cup white sugar and ½ cup powdered sugar.   Add 1½ t. vanilla and I beaten egg. Add ½ t. cream of tartar, 2/14 cups flour, ½ t. salt and ½ t. soda, mix well.   Drop by teaspoon onto greased cookie sheet, flatten   with glass bottom dipped in white granulated sugar.   Bake at 375 degrees 10 to 12 minutes or until slightly browned on edges. If you wish, may roll out on sugar-sprinkled surface, turning dough to sugarcoat both sides, cut with cookie cutter and proceed with baking.

OATMEAL COOKIES

In bowl, mix 1 cup flour 3/4 t   soda, ½ t. salt, 1 t. cinnamon and 1/4 t nutmeg.   Add 3/4 cup soft shortening or butter, $1 \, ^1/_3$ cup brown sugar, 2 eggs and 1 t. vanilla,   beat until smooth, add 2 cups uncooked oatmeal, 1 cup raisins and ½ cup chopped nuts, mix.   Drop by heaping t. onto greased cookie sheet. Bake at 350 degrees 12 to 15 minutes.

GRANDMA'S COOKIES

Cream together   1 pound butter, not margarine, 3 cups sugar and 2 whole nutmegs grated.   Add 4 eggs, beat until smooth.   Add ½ t. salt, 6 t. baking powder, 4 cups flour,   1 T. vanilla and   1/4 cup milk.   Mix well. Turn out onto well floured board and knead more flour in until dough holds it's shape very well.   Divide dough in half, roll out a half at a time, to ½ inch thick. Cut into large sized (4 inch diameter) cookies.   Bake on ungreased cookie sheet at 375 degrees, until delicate brown, about 15 minutes.

You may substitute 4 T. ground nutmeg for the grated whole nutmeg, but the cookies will not be the same.   This recipe has been in our family for several generations.

PEANUT BUTTER COOKIES

Cream together   1 cup peanut butter and   1 cup margarine.   Add   1 cup white granulated sugar and   1 cup brown sugar.   Mix well and add 2 beaten eggs, beat until smooth.   Add   1 t. vanilla, 1/4 t   salt, 2 t. baking soda and 3 cups flour. Mix well.   Drop by teaspoonfuls on ungreased cookie sheet, slightly flatten with crisscross pressure of table fork.   Bake at 375 degrees for 10 to 15 minutes.   Do not overcook as these scorch easily.

CHOCOLATE CHIP COOKIES

Cream together ½ cup soft shortening or margarine, ½ cup sugar, ½ cup brown sugar, ½ t. vanilla, add   1 egg, beat until smooth.   Add   1 1/4 cups flour, ½ t. baking soda, ¼ t salt, mix well.   Stir in   1 cup chocolate chips and 1 cup chopped walnuts.   Drop by teaspoonfuls onto cookie sheet.   Bake at 375 degrees for 10 to 15 minutes.

May add 2 cups crispy cereal or oatmeal to dough.

May add   1 cup raisins and ½ t. cinnamon and 1/4 t   nutmeg.

May add ½ cup of peanut butter with shortening.

This is an easy recipe to experiment with, let your imagination run wild. Here is a good example:

Place 1 T. of cookie dough in bottom of greased muffin cups, Top with a peanut butter cup, turned upside down, paper off.   Top the peanut butter cup candy with enough Brownie dough to fill muffin cups 3/4 full and bake at 350 degrees F. for about 18 minutes. May use peanut butter cookie dough in the bottom instead.

GRADUATION TREATS
Ingredients
24 miniature peanut butter cups
1 tube (6 ounces) decorating frosting in color of your choice
24 After Eight thin mints

24 milk chocolate M&M's in color of your choice or 24 semisweet chocolate chips
Directions
Remove paper liners from peanut butter cups; place upside down on waxed paper. Place a small amount of frosting on each peanut butter cup; center a mint on each. Using frosting, make a loop for each cap's tassel. Place an M&M on top of each loop. Yield: 2 dozen.

COOKIE DOUGH COOKIE BOWLS

1/4 cup butter flavored shortening
1/4 cup butter (room temperature)
1/3 cup white sugar
1/3 cup brown sugar
1 egg
1 teaspoon vanilla extract
1/2 teaspoon salt
1/4 teaspoon baking powder
1½ cups all purpose flour
1/4 cup miniature semisweet chocolate chips

Beat together shortening, butter and sugars in a large bowl; add the egg and vanilla; beat until well mixed.

Mix the flour and baking powder and gradually stir them into the batter; stir in the chocolate chips.

Put batter into a large plastic bag and flatten into a disk; chill for at least an hour. Preheat your oven to 375. Turn your cupcake (or muffin) pan upside down and cover every other one with foil.

NOTE: standard size cupcake pan requires a 4" circle of foil and the Texas size muffin pan requires a 6" circle of foil. Spray the foil with vegetable spray.

NOTE: I used the new no stick foil and didn't have to spray it at all.

Roll the chilled cookie dough (between two pieces of waxed paper) out to about 1/8th inch or about the same as pie dough. Cut circles and drape over foil, smoothing cracks together and trimming to fit.

Bake 10-12 minutes or until light brown. Remove from oven and let them cool on the pan for about 10 minutes. After 10 minutes, gently lift them off of the pan (use the tip of a butter knife to lift one corner first) but don't remove the foil until the cookie bowl is completely cool. Fill just before serving.

CANDY

Candy, ah my favorite subject. The only thing I know of that applies 5 pounds of weight to the hips for every 1 pound eaten.

Candy brings visions of Holidays Past, when we made candy to give as gifts. We learned many little tips towards successful candy making. Two of the most basic were the ways to prevent sugaring.

IF a recipe has butter as an ingredient, use part of that butter to thoroughly coat the sides of the kettle you will be cooking in. Also butter the thermometer and the lower part of the spoon handle. For good measure.

IF the recipe does not include any butter, after the mixture comes to a boil, remove spoon and thermometer and cover tightly with a lid.   Be sure to turn heat down enough to prevent boilover.   Wash spoon and thermometer to remove any sugar crystals.   It only takes one unmelted sugar crystal to sugar the whole batch of candy.   Remove lid and replace thermometer.

You can make good candy without a thermometer, but for consistently good results, I recommend a candy thermometer.   It should be checked by testing boiling water - - - 212 degrees F.   Adjust for altitude.

Candy is a fun project for a party, for kids or just to do on your own.   A couple of the recipes need at least two people to handle, such as the candy canes.   You can use the same recipe and make candy twists of different colors and flavors.   Candy and cookies are favorite things for children to begin cooking.   I learned the practical application of fractions by making recipes into goodies.

Any recipe using beaten egg whites will have better results if all utensils are washed in hot soapy water and scalded well.   No plastic utensils, please.   Egg whites achieve more volume if allowed to reach room temperature before beating.   A little speck of grease or egg yolk can thoroughly ruin a batch of Divinity or No-Fail Meringue. Cookies are usually easier for first time cooks to have consistently good results with.   Of course, the dough usually disappears as it's being mixed, if the beginner is very young.   A common mistake in making cookies is adding more liquid because "there must be a mistake, it shouldn't really be that thick".   Yes, it should be that thick.

Cakes, pies and puddings all have their little quirks.   Most are very simple to make and require little more time than a convenience mix.   I make up large batches of dry mix, store and dip out of as needed.   In one afternoon, I can make enough to keep us supplied a whole season.   Pie crust mix and biscuit mix are two that are used the most around our house.   The biscuit mix can be used in any of the recipes on commercial boxed mixes, plus a few things I have never found on commercial boxes.   Quick breads, coffeecakes, applesauce cake, all can be made from the biscuit mix.

TERMS AND TEMPERATURES FOR CANDY COLD WATER TEST:

Thread	230 to 234 degrees	Have ready small bowl
Soft ball	234 to 238 degrees,	of very cold (but not ice

cold)

Medium ball	238 to 244 degrees	water. Remove pan from

heat.

At once, drop a few

drops of

Firm ball	244 to 248 degrees	syrup into water. Form drops
Hard ball	248 to 254 degrees	into ball - its firmness
Very hard ball	.254 to265 degrees	indicates temperature of

syrup.

Light crack	265 to 285 degrees
Hard crack	290 to 300 degrees

CANDY MAKING TIPS

Allow plenty of time when making candy,   Many, such as caramels, take long cooking and stirring.

In humid or rainy weather, cook candies 2 degrees higher than the recipe directions specify.

Use a heavy saucepan, and an asbestos mat, if available, For candies made with cream or milk, since they burn easily.

A candy thermometer is almost a must to assure accuracy. I have made good candy without a thermometer, but I have also made some very rich syrup that I had intended for candy, also some Fudge that could pass for rock candy.

Temperatures rise quickly towards the last of the cooking time for candy. Watch it closely.

Usually it is best not to try doubling the recipes. Several small batches turn out better.

Store candies separately, brittles soften if stored with creamy candies and some sugar. Good luck.

PULLED MINTS

Mix in saucepan:

1½ cups sugar

½ cup water

2 T. lt. corn syrup

Cook, stirring, until sugar is dissolved. Cover and cook 3 minutes to allow steam to wash sugar crystals From sides of pan. Wash spoon. Uncover and place thermometer in mixture, but not touching bottom of pan. Cook without stirring until temperature reaches 260 - 262 degrees on thermometer. Remove From heat and pour into a buttered pan. When candy is cool enough to handle, pour 1/4 t   essence of peppermint extract into center and fold corners over.   Pull with buttered fingers until mixture is satiny and light in color, and will hold ridges and grooves.   Pull into long strips ½ inch in diameter and cut in ½ inch to   1 inch pieces.   Layer pieces in bowl, separating layers with waxed paper.   Cover tightly and store until creamy, usually 24 hours.

CANDY CANES

Follow the above directions until it's time to pull the candy.   Then about halfway through pulling, divide the candy, separating about 1/4 of the mixture. Add a few drops red food coloring to the smaller portion.   Two people are necessary to make these.   As soon as the candy begins holding it's shape, work the two portions together, laying the smaller red stripe along the white stripe. Roll back and forth between your hands to make a smooth cylinder.   For a large candy cane, do not make too slender, cut ends at an angle, twist the cane for the spiral stripe then curve the top over. Place on a sheet of waxed paper until cool.   We usually make lots of tiny canes For tree decorations and as gifts. May use spearmint or wintergreen extract For a change, or even cherry or lemon.   Can be made into all sorts of twists or sticks.   If they are not covered, it takes a long time for them to turn creamy.

BUTTERSCOTCH

Butter sides of heavy kettle, combine:

2 cups sugar

2/3 cup dark corn syrup

1/4 cup water

1/4 cup light cream or evaporated milk, undiluted

Cook until reaches 260 degree, add 14 cup butter or margarine, cook to 280 degrees, pour into buttered 8" square pan, cut in squares when almost set. Cool, break apart.

COCONUT/POTATO CANDY

In double boiler, combine:

½ pound marshmallows 1/4 cup butter or margarine

½ t. salt

Heat until marshmallows melt.   Remove from heat, add:

1 cup prepared instant mashed potatoes or regular mashed potatoes (omit salt & butter) 1 T. vanilla

Divide mixture into 3 parts.   Tint each   part a different color, add a few drops different flavored extract to each (red - cinnamon, green - mint, yellow - lemon, or your own favorites) to each part, add:

1 pound (about) confectioner's or powdered sugar

1 cup flaked coconut

A bit more sugar may be needed to make mixture hold it's shape.   These can be shaped in   1 inch balls, topped with pecan or walnut halves or candied cherries or formed into patties.   You may like to make ½ inch balls, let them firm up, then dip in melted chocolate.

MOLASSES TAFFY

Butter sides of heavy kettle, add:

1 cup unsulfured molasses

1 cup sugar

1 T. butter or margarine
dash of salt
Cook until mixture reaches 270 degrees, pour onto greased platter or cookie

sheet.   As edges cool, Fold toward center.   When cool enough to handle, press into ball with buttered fingers.   Pull until light colored and very firm.   Stretch into long rope ½ inch in diameter and cut into   1 inch pieces.   Wrap each piece in waxed paper or plastic wrap.

NO - COOK CHOCOLATE CHEWS   (an easy first recipe for children)

Mix 2 T. butter with ½ cup corn syrup, stir in 2 squares melted unsweetened chocolate and 1 tsp. vanilla.   Mix 3 cups powdered sugar and ¾ cup dry nonfat powdered milk together.   Gradually stir into first mixture, then knead thoroughly to blend.   Shape into ¾ inch roll and cut into 1 inch pieces.

FUDGE REPAIR

To soften, IF fudge is smooth but became too stiff before you poured it out, knead with your hands until it softens, press into buttered pan or shape into   1 inch balls or into a role and slice.

To Firm up, IF Fudge doesn't thicken enough, it was poured too soon, or not cooked long enough.   Add   ¼ cup milk, cook and stir until 236 degrees, proceed as recipe directs.   You may also just mix in enough powdered sugar to make stiff and proceed as above.

OLD - TIME FUDGE

Butter sides of heavy kettle.   Add:
2 cups sugar
3/4 cup milk
2   1 ounce squares unsweetened chocolate
dash of salt
1 t. corn syrup

Heat & stir over medium heat until sugar dissolves and mixture boils. Cook to 236 degrees, stirring only if necessary, but watch closely.

Remove from heat, add 2 T. butter or margarine and cool to lukewarm without stirring.   Add 1 t. vanilla and beat vigorously until fudge becomes very thick and starts to lose its gloss.   Quickly spread in buttered pan. Score while warm, cut when firm.   May add ½ cup chopped nuts before pouring..

EASY FUDGE

4 cups sugar
1 14½ ounce can (1 2/3 cups) evaporated milk

1 cup butter or margarine
Cook, stirring frequently, to 236 degrees.   Remove From heat, add:

1 12 ounce package (2 cups) semisweet chocolate pieces

1 pint marshmallow creme or   1 pound marshmallows

1 t. vanilla

1 cup chopped walnuts
Beat until chocolate is melted and marshmallows are blended.   Pour into buttered pan.   Score while warm, cut when cool.

FOR SOMETHING different, halfway through beating, add another package of chocolate pieces and some miniature marshmallows For a Rocky Rhode type candy, do not beat until melted, either drop onto buttered cookie sheet or wax paper by teaspoonfuls..   Let set until firm.   May also mix coconut instead of chopped nuts into Fudge.

PANOCHE

Butter sides of heavy kettle, add:
1½ cups sugar
1 cup brown sugar

1/3 cup light cream

1/3 cup milk   OR   2/3 cup evaporated milk, undiluted, in place of
                milk & cream

2 T. butter or margarine

Heat until sugars dissolve and mixture boils, stirring constantly.   Place

thermometer, cook to 238 degrees, stirring   only if necessary.   Remove From

heat and cool to lukewarm without stirring.   Add   1 t. vanilla, ½ cup nuts,

Beat until thick & loses gloss, spread in buttered pan, score, cut when cold.

FONDANT

Butter sides of heavy kettle, add:

2 cups sugar

1½ cups boiling water

1/8 t   cream of tartar OR 2 T. lt. corn syrup

Stir and cook until sugar dissolves and mixture boils.   Cook without stirring

until it reaches 238 degrees.   Immediately pour on platter, do not scrape pan.

Cool until Fondant Feels slightly warm, about 30 minutes, do not move.   Using

spatula or wooden spoon scrape Fondant From edge of platter to center, then

work until creamy and stiff.   Knead until smooth and Free of lumps.   Wrap,

place in covered container to ripen 24 hours.

For vanilla fondant, knead in 1 T. soft butter and 1/3 t. vanilla.

For mint Fondant, knead in 10 drops mint extract and 4 drops Food coloring.

Shape and decorate.   Or, stuff dates, prunes or Figs with Fondant, roll in

powdered sugar, or place walnut halves together with Fondant. JORDAN

ALMONDS - Melt Finished fondant over warm water, dip blanched almonds.

CHOCOLATES - Make Fondant centers a couple of days early, then Fondant won't be so inclined to leak through chocolate.   May form Fondant around cherries.   Don't attempt to dip chocolates on a damp or hot day.   A cool (65 degree) room is best.

Use at least 1 pound grated candy making chocolate, may use chocolate chips with 1/3 T. shortening added.   Place over <u>hot, not boiling</u>, water (115-120 degrees) with water touching top pan.   Stir constantly until melted.

Exchange hot water for cold water in bottom of double boiler,, stir and cool chocolate to 83 degrees, exchange cold water for 85 degree water.

Working rapidly, drop center into chocolate, roll to coat, lift out with fork. Draw fork across rim of pan to remove excess chocolate.   Drop onto wax paper, bring string of chocolate across top for decoration.

IF chocolate becomes too stiff, heat as at first. May dip nuts, caramels, candied Fruit or anything you want chocolate coated.

DIVINITY

In 2 quart kettle, combine 2 cups sugar
½ cup lt, corn syrup ½ cup hot water 1/4 t   salt

Cook and stir until sugar dissolves and mixture boils. Cook to 250 degrees without stirring.   While syrup cooks, beat 2 egg whites stiff.   Remove syrup from heat and pour hot syrup slowly over beaten egg whites, beating constantly, at high speed on mixed.   Add 1 t. vanilla and beat until mixture Forms soft peaks and begins to lose its gloss.   Add ½ cup chopped nuts if desired.   Drop divinity from teaspoon onto waxed paper, twirling top.   IF divinity becomes too stiff to twirl, add a few drops hot water.

CARAMELS

Butter sides of heavy kettle.   Add:

1/3 cup sugar
3/4 cup dark corn syrup
½ cup butter or margarine
½ cup cream or evaporated milk, undiluted

Bring to boil, stirring constantly.   Slowly stir in another ½ cup cream. Cook over low heat, stirring as needed to 242 degrees, stirring almost constantly toward   the end.   Remove From heat, add ½ t. vanilla, may also add ½ cup finely chopped nuts, if desired.   Pour into buttered pan.   Mark when cool, cut when cold.   Wrap in plastic wrap.

SUGARED WALNUTS

Heat 2½ cups walnut halves in 375 degree oven 5 minutes, stirring once.

Butter sides of heavy kettle, add 1/3 cup sugar, ½ cup water,   1/3 t. cinnamon & ½ t. salt.   Cook
to 236 degrees, remove From heat, beat 1/3 minute,   Add 1½ t. vanilla & nuts. Stir gently.

SALT WATER TAFFY

Mix in heavy kettle:
1/3 cup sugar
2 T. cornstarch
Stir in:
¾ cup lt. corn syrup

½ cup water

½ tsp. salt

2 T. butter

Cook and stir constantly until mixture boils and sugar is dissolved.

Continue cooking without stirring until mixture reaches 260 degrees. Remove from heat, stir in 1 t. Flavoring or extract, use any Flavor you like, and a Few drops Food coloring. Pour into greased pan. Let stand until cool enough to handle. Grease hands and pull until it has a satin-like appearance and light color. Roll out like a pencil between both hands. Cut into 1/3 inch pieces. Wrap in waxed paper.

PEANUT BRITTLE

Combine in large heavy skillet:

2 cups sugar

1 cup lt. corn syrup

1 cup water

Cook slowly, stirring until sugar dissolves, then cook to 236 degrees. Add 2 cups blanched* Virginia peanuts or raw Spanish peanuts, ¼ t. salt, cook to 295 degrees, stirring constantly. Add:

1/3 t.butter or margarine

1/4 t.soda

Stir to blend, mixture will Foam up. Pour onto buttered cookie sheet. Cool partially by lifting edges with spatula. Keep spatula moving under mixture so it won't stick. Turn over while still warm but firm, pull edges to thin in center. Break into pieces when cold. *Blanch by covering with boiling water 5 minutes, then run under cold water. Remove coating.

PEANUT BUTTER CUPS (easy first recipe)

Melt:

1 cup chocolate chips & ½ cup butter or margarine

Smooth small quantity in bottoms of small paper cups, reserve 2/3 of mixture.

Mix:

1½ cups peanut butter
1½ cups powdered sugar
1/3 cup brown sugar
1t. vanilla

Blend well, divide into small paper cups lined with the chocolate mix. Carefully remelt the reserved chocolate, spread over peanut butter filling.

EASY CANDY   (easy First recipe)

Butter sides of heavy kettle, combine:
1/3 cup margarine
½ cup lt. corn syrup
½ pound powdered sugar

Cook over low heat until bubbly. Quickly stir in:

½ pound powdered sugar

1 t. vanilla

Remove From heat, stir until mixture just holds shape.   Pour into greased pan and cool to lukewarm.   Knead until smooth.

BON BONS - Form around nuts or candied Fruit.   Roll in colored sugar or sprinkles.

MINT PATTIES - Instead of vanilla, use mint extract.   Add red or green food coloring.   Form into patties, lightly press fork across top For decoration.

FILLED FRUIT OR NUTS - Fill pitted prunes, dates or apricots, roll in sugar. Place between nut halves.

CHOCOLATES - Make any of the above, chill, dip in melted chocolate to cover.

ALMOND BUTTER CRUNCH

Melt 1/3 cup butter or margarine in heavy kettle, Add 1 1/3 cups sugar, 1/3 T. lt. corn syrup and 3 T. water. Cook stirring often, to 300 degrees. Watch carefully after syrup reaches 280 degrees. Quickly stir in 1/3 cup coarsely chopped blanched almonds (toasted), spread in well-greased 13 x 9 inch pan. Cool Thoroughly.

Turn out on waxed paper, spread top with 2 4½ oz. milk chocolate bars, that have been melted, sprinkle ½ cup finely chopped blanched almonds, toasted, over chocolate. Cover with wax paper, invert, and repeat with 2 4½ oz. milk chocolate bars, melted and ½ cup more finely chopped almonds. Chill. Break into pieces.

CHOCOLATE-COVERED CHERRIES

Mix 1 can sweetened condensed milk, ½ cup soft butter or margarine, 1/3 t. vanilla together. Add 1/3 pound powdered sugar. Put another pound of powdered sugar on a cookie sheet. Dump mixture in center and work like bread dough. Cool mixture in refrigerator. Remove small amount of mixture at a time, break off small pieces and form around drained Maraschino cherry. Freeze on cookie sheet. Remove few at a time from freezer, dip in chocolate.

Melt 2 12 ounce bags of semi-sweet chocolate chips for dipping chocolate. May wish to add 2 T. butter to chips as they melt.

SUGARLESS CHOCOLATE FUDGE

Combine in kettle, 1/3 package sugarless chocolate pudding mix (not instant)

½ cup real sour cream, 1/8 t. chocolate extract, ½ t. vanilla, ½ t. almond extract, Granulated artificial sweetener = to 3 T. sugar.   Blend well, place over low heat and add 2 T. butter.   Heat and stir until butter melts and mixture is smooth. Pour into non-stick spray coated 8" square pan, spreading evenly. Chill until firm.   Cut into 16 squares.   33 calories per square.

SUGARLESS GUMMIES

Melt 2 8-ounce jars sugarless jam or jelly, any flavor, over low heat, add 1 .3 oz. pkg. sugarfree gelatin, stirring until dissolved, remove From heat.   Soften 5 envelopes unflavored gelatin in ½ cup cold water, add to the jam, stirring well. Bring to rapid boil, boil 5 minutes, stirring constantly.   Remove from heat and pour into 8 inch pan.   Cover and let stand at room temperature overnight. Gently run knife around edge and turn candy out onto a cutting board.   Cut into 1 inch squares, long slender strips or whatever shape you prefer.   Wrap with plastic wrap. Possible combinations: Pineapple spread-lime gelatin- dash of mint extract, Raspberry spread- raspberry gelatin, Strawberry spread- strawberry gelatin, Orange marmalade spread- lemon gelatin, try your favorite flavors.

SWEET SPICY NUTS

Toast 4 cups shelled nuts of your choice with 1 cup butter or margarine, in skillet over low heat until lightly browned.   In a bag, mix 3 cups powdered sugar, 3 T. cinnamon, 2 T. nutmeg,   1 T. allspice, 2 t. cloves.   Drain nuts on paper towels, dump in bag and shake until nuts are well coated.   Dump into colander or wire strainer to shake off excess coating, cool, store in covered container.

EASY CANDY-COATED TREATS

In small saucepan, melt 1 can ready-to-spread frosting or 2 cups of a standard butter-powdered sugar- water or milk- flavoring frosting, over low heat, stirring occasionally. Dip chunks of any fruit, fresh or well-drained canned or even dried fruit, nuts, pretzels, candied fruits or almost anything edible into melted frosting. Allow excess to drip off, place on waxed paper at room temperature to dry, about 6 hours. If frosting thickens too much, reheat. Dry items work best For dipping. A quick treat for kids to make.

MARZIPAN

Finely grind 1½ cups blanched almonds, knead in 1½ cups powdered sugar, 1 egg white 1 1/4 teaspoons almond extract and dash of salt. Knead well to form a stiff paste. Using 1 or 2 tablespoons of paste at a time, form paste into Fruits, vegetables or other shapes to suit your fancy. Use a small clean paint brush and food coloring to paint the finished shapes as you wish. Let dry at least 30 minutes before serving. Will keep up to six weeks if kept cool.

CHOCOLATE NO-BAKE FUDGEYS

Bring to a boil:

2 cups sugar

½ cup milk

¼ cup butter

½ cup cocoa

Boil for 1 minute. Remove from heat and stir in:
3 cups quick cooking oatmeal and 1/3 teaspoon vanilla. Drop by spoonfuls onto waxed paper or greased surface. May add ½ cup peanut butter with the oatmeal flakes.

COCONUT PIE CRUST

Combine 2 ½ cups shredded coconut with 1/3 cup melted butter or margarine. Press evenly into ungreased 9 inch pie pan. Bake at 300 degrees about 20 minutes or until golden brown. Cool. Use as you would a crumb crust.

MARSHMALLOWS or MARSHMALLOW CREME

Mix 1 envelope plain gelatin and ½ cup sugar together in a saucepan. Add 1/3 cup cold water. Place pan over boiling water and stir until dissolved. Add a dash of salt. Set aside.   In a large bowl, pour 2/3 cup white corn syrup and 1/3 teaspoon vanilla. Add the gelatin mixture and beat at high speed until mixture becomes thick and of a soft marshmallow consistency, about 15 minutes. For marshmallow creme, stop at this point and pour into a wide-mouthed jar, cover and store in a cool place. May be used in any recipe calling for marshmallow creme.

For marshmallows, beat until very thick. Have a plate with powdered sugar on it near the bowl. Drop tablespoons of the mixture onto the powdered sugar and roll to cover well. Place on waxed paper to dry.

ALMOND PASTE

In food processor or blender, Finely grind 2 cups blanched almonds. Add 1 cup sugar while grinding. Process until smooth, adding ¼ to 1/3 cup orange juice to make smooth paste. Use in any recipe calling for Almond Paste.

APLET-TYPE CANDIES

Heat 2 cups unsweetened thick applesauce. While it's heating, soak 2 T. plain gelatin in 8 T. cold water. Add gelatin to the hot applesauce and stir until dissolved. Cool slightly then add 1 cup chopped nuts and 1/3 T. lemon juice, stirring well. Pour into a flat pan, let stand overnight. Cut into bite-sized squares and roll in powdered sugar.

May use any thick Fruit puree or sauce in place of the apples. Apricots, peaches, berries or even melon all make interesting candies.

CHOCOLATE PEANUT BUTTER BALLS

Mix 4 T. melted butter or margarine, 2 cups powdered sugar, 1 cup chopped nuts, 1/3 cup coconut. 12 chopped maraschino cherries, 2/3 cup chunky peanut butter and 1 t. cherry juice very well. Roll into small balls, refrigerate until cold. Melt 2 large chocolate bars over hot water in double boiler. Dip balls in melted chocolate and set on foil until firm.

CHOCOLATE AMARETTO TRUFFLES

Melt 2 cups chocolate chips (12 ounces) over hot water, stir until smooth. Remove from heat and blend in ¼ cup sour cream, add 2 T. almond flavor liqueur, (may use I t. almond extract instead) mix well. Chill until firm, drop by teaspoonfuls onto waxed paper, form into balls, roll in chopped almonds. May dip into melted chocolate, also.

CHOCOLATE CREAM MINTS

Melt 2 cups chocolate chips (12 ounces) over hot water, stir until smooth. Remove From heat and blend in ¼ cup sour cream and 2½ T. mint flavor liqueur, (may use ½ t. mint extract, instead) mix well, chill. Form into balls, as above, or pipe through pastry tube for plain or fluted kisses. May dip into melted chocolate, if desired.

Drinks
Wines, Cordials, Liqueurs
And others . . .

WHITE WINE COOLER

Half-fill large pitcher with ice cubes. Add 2 cups dry white wine, 1½ cups white grape juice and 1½ cups ginger ale. Stir, add 12 melon balls and a few orange slices.

PINK WINE COOLER

Substitute cranberry juice cocktail for the white grape juice.

LINGONBERRY LIQUEUR   (Low-Bush Cranberries) or BUSH MEDICINE

Very good for sore throats, coughs, flu symptoms, if made with Lingonberries, only,

First day: Crush 3 pounds Lingonberries, let stand 24 hours.

Second day: Add a Fifth of 190 proof grain alcohol, (Everclear), cover, let stand 24 hours.   Boil 6 cups sugar with 3 cups water For 5 minutes, refrigerate.

Third day: Strain juice (I use a colander and press mixture against the sides with a wooden spoon, the pulp doesn't hurt the liqueur, just shake before serving).   Add syrup, stir well and bottle.   Should age at least 3 weeks, but can be used immediately.

   Variations:

Use 12 cups blueberries, blackberries, strawberries or raspberries instead of the Lingonberries.

3 pounds of crushed peaches, apricots or other fruit, works quite well, only add the alcohol immediately after crushing.

May use vodka instead of grain alcohol, but liqueur will be very mild.

BERRY OR FRUIT CORDIAL

In quart sized jar, combine 1 cup berries or chopped fruit, 1 cup sugar and 1 cup vodka. Shake well, set aside. Shake once a day for 1 month, strain and bottle. Best kept in cool, dark place.

Liqueur or cordial make very nice gifts and are a real treat. May be served over vanilla ice cream as a dessert. Use in place of flavorings in candy for a really different candy.

WINE

In 4 or 5 gallon crock or plastic container, combine;

1 box dried currants, 5 pounds sugar, 3 T. dry yeast, 7½ pound soaked brown rice,

and 3 thinly sliced lemons. Add 3 gallons warm water, stir well. Cover loosely.

Set for 28 days, stirring every other day. Add 1 more T. yeast, mash berries.

Let set at least 10 more days, there should be no bubbles around the edges. Strain and bottle.

May omit the oranges and lemons, raisins may substitute for the currants. Experiment with other types of berries. I have had good luck with blueberries, raspberries, strawberries and lowbush cranberries (lingonberries). I have also mixed berries.

I add the pulp from making liqueur or jelly, also. Write down any changes you make, so you can make your own special wine exactly the same, next time. 5 pounds of sugar is approximately 11 ¼ cups. This makes a very potent wine.

DRY RHUBARB-CRANBERRY WINE

Chop up about 4 quarts of rhubarb, thinly slice 1 1/2 lemons, cover with boiling water, let stand 48 hours. Strain. Cook 2 quarts lingonberries (low-bush cranberries) in 1 quart water until berries pop open. Strain.
Combine the strained juices and add;
3 quarts warm water, 5 pounds sugar and 2 T. dry yeast dissolved in 1 cup warm water. Mix together thoroughly. Place in non-metal container large enough for the juice to ferment without running over. Cover loosely and let stand until it quits working, about 1 month. Siphon off carefully and bottle. Let stand until wine is clear. Decant carefully so no sediment is disturbed.

ORANGE FLAVORED BRANDY

Thin peel 1 orange, place peels in quart jar. Add 1 cup sugar and 1 bottle of Brandy. Shake to dissolve sugar. Place in the dark for 24 hours, remove peel. Replace in brandy bottle or other dark bottle.
Sliver peel and use as Flavoring in fruitcake or other items of your choice.

CREAM LIQUEUR

In blender, combine 1 ½ cups Irish whiskey, 1 2/3 cups sweetened condensed milk, 1 cup whipping cream, 4 eggs, 2 T. chocolate syrup, 2 t. instant coffee granules, 1 t. vanilla and ½ t. almond extract. Blend until smooth. Store tightly covered in cool place or refrigerate up to 1 month. Stir before serving.

RUSSIAN TEA MIX

Mix 2 cups instant orange breakfast drink powder, 1 cup instant tea powder, 1 t. cinnamon, 1 t. cloves or allspice, 1 T. powdered lemonade and 1 ½ cups sugar. Store in covered jar. Use 2 T. mix to 1 cup boiling water.

SPICED CIDER

Squeeze 3 oranges and 2 lemons. Reserve juice. Boil rinds in 6 cups water, with 1 T. whole allspice, simmer, covered, 2 hours. Strain, add 1 1/2 cups sugar, stirring until dissolved. Add 1 gallon cider and reserved juices. Heat, but do not boil. Serve.

HARVEST SWITCHEL (Old Time)

1 gallon water, divided

2 cups sugar

1 cup molasses

¼ cup cider vinegar

1 t. ginger

Mix 1 quart of the water with the rest of the ingredients. Heat until dissolved. Add remaining water and chill.   Serve chilled, very thirst quenching.

MODERN SWITCHEL

1 gallon water, divided

2 T. instant tea

1 cup lemon juice

1 T. vanilla

1 T. almond extract

1 ½ cups sugar or less, to taste

Mix 2 cups warm water with the rest of the ingredients, stir until dissolved. Add remaining water and chill.

SANGRIA

Mix 3 bottles red wine, ¼ cup brandy, ½ cup powdered sugar until sugar dissolves. Add slices of lemon, oranges and apples. Let stand 4 to 6 hours, add 2 bottles soda water before serving.

HOT CHOCOLATE

Melt 1 1 ounce square semi-sweet chocolate for each 8 ounce cup of chocolate you are making. Beat in 2 T. brown sugar and 6 ounces hot half 'n half or whole milk. Top with sweetened whipped cream. May add a small dash of cinnamon or nutmeg to the hot chocolate. Add 1 t. vanilla for richer flavor.

HOT CHOCOLATE #2

Combine 3 T. cocoa powder, 5 T. sugar, dash of salt and 3 T. HOT water in a small pan. Mix well, add 2 cups milk and cook, stirring constantly to prevent scorching, until very hot. Remove from heat and add ¼ t. vanilla. May serve with a dollop of flavored whipped cream.

Variations:

Canadian: add ¼ t. maple extract

Irish Mint" add ¼ t. mint extract

Orange: add ¼ t. orange extract

Swiss Mocha: add 1 t. instant coffee

Viennese: add a dash of cinnamon and a dash of nutmeg. Serve with cinnamon stick.

WHEN YOU ARE DESPERATE FOR COFFEE, BUT ARE OUT (I don't drink coffee)

Dig Dandelion roots, wash, slice and dehydrate until very dry. Roast until the pieces are quite browned, then grind. Brew or steep until a desired degree of color and taste is reached. This is kind of a last ditch effort for a coffee substitute, but may extend your coffee supply, if there is no alternative.

I have not included a regular recipe for coffee in this book as almost everyone makes better coffee than I do. I can make camp coffee, which is to bring a pot of water to a boil, throw in a couple of handfuls of grounds and remove from the fire. Either let set until the grounds settle or add a bit of cold water to settle them. Prepare to strain through your teeth as you drink.

Mead (pronounced /'mi 'd/ or pronounced /mi'ad/) is an alcoholic beverage, made from honey and water via fermentation with yeast. Its alcoholic content may range from that of a mild ale to that of a strong wine. It may be still, carbonated, or sparkling; it may be dry, semi-sweet, or sweet. Mead is often referred to as "honey wine."

Depending on local traditions and specific recipes, it may be brewed with spices, fruits, or grain mash. It may be produced by fermentation of honey with grain mash; mead may also be flavored with hops to produce a bitter, beer-like flavor.

MEAD
This is more of a Melomel than a regular mead. Just follow a standard rule of 1/2/1, that being:
1 lb pure honey , the darker the better
2 q. distilled water, or 1/2 water, 1/2 fruit juice - which is what I do
1 TBSP dry active yeast
Pick the fruit you want to use.   Boil these down and squish the juice out of them then set it aside. You can use canned juice.

Next, melt your honey down in the water until it's all liquid, add the yeast then the juice. Stir until it's completely liquid and there's no trace of yeast or honey. Strain into a separate container just to get any residue out.

Allow to cool only slightly then pour into jars/bottles with lids that can be easily removed. Allow to cool completely before placing the lids on. Every day you will want to loosen the lid and let the trapped air out. Failure to do so will make a really big mess, I promise.

After two weeks, your "moonshine" should be ready to go. Don't let it ferment for very long. I use a smell test! LOL! I once let a bottle set for a year before drinking, 3 sips and everyone was toast!

LIGHT MEAD
A light type of mead, good to drink with dinner. Serve chilled
Makes 1 gallon
For this mead, use clover honey or similar. Do not use oil seed rape, which looks like lard: it is no good for mead.
1 gallon water
2 ½ lb light honey
½ oz citric acid
2 teaspoons yeast nutrient
1 heaped tablespoon light, dried malt extract
½ teaspoon grape tannin
Yeast - Sauternes

48 hours before you begin the mead, make up a yeast starter, using the Sauternes yeast, so that it is actively working when required.

Heat the water to 57-60 degrees C. (140 degrees F about) Stir in the honey. Keep at this temperature for 5 minutes.

Pour honey water into a bin. Cover bin. Let it cool to about 30 degrees C (88 degrees F. about).

Add other ingredients, including actively working yeast. Stir well. Cover the bin and leave it in a warm place, about 18-20 degrees C, for 4 to 5 days. Stir it daily.

After 4-5 days, siphon liquid off sediment into a 1 gallon jar. Fit an air lock or cover top with a piece of polythene secured with a rubber band.

Keep jar in a warm place. Rack every 2 or 3 months - i.e. siphon mead off the sediment into a clean jar, replacing air lock or polythene cover until fermentation has ceased completely.

When mead is stable and clear it can be bottled. Thoroughly wash 6 bottles. Siphon mead into the bottles. If you want to keep the wine, cork the bottles with straight sided corks and lay them down on their sides. If it is going to be used in a few months, use a flanged type cork but leave bottles standing upright.

Should be ready to drink in 9 to 12 months.

MEDIUM SWEET MEAD

A medium to sweet mead

Makes 1 gallon

1 gallon water

2 lb Australian or Tasmanian Leatherwood honey

2 lb general flower honey, English or clover

½ oz citric acid

1/4oz tartaric acid

½ level teaspoon grape tannin

3 teaspoons yeast nutrient

2 tablespoons light, dried malt extract

Yeast - Sauternes

48 hours before you begin the mead, make up a yeast starter, using the Sauternes yeast, so that it is actively working when required.

Heat water to 57-60 degrees C. Sit in the honey. Keep at this temperature for 5 minutes.

Pour honey water into a container. Let it cool to about 20 degrees C

Add other ingredients, including actively working yeast. Stir well. Cover container and leave in a warm place, about 18 degrees C, for 4 to 5 days. Stir it daily.

After 4-5 days, siphon liquid off sediment into a 1 gallon jar. Fit an air lock or cover top with a piece of polythene secured with a rubber band.

Keep jar in a warm place. Rack every 2 or 3 months - i.e. siphon mead off the sediment into a clean jar, replacing air lock or polythene cover until fermentation has ceased completely.

When mead is stable and clear it can be bottled. Thoroughly wash 6 bottles. Siphon mead into the bottles. If you want to keep the wine, cork the bottles with straight sided corks and lay them down on their sides. If it is going to be used in a few months, use a flanged type cork but leave bottles standing upright.

Should be ready to drink in 9 to 12 months but if kept it will improve and mature.

BALLOON WINE

Balloon wine enables novices to prepare homemade wine without purchasing expensive specialty supplies. Making wine out of grape juice requires fermenting the juice with yeast and sugar. A balloon traps the gases produced during the fermentation process. The results of this wine-making technique lack the subtle flavors found in traditionally made wines, but the alcoholic content is usually higher. (See Reference 1)

Difficulty: Moderately Easy

Instructions

Things You'll Need:

1 pkg (1/2 tsp.) active dry yeast

4 cups granulated sugar

24 oz. (Two 12 oz. cans) frozen Welch's grape juice concentrate mixed with 72 oz. water or 96 oz. (3 qt.) ready-to-drink Welch's grape juice

1 1/2 gal. bowl

Long-handled spoon

Funnel

1 gal. jug, sterilized

1 balloon

1 rubber band

Step 1

Mix together the grape juice concentrate and water (or the ready-to-drink grape juice) with the sugar and yeast in the 1 1/2 gallon bowl. Stir thoroughly to combine using a long handled spoon.

Step 2

Place the funnel in the top of the gallon jug. Carefully pour the grape juice mixture through the funnel and into the jug.

Step 3

Place the balloon over the opening in the jug, securing it to the mouth of the jug by wrapping the rubber band around the balloon.

Step 4

Place the jug in a dark place. Leave the jug alone until the balloon inflates and then completely deflates, signaling that that the sugar has fermented into alcohol. The process may take several days. Remove the balloon and serve the wine.

Tips & Warnings
Substitute any type of juice on hand for the grape juice (except for citrus juice) to make different flavors of alcoholic beverage. Do not serve this to children, as it contains alcohol.

This is for informational use only.   Check local and federal laws before attempting this.
THE BASICS OF MAKING MOONSHINE & WHAT YOU NEED TO KNOW
HOW TO MAKE MOONSHINE & MOONSHINE INSTRUCTIONS:
Ingredients:
1) Corn meal
2) Sugar
3) Water
4) Yeast
5) Malt extract
Now you also need the following for you to be able to know how to make moonshine:
1) A Mash Tub, or Fermenter
2) A Still
3) A Condenser
Now, not everyone has copper stills lying around in their own backyards. However, most kitchens have a pressure cooker, a kitchen sink and a stove. And of course you will need a 20 gallon drum. However, a new, metal garbage can will do the trick, if you can't find anything else. Note I said new!!!   With a few other minor adaptations, you
have yourself a homemade moonshine still and...
So, you will need:
1 x 5lb bag of cornmeal
1 x 5lb back of white, granulated sugar
10 gallons of hot water - at 120 degrees F.
1 cake of yeast
1 pint of malt extract
HOW TO MAKE MOONSHINE & MOONSHINE INSTRUCTIONS:
1) Fill your 20 gallon container with 10 gallons of water. Make sure that it is at 120 degrees Fahrenheit.
2) You now need to scald the meal by adding it to the water, a little at a time, followed by the sugar. Stir well.

3) You will now need to set the drum or garbage can on a very slow fire. Make sure that you do not scorch your mash and the temperature must be kept below 145 degrees F. else the heat will prevent the starch from being converted into sugar. Leave for about half an hour.

4) When your mash is a very thin gruel like consistency, take it off the heat and cool it down by cooling the outside of the container with water. You can do this by placing the container in the sink or the like, and filling up the sink with water to bring the temperature down.

5) When your mash is cool enough to stir your finger through it without being burned, we need to check that there has been enough conversion from starch to sugar. To do this we need to do the iodine test.

6) Take a small amount of mash and place a drop of iodine on the top of it. If it turns a dark purple we know that there are still starches present that haven't been totally converted into sugar. If this is the result, put the mash back on a low heat for another half an hour. If there is only a light purple, then we can continue to the next stage of learning how to make moonshine.

7) We now add about a pint of malt extract and a cake of yeast that has been well crumbled and mixed in a little cup of warm water to dissolve first.

8) You may find that your mash is very thick at this stage. It is fine to add some warm water to the mash to thin it out. Don't add hot water as this will kill off the yeast.

9) Place your drum of mash in a warm place - about 65 degrees and leave it for 3 days. At this stage you may cover it with a cloth if you have a danger of rats or insects falling into your mash. However, if you don't have these dangers, leaving it open will encourage wild yeast to enter your mash, giving it a distinct flavor.

10) You will see your mash rising in the drum with a foamy head to it. This is normal. When the froth stops growing, your mash is ready. Too much acid in your mash while it is fermenting will result in vinegar. Therefore, you will need to check your mash with litmus paper to see if your mash is still safe. If you find that the litmus paper turns blue on contact with your mash, or only a slight tinge of pink, it is fine.

11) So, in the next process of learning how to make moonshine you will want to build your still, while your mash is fermenting. Take the old pressure cooker and drill a 1/4 inch hole into the lid of the pressure cooker/pressure canner. Now take your copper tubing and get it through the hole, making sure that it is projecting no more than an inch into your pot. The tubing should fit in very tight, without the possibility of it coming out under pressure from the gases.

12) Now we need to run the copper tubing from the pressure cooker on the stove to the sink. At least 3 feet of the copper piping should be left in the sink.

13) To condense the vapor into moonshine, we now need to convert a thermos

jug for this purpose. Take a 1 gallon thermos jug with a tap/faucet and remove the tap. Now take the excess copper wire beyond the three feet that is sitting in the sink and coil it by wrapping it around an object multiple times so that it will fit snuggly into the jug. Have an extension of copper wire coming out from where the faucet used to be.

14) During the distilling process the thermos jug will be placed under an open cold tap where the jug will always be filled with cold water, and excess water will flow through the space where the faucet used to be, flowing over the copper extension through this gap.

15) In learning how to make moonshine you will soon notice that after 3 or 4 days the foam on the mash has stopped frothing and being active and you are left with a light golden-brown liquid called still-beer. We will use this to fill up our pressure cooker.

16) Fill the pressure cooker up to only 4/5ths of its capacity, but make sure that you strain it first using either a clean, open-weave tea towel or some cheesecloth.

17) Place the lid on the pressure cooker and heat up the still-beer over a very low heat. Make sure, that at this point you have the water running through your thermos jug and you have a receptacle below the end of the copper tubing to catch the alcohol vapor.

18) Allow at least 1/2 cup of moonshine to accumulate in the cup and then throw it away down the drain. This is a vital step when learning how to make moonshine. NEVER drink this first distill. It is not just paint stripper to your insides, but is highly toxic to your system and you are putting your life in danger by drinking this liquid. People have lost their sight, damaged their organs and worse, even died, from drinking this first distill. It can be used as disinfectant or to clean grease and oil off tools, just don't drink it.

19) After each lot of still-beer in the pressure cooker has been distilled you will be left with about a gallon and a half to two gallons of alcohol known as 'low wines'.

20) What you need to do now, is to re-distill this liquid as it contains too much water. The pressure cooker needs to be rinsed out and dried before we add our low wines back in to the pressure cooker.

21) Again, place over a very low heat and wait for the vapor to emerge. Again we have to throw the first lot of vapor away. About 1/2 cup again. When the first appearance of a white liquid emerges then we know that we are the path to having made our first batch of hopefully, drinkable moonshine!!!

22) However, before we get too excited, what we have made is probably rocket fuel, as it is about 140% proof. What we need to do is to find a hygrometer, and mix enough water with the whiskey to get it down to a more drinkable 100% proof. If you don't have a hygrometer, do it the old fashioned way. Take

a quart jar and fill it half with moonshine. Now shake it gently and sit it on a flat surface. If there are bubbles half above and half below the liquid, then you have the right proof.

A final word about learning how to make moonshine, don't be tempted to use plastic tubing to replace the copper tubing as the heat and activities of the distillation process will cause chemicals from the plastic to be leached into your moonshine. Lastly, use your common sense when making this stuff, and adopt safety procedures at all times, knowing that what you are working with is a volatile substance, that needs attention and concentration at all times. It's inattention that caused most old stills to explode. Instead of discarding the first distill of each step in the cooking, save it and use for fuel, cleaning or sterilizing. Just don't drink it. I can't stress that fact too often.

Assorted Info
Shelter, Oven
&
Chinking

SIMPLE SHELTER CABIN
Something to think about if you need a fairly fast to construct roof over your head, is a trappers cabin. Most of the guys here, flatten 2 sides on a standing

tree so it is L shaped, to use as a corner post for the cabin. The top of the tree can be left or not, but it usually eventually dies from have two slabs cut off. Stack small logs with the ends butting against one of the flat sides and spike into the end through the standing tree. You may need to spike in a couple of spots to hold it steady on the log below each log, but don't go too close to the end. When you have as many logs high as you can manage, cut the ends straight down to even that end of that wall and place an upright post with 2 sides flattened, L shaped again, and spike into place through the upright into the ends of the logs. Then do your next wall in the same manner. This building doesn't have to be square, and if you want to take the time to measure and cut to length, you can use all standing trees for the corners. This makes the building blend in with the surrounding trees better. Place a ridgepole (may be 3 small trees bundled together, with one butt end on opposite end of the bundle) across the top, preferably after placing a couple more logs on the 2 opposite ends to make a slightly pitched roof. If you have managed to span a fairly large distance, you may need to add a purlin between the ridgepole and side wall to help support the roof. Place smaller poles across from the ridgepole to the side walls. Try to have a few inches of overhang, if possible and chink between them, where they cross the wall with moss now. It's very difficult to add the chinking in this area later. If you have a piece of tarp or plastic that has no holes in it, or very few, place that over the poles, then cover with heavy moss. If you will be able to have a source of heat in this little building, you will need to put some sort of chimney surround to keep from burning the place down. In a pinch, you can use a 5 gallon metal can, cut one end out and cut a hole in the middle of the other end the size of the pipe going through it, nail the can with the open end down, to a couple of the roof poles, then fill in around it to the best of your ability with the materials on hand. If you have a barrel cut in half and can cut a hole the size of the pipe going through, even better. Chink between the logs with moss or old clothing or whatever you can find. It is best to have a fairly level area to do this, but during the winter, you can peel the inside of the wall logs and work at leveling the floor a bit, since it is just dirt. It is best to mark where the spikes are, in the walls, so that if you have a window, you don't cut into a spike when cutting out a window opening. Usually it works best to leave a full log across the bottom of the doorway, and step over it, to keep the wall stronger. Most trapper cabins have a fairly low doorway, as they don't want the heat to escape every time the door is opened. Some of these cabins last for several years, depending on use and maintenance. They do require a source of spikes or other method of fastening the logs together. In bygone times, the logs were sometimes pegged together, but that requires the use of a good drill to make the holes, or rather a handheld auger. This is a very basic shelter, but it might save a life. Build some on a small scale with the kids, for practice.

If you don't have plastic or tarp to make the roof a bit waterproof, you can peel bark from trees and lay on the poles like shingles, with each layer overlapping the lower layer, then cover with moss to hold it down and insulate a bit. Birch bark is very good for this as it does not rot and is waterproof if done carefully.

If you want to make a shed type building with no ridgepole, place all butt ends of the logs at one end and the tree top ends at the other end on both sides to make a tapered wall, high in front and low in back, then roof accordingly as directed above.

Variation: Instead of using a standing tree for the corners, you may nail a 2x4 or 2x6 board in an L shape and stand on end. Nail through into the ends of the logs as you stack them. You will have to start with logs on both sides to keep it from falling over. But you can use 2 16 penny nails in the end of each log to hold, instead of spikes. Proceed as above to build the cabin or shed. For looks, you can split a log in quarters and use to fill the L shaped corners after the walls are up.

BUILDING A COB OVEN

So what is cob? Cob is an earth based building material, normally fashioned from mud, clay, straw, grass, rocks, or whatever else you have on hand. Think adobe, mud hut, just on a smaller scale. To build your oven requires only time and manpower, all the materials can be found in nature. Straw/grass can be cut & dried from any field or roadside. Rocks…well everybody can find rocks, they're everywhere. Mud/clay, this is the part you might have to hunt/dig for. Most regions of the US have natural clay deposits; you just have to know how to find them.

Once you find your clay, dig a lot of it and move it to your chosen building site. Start a "pit" to mix the clay and mud, add the straw/grass as a binder. Mixing works easiest when done by foot traffic, so pick a few people to stomp around in the goo. Send everybody that's not mixing on a rock hunt, the more the merrier. Find as many as possible, the bigger the better. If you can find a pile of discarded bricks even better!

Now you've got your rocks, you've got your clay/mud/straw mix (cob), now to get building. Start by stacking your most stable rocks in a ring, fill the inside with the smaller ones and dirt, and pack it down good. Once you get up to a workable height, make a level platform with your flattest rocks (or bricks if you have any). This will be your cooking surface, make it as nice a possible using your best materials. Build a ledge on one side; this will be the entry/exit for your oven. Now, build up a dome shape using sand or something you can remove later without too much trouble, size it to hold a small fire and what you will be cooking. Cover this with paper, straw, old fabric, or what you have, just something to keep it from sticking to the next layer.

Now comes the cob. Cover your dome with a generous layer, several inches thick. Form into whatever final shape you desire, most of these I have seen are simple mounds, but here's where the artist in your group can flourish. Let them have free reign to finish the final coat, adding whatever decoration they might fancy. Allow this to dry for a few days, maybe up to a week. Then dig out the inner dome, smooth the inside faces of the oven while you're at it. Let this dry for another day or so, and then build a series of small fires inside the oven to help speed up the curing process. While working through this stage, fashion a door for the oven, this will help speed the cooking process by controlling heat loss.

You can cook with the fire inside of the oven, or dig out the coals and let the residual heat do the job, this will allow for more food to be in the oven at one time. Remember, wood burns at over 400 degrees, so once you have your oven fired and warmed up; this will be the temperature range you will be working with. Plan ahead on how you will be cooking, as the oven will hold heat for a long time.

LOG CABIN CHINKING(can be used for stove or oven, also)
Basic formula:
2 parts clay (or dirt)
1 part sifted wood ashes
1/2 part salt
Water to mix
Only use enough water to hold the mixture together and hold it's shape. I just used it to cement my chimney to the stove.

FUR SEWING
Dampen a tanned fur on the hide side. Let it set long enough to stretch easily without tearing. Stretch the fur, hide side up, and tack or nail it down on a board or the wall or floor. Allow to dry. After the hide has dried completely, draw your pattern on the hide side as though it were the wrong side of fabric. Cut out the pieces with a razor knife or scalpel, being careful not to cut

through the fur. Always pay attention to the direction of the flow of the fur, for the best results, you want the fur to flow up to the peak of a cap, down toward the fingertips on mitts. If there are flow arrows drawn on the pattern pieces, follow them. Leave about an 1/8 inch or less, seam allowance on the pieces or less.

Sew from the wrong side, use dental floss and a leather needle for best results. A leather needle has a 3 sided point to cut through the leather of the hide. Use small stitches and whip stitch the seams, keeping the fur tucked inside so it isn't gobbed in the sewing. When you reach the end of a seam, back stitch and tie firmly. A drop of glue on each end of the floss will help keep it from raveling out.

If you don't prestretch the tanned hide, it will stretch so badly after the item is worn, that it will be shapeless and not fit correctly.

LAUNDRY SOAP

Shave a bar of soap, can be Fels Naptha or regular bar soap. Heat 6 c. water and shaved soap, mixing both.

Stir in 1/2 C. washing soda and 1/2 cup borax. Wear rubber gloves for soda handling.

Mix until dissolved, bring to boil and boil for 15 minutes.

Remove from heat. Consistency should be like honey.

In bucket: add 1 quart hot water. Then add soap mixture and stir.

Add enough cold water to this to make 2 gallons overall(includes previously mixed soap mixture and water.)

Mix well and let sit for 24 hours. This will gel.

Stir before use. You can distribute these to empty laundry detergent containers and shake well before using.

Or:

1 bar grated Fels Naptha, Heat on the stove in a large pot of water until melted. (About 1 gal of water)

1 C. Laundry Soda,

1 C. Borax

Add the hot fels mixture to a 5 gal bucket, mix in the soda and borax, fill about 3/4 full with hot water. You can add one or two tsp. of essential oils. Then cover the bucket with a lid and store it in the garage. It gels. Keep a small plastic bucket full in the laundry room and use a 1/2 cup dipper to measure into the washing machine.

Hand soap:

Grate or finely chop a bar of soap. About 4 oz.

Bring 4 cups water to boil, remove from heat and add soap. Stir until dissolved.

Mixture will be very liquidy.

Cool for at least 15 min. Stir again. Will be slightly thicker.

Allow to cool for several hours or overnight. If too thick, reheat and add a bit more water. You can play with this until you get the consistency you prefer.

Pour into liquid soap dispensers or into an empty liquid soap dispenser.

You can also run this through a blender before repackaging.

Essential oils or baby oil can be added, too.

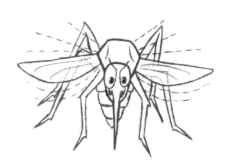

Earth Battery,   (thanks to Wilderness Joe)
Drive alternating copper & galvanized rods about 2' deep & about 2' apart into the ground.   Connect all of those rods together with electrical wire. Use 1 of those cheap electric multi meters to see when you reach 12 volts, check the amperage as well. To get more amps. run more sets in parallel until you get enough power. An inverter can easily turn this 12 volt source into regular 110 volt AC.   One end of the wire will be - the other end will be +.

Life and Times of an Unwilling Alaskan Woman

I was devastated by the sight of our new home-to-be.   There it sat, a gaunt, homely house with 3 or 4 bare leafless trees on a barren hillside.   Slightly above it was a large old barn and a pole corral.   Nothing looked alive, including the horse standing hipshot in that corral.   She was a nondescript whitish grey that blended in quite well with the dusty sage and dirt.   How could we move from the perennially green and vibrant rain forest of the Oregon coast to this dead looking place and only a couple of days before Christmas?   Even worse, I only had one semester to go until graduation from

High School.   Nobody moved after 11 ½ years in one school, before completion of term.   Forget that I left behind only one friend made in all those years.   Forget that at 17, I had only gone on one date and that was a fiasco.   I didn't want to be here.   I didn't know how to ride a horse and now was expected to become a cowboy, overnight.   Well, Daddy had been disappointed before, he was about to be, again.

I was born 9 months, 2 weeks after Pearl Harbor, so it doesn't take much imagination to figure out what brought me about.   My father wanted to leave behind a male heir when he went off to fight.   I didn't turn out to be male and he didn't get to go fight.   He never quite forgave Uncle Sam or me.

We lived in a small town, across the road from the school, until the year before I was to start school.   Then we moved 14 miles from the nearest school, most of it up a twisting rut on the side of a steep hill that passed for a road.   There we lived for the next twelve and a half years.   It was beautiful, a wild area, one thousand acres of prime timber land surrounded by a National Forest.   Once school was out in the Spring, we usually never saw another human until school started in the Autumn.   My younger brother and sister knew no other life.   It was heaven for us, no neighbors to complain about us, no matter what outrage we committed.   Our mother worked like a slave to keep everything in order.   There were no modern conveniences.   No electricity, no telephone, no running water other than the water we ran and carried from the spring.   No radio, no washer, dryer or refrigerator.   She spaded our two large gardens by hand, every Spring, canned and cured the produce and meats raised by her own hand.   If we didn't grow it or kill it, we didn't eat.   This was all "woman's work" and my father was not about to do any of it.   Why should a man have to do anything like that, when there were women?   She scrubbed all clothes on a scrub board.   She did not know how to drive so there was no running to the store for groceries.   Life there was very hard on her, but for children, it was marvelous.

School was difficult.   I did not know how to make friends with other children.   I loved to read though, so books became my life. My mother usually read to us in the evenings before bed, she would read as long as her back was being rubbed.   I got very good at rubbing a looooong time.   As I grew older and started doing chores before and after school, I seemed to always have a slight barnyard odor that the town kids never had, so noticed immediately. This increased   my distance from possible friends, in a literal sense, you might say.   When every drop of water used in a home is carried by hand and heated on a wood stove, water is used sparingly.

My mother was very artistic and always encouraged any drawing I wanted to do.   Then, when I was 13, she and I took up taxidermy.   That was my training as an artist.

My father would disappear days and weeks at a time, leaving us stranded with no means of help in an emergency. After my brother had a bad accident, my mother decided to learn to drive. She and I learned together.

Shortly after learning to drive. My little world was turned upside down when my father decided to get out of the timber industry and traded our lovely timberland for a ranch. We had raised a few cows, sheep and goats, but they were fairly tame animals that could be herded on foot. No horses required. Now we were to have several thousand acres of nothing but sagebrush, some juniper and scant grass that wasn't even a decent grass colored green. On this mean looking ground were several hundred head of cattle with dispositions to match the look of the land. Someone was going to have to ride horses and work cattle,, on a large scale. Guess who.

I didn't want to be a cowboy. I wanted to be the one having a good meal waiting for the crew when they came in at the end of the day. Didn't think I was going to get to do both, help get the meals and be one quarter of the crew.

I should have known that the safe stereotype woman's role wouldn't be available. As far as my father was concerned, a woman's place in life was to make life easy for men. I never had to contend with lack of opportunity to work at traditionally male jobs. His idea of my having an easy time of it was to let me leave the hay fields a half hour early to prepare the noon meal for the hay crew. Everyone would eat. The men would relax on the lawn in the shade while the women cleaned up after the meal. then it was back to the hay field. I got off early again, to fix the evening meal. After the evening meal, the men relaxed after their hard days' work The women cleaned up, did the baking for the next days' meals and the laundry. The boys got paid $250 a month but since I didn't work as long in the fields, I got $35 a month.

Since I didn't know how to drive heavy equipment, I operated pitchfork, up on the stack, arranging the loose hay to make the stack water resistant. The men sat on their butts on the big tractors all day and not one volunteered the information that a tractor is not much different than driving a pickup or car.

After one summer of this and several heat strokes later, I decided to change things a bit. An elderly man that worked for us agreed to teach me to operate the Farmhand tractor. This was the one essential piece of equipment for the haying operation and my father had to pay premium wages to the man that could operate it. I not only learned how, I learned well and improved on it. One of the neighbors offered to hire me at top wage when he saw that I could stack without the extra person needed on the stack to arrange the hay. My father wouldn't allow me to work for the man, but I never had to operate pitchfork again.

My learning to operate horse didn't turn out as well. Everyone kept telling me I was supposed to be smarter than the horse. I don't think so. We owned

28 horses and all but one threw me at least once.

My father bought $25 horses at the dog food factory, when good horses were selling for $250 Those horses were usually there for a reason. It was not their good nature.

I not only   was thrown from 27 of our horses, but 2 of the neighbors' as well. It wasn't that I didn't learn to ride, it was just that there were so many opportunities.

I finally learned to stay on most of the horses. My own horse was a beautiful golden palomino mare. I painted a portrait of a neighbor's stallion in exchange for stud fees from his Appaloosa. That Spring, I would take my soon to foal mare out along the highway right of way to eat the fresh early grass. I not only could ride, I was downright cocky about it. I would saddle her loosely and use only a halter to make it easier for her to eat. I would lie along her back, my head on her rump, my feet crossed under the saddle horn and read a book while she ate. We spent many pleasant hours this way, over several weeks.

One day she stuck her nose into a bush for a particularly nice bit of grass and found a roadkill rabbit. She shot straight into the air, I didn't fall off. My feet were stuck under the saddle horn. She bucked along the nice soft roadbed, up the driveway to the edge of the pavement. I finally got my feet loose and fell off over her head. I landed on the back of my neck and top of my shoulders. Her front feet came down on either side of my face, pulling hair and pinching skin beside my ears. Her hind feet hit my backside and we went back down the driveway with me curled in a ball rolling under her big belly, being hit front and back by her legs. She never stepped on me the whole way down.

My grandmother was watering the front yard while this was happening. I don't know how much she saw of it, but as I lay there, still seeing stars, she asked me if I was okay. I said "Sure, I'm fine." I couldn't move for several minutes and my back and neck have never been quite the same. I had landed the same way on frozen gravel a few months before. A car accident that separated the muscle along one side of my spine didn't help either. I had to wear a full body brace for a year after that one. I was told I would need to wear it for life, but they didn't know me. I did, but for pregnancies only.

We learned to doctor sick animals, forcing huge pills down tiny calves if they had scours, brand, mark, give shots for assorted ills and dodging irate mothers while doing this. Most cows are very protective of their young and to have several hundred pounds of mad cow stomping on you as you try to repair their darlings is not fun.

It's even worse to have to doctor one of the cows in the field. One evening my sister and I were dressed to go to a dance, but decided to check a heifer one more time before leaving.   Our father was drunk, so we couldn't depend on him to watch out for her.   She had wandered from the area we thought she was in and it was dark by the time we found her.   She had bogged down in an irrigation ditch, in labor, but had about given up.   She was half drowned and if we went for help, would probably not survive until we got back.   My sister held the heifers' head up out of the water, I worked the calf's front feet free and started pulling.   The heifer started giving some help and the calf came with a sudden whoosh of amniotic fluid.   I landed on my rump in the ditch with the calf on top of me.   The heifer knocked my sister back into the mud also, so we were both muddy and I was also bloody and gooey.   Sis and I had to do some major cleanup before going to the dance.

The seeds from Foxtail grass work into the flesh under the tongue or in the throat of cattle, causing pus pockets to form.   We would have to catch the animal, lance the infected lump and clean it out.   With no anesthetic, they do not take kindly to this treatment.   I can't blame them, but my brother, sister and I didn't get anesthetic either, and were doctored the same way.   Luckily we were all a sturdy lot and survived in spite of our self-doctoring.   So did most of the animals.

Not only did we become cowboys, our neighbors were real Indians.   The family living near us were Klamath-Modoc and French.   The kids were about the same ages we were and they had lots of cousins.   Even though some of us (me) were of the ripe old age of nineteen, we still played cowboys and Indians on horseback.   The slight twist to this was, the Indians usually played the cowboy parts.   Several other kids would join in and we would ride like banshees over the hills.   We certainly livened up several tourists vacations and one new family moving into the area from the east coast.   They had been expecting wild Indians from the time they crossed the Mississippi.   There were about 40 of us the day they thought they were under attack.   We didn't even know they were there, until we saw some silly people dressed in suits and dresses diving for the bushes and the full irrigation ditch.   What a first impression we made on each other.   I haven't changed mine, of them.

By this time, we had learned how to ride, brand, castrate, earmark and doctor anything needing it.   Fair warning.

The new school had turned out to be a very pleasant surprise.   That year it was the smallest public high school in the State of Oregon.   Everyone was friendly.   All the students had chores to do, no one noticed if anyone smelled a bit barn-ish.   We did have electricity, a phone and running water through pipes into the house.   Bathing was a much easier task and all of us were a little prune skinned from indulging long and often.   To top it all, there was a paved highway, less than a half mile from the house.   No more leaving at quarter to seven in the morning and returning at six at night to go to school.   Money was a scarce commodity for all the students, so whenever there was a dance or movie, most of the Senior class could fit in one car and attend. I had never done any of these things before and loved it.

I didn't know it, but my childhood would give me the skills I would need to thrive in Alaska, ten years later.

Home Ec was supposed to help teach girls homemaking skills and what to look for in a husband. I must have been absent the day they covered telling toads from frogs. I didn't just kiss the damn toad, I married him. Being too stubborn to admit a mistake, I kept trying to treat him the way I wanted treated so he would become the loving, kind prince that would love and care for me and our children and we would live happily ever after.

By the time I caught on, I was pregnant. By the time we had been married 3 years, we had 2 children, a girl and a boy. Poor kids, it's a wonder they weren't pollywogs.

Somehow I was convinced that a child needed it's natural mother and father, no matter how unnatural either parent might be. I had the example of my grandmother staying with my grandfather, even though he drank himself under the table too many times and beat her at least once. Toad thought he could do that, also. I waited in a chair beside the bed with a hatchet in my hands, until he woke up sober, then graphically described what would happen to him if he ever hit me and his chances of surviving if he ever turned his back or went to sleep, afterwards. There are no social drinkers in my immediate family on either side, that I know of. They are either drunks or teetotalers. I made up my mind when I was about 10 that I was not going to be one of the drunks. Then there was my mother, putting up with my father's drinking and girlfriends. Years later, I found that I knew more about his girlfriends than she did. I thought all men were like that. The male of the species was Lord and Master, no matter if he were barely capable of dressing himself or getting his shoes on the right foot. Other women must have liked that though, he always had another woman on the side.

We moved 19 times in the next 6 years, usually late at night. I got to be very fast at packing and learned to put all the important things in the first load. Usually it was the only load. The Toad had an aversion to work but was not about to have HIS wife work, unless he got her the job the day after she had all her upper teeth pulled, then she could cook in an upscale restaurant. One year our total cash income was $236.00 and I still have the tax return as evidence. It was a good thing I knew how to can and preserve garden produce, meat and fruit. I was also a good shot. We didn't starve, but it is a wonder.

A long term friend of my parents came to visit, from Alaska, while we were there. In an off-hand remark, they mentioned if we were ever in Alaska, to drop in and spend some time at their place. If they had known my husband at all, they would never have made the offer within his hearing. But the poor dears thought they were safe and went happily back to their home in Wrangell, Alaska. The Toad cured them of ever making any kind offers to anyone. We moved to Alaska, into their tiny 12' x 18' cabin. Everyone learned the true meaning of togetherness.

Five weeks later, we rented a trailer house. We went back to Oregon to get our pickup and household goods. The Toad flew back to Wrangell and the kids and I packed all I could into the bed of the old pickup and started out to catch the ferry in Seattle.

The rear axle broke on the freeway in Portland, Oregon. We finally got it repaired but the delay was just long enough that the ferry was still in sight on the horizon when we pulled in to the dock in Seattle.

Being always short on money, I thought maybe I could catch the ferry at Prince Rupert in British Columbia and still be able to have the family together. (Never said I had much sense, did I?) I didn't have a map, so turned onto any road that sounded like it was going the right direction. We crossed the Canadian Border at some little outpost, just before the changing of shifts, one morning. I had no proof of ownership or insurance for the pickup. I had built the rack and packed everything loose. There was a 23 cu. Ft. freezer full of meat (mostly venison). Layers of clothing and blankets cushioned all the canned goods I had put up at my parents, just before starting North. Rifles and pistols were on the bottom of the whole load. The Border Guard wanted to check my load, so pried some nails loose that held the tarp down over everything. He peeked inside, said, "OHMYGOD" and nailed the tarp back down.

He looked at me, missing my front teeth (due to an accident with a wringer washer) my children's white faces, my cat hiding under the seat (no health certificate for her) another look toward the back of my pickup and told us to hurry up and get going. I assumed he meant North, so I drove on into Canada. We stopped at each and every service station and rest stop along our way as we were suffering from a nasty bout of possible food poisoning.

We parked on the dock in Prince Rupert and watched our ferry chug on by. That was not a stop on its' way. The one for the next day had run aground on an island. The one for the day after, was in dry dock. I livened up our stay in Prince Rupert by having a miscarriage. The first words my Toad bellowed at me from the dock as we pulled in to Wrangell, were, "Who you been messing around with?" Don't I wish.

The people the Toad had made the same offer to, in Oregon, started arriving and soon our 2 bedroom trailer housed 5 adults, 3 children under the age of 5 and the cat. We moved to a larger house in town, most of them moved with us. More moved in. A year later, we moved to Fairbanks, Alaska.

Two of our household moved with us. They stayed a few months and went back to Wrangell. I wanted to go back, too. Our move to Fairbanks was prompted by a conversation the Toad struck up with an unsuspecting fellow on the ferry. Another person that learned the hard way, not to casually invite someone to drop in, if in the area.

I hated Interior Alaska. We arrived in October of one of the worst winters ever recorded, 1970-1971. There was snow on the ground when we arrived and it kept increasing until there was over 145 inches. Where we ended up living, in a swampy area off Badger Road, the temperature dropped to minus 82 degrees. Although the official temperature was less, in town but did drop to minus 81 up at Prospect. As far as I was concerned, all the tales of the frozen North were true. Anyone would have to be a fool to live here. Well, I never claimed I wasn't, did I?

My parents sent us the money to come spend the Holidays, a couple of years later. I went, fully intending on never coming back. After 2 days in Oregon, I was more than willing to come back and never leave Alaska again. I had conveniently forgotten the Toad's family. They still lived in Oregon. Toad's idea of spending half the time with each family, was, nights were spent with my family and all waking hours with his. If you have never seen a family of screaming fighting toads, you've been very lucky.

I also had forgotten how small towns are. Everyone thrives on knowing everyone else's business, true or false. False makes better stories.

I loved the easy going lifestyle of Alaska. As long as you don't bother me, I won't bother you, should have been the State Motto. Now it has changed a lot and not for the better. The small town mentality is creeping in. suddenly everything has to be studied and regulated to death. I'm glad I got here soon enough to still find what I needed. A spine.

Finally, after 13 years and a few thousand miles between my family and I, so they wouldn't know of my shameful admission of failure, I left the Toad. It was either leave him or kill him. A friend of ours had a vacant apartment and having learned a few of the Toads' bad habits, I asked if I could move into it. He said yes. He saved the Toad's life.

I immediately started work as a cook at the hospital to pay for a divorce. It had to be paid in full before the attorney would even file the papers. If I could have hung in there another year, do it yourself dissolutions became available.

Six months later, I finally got up enough courage to tell my parents I had left the Toad. As he and the children had gone back to Oregon, I figured maybe I should tell them before they ran into him. The return mail had a letter from my mom saying, "Congratulations, what took you so long to get smart?"

My landlord and I became lovers and when he offered me the summer at his mining camp, I quit my job in a flash.   We had a perfect summer.   His youngest son and I both learned to operate dozer, I was hooked.

The mining camp consisted of a small ancient log cabin, a tiny bunkhouse and zillions of mosquitoes.   Charlie owned a small dozer and made a set of riffles for an antique sluice box that we lined with carpeting.   The floor of the cabin was pretty bad, so we put a layer of carpet down in it, too,   As the summer progressed, the layers of carpet built up until the swinging door could not be closed.   So a rotting screen door, held together by cardboard stapled inside is all there is between us and the bears.   My talents as a housekeeper leave a lot to be desired.

Our first summer consisted of a series of trial and error attempts at finding the perfect setup for our mining.   Some worked, a lot didn't.   We needed a small scale setup with low overhead.   We settled on a small pond with gravity flow water (which is no longer legal) coming through a pipe under the dam.   A valve on the pipe controlled the water flow.   We set the sluice box with a slope of 1 inch   per foot drop.   The dirt was simply pushed over the side of the dump box; the water washing it down over   the slick plate and through the sluice box.   The dozer, carpeting and us were the only things different than when this area was mined almost a hundred years ago.

Maybe I never learn or else I finally got smart, but   we got married the next year.   Maybe I finally learned to tell the difference between frogs and toads. Mostly this one is a Prince although in a few instances, he has displayed some toad tendencies.

The third summer, Charlie had a job offer halfway through the summer. He went to Prudhoe Bay and I stayed at the cabin and finished the mining season by myself.   I didn't do this without some apprehension.   It was still wonderful, but without someone to show the nuggets to, I quit picking them out of the box.   Gold is fun, but it is still just pretty rocks.

When I started a garden site in a nice spot near the cabin, I was amazed at the amount of junk I found in the ground.   I found lots of large heavy pieces of metal that some poor soul had thought was important enough to pack in from the Yukon River at Rampart to the north, or, later, from Manley Hot Springs on the Tanana River to the south.   I had no idea what most of it was used for but I use it to hold the tin on the sod roof of the cabin.   We never find much gold, only what the old timers left, but always have a beautiful garden.

My days settled into routine after Charlie left for work.   The dog would wake me to go out, unless there were bears around.   Then he could wait all day.   He was a large German Sheppard that was supposed to be our watchdog. That's what he did, too, he watched.   He knew he wasn't brave and never pretended to be.   His name was Dum-Dum and he earned it, repeatedly.   He was probably the only dog in the world afraid of mice in the house. My blind cat, Missy, would let me know if there were bears around.

After feeding the dog and cat, Dum-Dum and I would walk up the creek to work. I would start the dozer, push a small amount of dirt into the slick plate and then open the valve to let the water start washing. There was usually only about 15 minutes of water pressure enough to actually do the job, so I didn't overwork. As the dirt washes out, I push small amounts in. when the pressure starts to drop, I stop pushing and let the water clean out the box. Hopefully, the gold has dropped into the carpeting under the riffles in the sluice box. I shut off the water, push the tailings away from the bottom of the box into the previously worked area. The silt and much that accumulate in the first settling pond is spread over the gravel tailings. By next season there will be fireweed growing on it and wild rhubarb starting. Within a few years the willow and aspen are as tall as I am and excellent moose browse.

We had a water tank hanging from the eaves of the cabin, to catch rain water. The sun would warm it during the day and I would take my shower out there, listening for the sound of an approaching motor so I could make it indoors. One day, as I was finishing rinsing my hair, wrapping a towel around my head as I turned to go into the cabin, I saw feet. There were a pair of unfamiliar work boots, just visible under the edge of the towel. I hadn't considered pedestrians. Not something that usually wanders by 142 miles from town. I kept the towel around my head and over my face and walked right on by the feet, not acknowledging his presence. I figured he had already certainly seen the rest of me, but I didn't have to let him know I knew it. I went on into the cabin and did not look back out or try to see who it was, but we did build a shower house right after that. Charlie still walked nude from the door of the cabin to take his showers until the day the new neighbor's sister and young son came to visit and went to the sound of running water in the shower house instead of to the cabin door. Don't know what they expected, but I guess a naked Charlie wasn't it.

I am not sure whether the moose or the bears startle me the most. Each can do a lot of damage to a person. There have been scares as well as fun. Some involved moose, some were people and some were bears. One summer there were 6 different bears that I saw, at the cabin, within a 5 day period. One finally had to be shot. He stayed around the cabin for 3 days, never quite in sight, but always pacing through the brush near us. My daughter was 8 ½ months pregnant at the time and staying with me at the cabin. Every time we left the cabin, whether it was to work, to the garden or to the outhouse, he was there. The sound of his teeth clicking together was an unnerving accompaniment as we walked. Never out where we could get a clear shot, though. We tried yelling and firing shots in the air, that bear would not leave.

Finally, one morning about 4am, the blind cat jumped on my daughter on the couch and woke her up. The bear was in front of the cabin on the road. Both pulled my covers off, to wake me. If they were going to be scared, I could be awake and share it with them. We turned the radio up full volume and the bear started for the door. Don't know if he didn't like our choice of station or what, but his fur raised and his teeth were clicking. I started to open the door to shoot him, my daughter was getting a bit more than excited and I thought we were going to have a home birth, right then and there. So I shot the bear through the screen door.

Our cabin is 14' x 20' and with the door closed, the sound of the pistol was something else. The cat hated me for hours until she could hear again. The door is a false sense of security at best, being the old rotten screen held together with cardboard to keep the breezes and some squirrels out.

Usually the bears that come around the cabin are black bears. But the only people ever hurt or killed in our area have been by black bears. The grizzlies usually don't come back after they discover smelly humans in the area. A young man was killed as he stepped out of his pickup and partially eaten by a black bear, near one of our old trailers many years ago. Black bears can be any color phase, they are still called black bears and are all possibly dangerous. Being in direct competition with grizzlies here, they have to be aggressive to survive, unlike the Lower 48 black bears that all the aggressive ones were killed off a few hundred years ago.

My daughter scrupulously washed every food container and dish, we burned all trash and still the bears come around. At least they don't seriously try to get in, or they would succeed.

My worse scare with a human was the man that shoved the door open and knocked me down with a shove in my chest about 2 am one night. I had a shotgun in my left hand and was raising and cocking it as he was reaching at me again. I don't know what he intended on doing, but I wasn't waiting to find out. He did recognize the sound of the hammer going back, because he stepped back and started yelling at me to get out, they were moving in. That was the first time gold had reached almost $900 an ounce and they were planning on just moving in and working my claims. I told him to check with the State Division of Mining before he made a fool of himself. These were legal claims. There were 3 more men with the trucks and equipment in my yard, which is what had woke me to start with. A very good thing I was a fast dresser. He was still yelling that they would be back with the Troopers since I pulled a gun on them, I told him I would be right there. Never saw any of them again.

I spend about half of the summers by myself, mining. I am basically a lazy person, so have worked out the easiest ways of doing everything. No job is too small to put off until tomorrow. The things that just can't be put off, are done with the least amount of effort. This way, I manage to raise a large garden, do the mining and still go gadding about.

I find myself living in much the same manner that my mother did, but without the hardship of it. I pack water, but use the pickup to do so. I raise and can or cure a lot of our food, also because I want to. I butcher, can, cure and make sausage from bear, moose and caribou in season, because I like knowing what type of chemical is being added to my food. I do all these because I enjoy it. I also have a generator, if I want electricity. I can take my laundry to town, if I want instead of hauling washing machine and generator to the stream. I don't HAVE to do any of this to survive. Quite a difference from earlier times.

Instead of walking through the brush marking out claim lines by hand, I paint one pad on the dozer track. Then I measure the distance for that line to come up again and figure how many times that painted pad must come up to equal one claim length. Then I sit on a nice soft seat, run the dozer around the claim and have the lines marked. See? Basically lazy.

There are three layers of carpet in the cabin now. Four in some high traffic areas. When the house or cabin get to be a health hazard, I'll sort things out a bit. Not too much, though. I keep house in town the same as at the cabin, I ignore it.

I can find any number of reasons and excuses not to do housework. I read and comment on proposed changes on Laws and Regulations in the mining industry, trapping, hunting and gun industries. It may not do any good, but I can't gripe and complain if I don't at least try. I fill out affidavits of annual labor for myself and some of my friends that mine or own mining claims. There is always something more important than housework.

I had tended to be more than a bit anti-social before I met Charlie. I preferred solitude and animals to most humans. Of course, a person that would marry a Toad isn't hitting on all cylinders anyway. Charlie taught me a lot more than how to operate a dozer and a road grader. He also encouraged me to actually talk in front of other people. There were folks that had known me for years and never heard me speak. Probably thought I was mute. Now they wish I were. He is my best friend, too.

We have been married a little over 12 years now and still even like each other, besides loving each other. Instead of going away on vacation, we go mining. We probably spend a lot more at that, than we would on vacation. But we both love the lifestyle.

It is exciting to look out the cabin window and see a cow and tiny calf moose walking through the garden. The calf is as curious as any baby is. It pulls up every row marker as it comes to them, carrying it in it's mouth until it reaches the next one and pulls that one, too.   Who is going to shoo them away?   Not me.

To walk out to the garden for a fresh salad and have three huge bulls and two cows moving as silently as ghosts through the birch and willow behind the cabin is wonderful.   It is also after hunting season.

I love walking up the creek to the area we are mining and see the moose standing in the pond, eating the browse along the banks.   The cows seem to feel safer raising their calves around a human dwelling.

As summer draws to a close, the nights become dark again as our daylight hours lessen.   The aurora shows in all it's splendor, far from the lights of any town.   The occasional satellite wanders through without notice.

This small mining venture was planned to be our retirement plan in a couple of years.   The way the mining industry is being attacked, we will be extremely lucky if we are able to mine at all by then.   I have lived all of my life in close proximity to the out-of-doors and wilderness and am probably more qualified than someone fresh from a city and college to relate to my surroundings.   I am very conservation minded, but I also believe in common sense.   Forests that are not harvested or managed, degenerate and die.   So do animals.   It is amazing to me that areas that have been mined extensively for almost a hundred years without any restrictions or regulations can leave an area so unharmed that it is selected as a Wild and Scenic River by the Federal government.   Then all mining promptly shut down on it so that no damage will occur.   Does that sound like common sense to you?

This country was founded as a Republic, not a democracy.   It was founded on the belief that a person should be able to keep what he or she has worked for, to improve their lot in life.   It was not founded on the principle that everything belongs to "The People".   That is Socialism.   Socialism is not even working in the socialist countries, why are people trying to make our country that way?   If I have the courage or stupidity to risk everything I own in an attempt to better my circumstances, that is up to me.   I do not want nor need someone telling me not to.   It is my risk, let me live with it.   Whatever happened to good old hard work, earn it by yourself, for yourself?   What happened to being responsible for our own actions?   Everyone seems to want someone to do it for him or her.   Television entertains them without having to think or use their imaginations.   A book at least requires forming the pictures in the mind as the story is read.

Tune in, in another 45 years and I'll tell you the rest of the story.   April, 1988

Post Script:

It is only 12 years later, not 45, but I will bring you up to date on the happenings since I wrote this.

My dear Charlie died of a massive heart attack on his way to work, December 28, 1988, one day after filing for early retirement. He did not get to enjoy one single day of what he had worked all his life for, He died about 8 months after I had wrote this and I still miss him. Our main differences had always been over our kids. His could get away with whatever they wanted to do, mine had to follow the rules. I preferred the way mine did, but it was hard letting his run roughshod over everything and everyone. He and I had other differences of opinion and we discussed them, the kids were the only arguments and they were dillies.

I had never been a touchy-feely sort of person, except with Charlie. Maybe growing up around groping drunks will do that, there was never open affection shown around our home. With Charlie's death, I started becoming physically ill whenever anyone would touch my arm or hug me in sympathy. I retreated a bit into the anti-social mode. Several months after his death, I was feeling a return of desire for sex, but did not want anything to do with anyone on a more personal level. An acquaintance and I talked it over in a dispassionate manner, he never wanted a personal relationship either so we decided to just be in it for a strictly physical relationship and nothing else.

This worked quite well for several months. We had been trading labor and knowledge on building projects, I did dozer work for him on his property and he helped on the construction of the cabin on mine. Then a friend was diagnosed with terminal cancer. She wanted to go to Greece for an alternative treatment and asked me to accompany her. We were gone almost a month and she went into remission. When we returned home, I found things had changed. I now had a room mate. He rented out his own home and was firmly moved into mine. He also decided he liked living with someone and wanted to get married. That totally blew it. Things went swiftly downhill from there.

As that was dragging through it's final phases; I was working on the mining with some nice men. One had been divorced for 8 years and was firmly anti-marriage. He and I got along well working together and I started to have feelings I thought were gone forever. I even enjoyed having him hug me in greeting. Then things progressed beyond that point, I really enjoyed.

I couldn't believe I fell in love. I didn't want to admit it to myself, let alone tell him, but I did. He and Charlie are the only 2 men I have ever told I loved, in a romantic way. It is not an easy thing for me to do, this loving business. The physical stuff is easy.

I was Secretary of the Alaskan Independence Party for many years. Not that I actually have any secretarial skills, but I draw a mean cartoon so did make a lot of people not real happy. I successfully ran for defeat by nominating someone else for my job when it started to get popular to be in our Party.   We even got a Governor elected.

I took 3 semesters at the University of Alaska, Fairbanks, in metal smithing and now can make jewelry and small sculptures with what gold I find.   Just as I was getting set up to start working at that on a more commercial scale, I had to sell all the gold we had saved, to pay Charlie's kids.   So I am pretty much out of that business for a while. Probably forever.

I renewed my taxidermy skills from many years ago.   Did some, while living in Wrangell, but the supplies were part of the items left behind during the move up here.   So now my house has the addition of assorted animals in various stages of undress.   Mostly bears.

I started work as a Class A Assistant Guide for a friend a few years ago. Might as well put all my years of hunting to some other use besides just putting meat on the table.   Every spring, we do the black bear hunts and in the autumn, it is grizzly and moose hunts.   I have just passed my Registered Guide exam and am now licensed for myself.   Guess I can add this license to the Boiler Operator license, the Taxidermy License and the Sawmill Operator rating.   Like I said before, anything to keep from doing housework.

I do like building cabins though.   So will start on a new project this spring on 80 acres I recently purchased about 60 miles northwest of Fairbanks.   I want to do another underground building.   I have drawn up plans of sorts, this time.   Didn't do that, on the last building project and was told many times that I needed to have plans.   I do, they are just in my head.   My first cabin is only partially underground in a very steep hill.   It is 14 feet into bedrock at the back of the building.   It is easy to heat in the winter and very cool in the summer.   I made extra storage out on the sides that are underground, they don't show from the outside of the building.   That is the nicest part of building underground.   Who cares if something sticks out?   Besides, out of town that far, there are no building codes.

My daughter has 3 kids, my son has a yearling and twins on the way.   They both live here in Fairbanks.   My oldest stepdaughter remarried in August and lives near North Pole.   She has 2 kids.   Other stepdaughter has 2 kids and lives in Hawaii.   I really enjoy   grandchildren, can always tell them to go home, their folks want them.

In the last 12 years, the small family mining ventures are almost gone.   The State and Federal regulations have made it an impossible dream to   earn a living in that manner.   Now the mining in Alaska is mostly by large companies that actually will ruin the areas they work.   I still own the claims, but they are for sale.

I have a different outlook on life now, than I did before Charlie died.   I do more spur of the moment things and do not think I have to pay so much attention to what anyone else is going to think about my actions. I have gotten more selfish; I am certainly living more for myself and doing what I want, now.

February 04, 2000

Post - post script

Okay, another update.

Boy, was I mixed up on that so-called relationship and as for telling the guy that I loved him? I must have been delusional. Now I don't trust anything I might think I feel for anyone. What a jerk he turned out to be. So, with that said, I will continue.

The plan to build a bed and breakfast to have income in the winter months for aurora viewing did not materialize. The hunting business also didn't since it turned out everyone in our group wanted to do it, but I was supposed to foot the entire bill for everything and I had already spent all I had buying the property. My "partners" never came through with the financial help needed. They were willing to live here on my property, just not invest anything in making it work out. They still live here. Free.

We lived in a single story of what was supposed to be a 2 story house, until my Mom had to move up here for her health. She sent up the money to build her a nice home and we did all work on that project. Mom couldn't live on her own and my relationship had hit the skids big time with the jerk. So I moved her and I down to her house and we settled in. My daughters' house sold and with my part, I started building a shop down below my Moms' house on the hill here. We started it in August and my daughter and 3 kids moved into it on October 5th, so it wasn't exactly code or fancy, but it was warm. We started her home farther up the hill in June and had it enclosed and ready for roofing by the end of August. The jerk had volunteered to roof it but kept putting it off until late September as the first snow was falling and then said no, too cold. A neighbor showed up and climbed up, said lets get it done, and they roofed it in a few hours. Unfortunately, no place was cut or set for a chimney and heat to work on it during the winter, so they had to stay another winter in the shop. 1 adult, 3 teenagers, 2 dogs and 8 cats in a 16' x 24' 2 story building.

The following summer, we insulated and finished the walls in her house, but still no chimney until late Autumn again rolled around. We had found someone not afraid of heights to go out and fix that, when the jerk showed up and did it.

I built an addition onto Mom's house finally, so I would have a bedroom and space to call my own. It is actually a small efficiency apartment.

Earlier this summer, my daughter decided we needed some sort of income and a friend gave us a trailer house frame. We built a little snack shack on it as they have different regulations than other food service that are not on wheels. It is doing fairly good, considering the "Insurance" signs at the driveway.

Mom died after a 5 day stay in the hospital in June, this year. She had been doing very well, right up until the evening we rushed her in. I miss her.

September 2011

This is a totally biased opinionated version of my life, told strictly from my point of view. If I have offended anyone, too bad, get over it.

Index

16206188R00140

Made in the USA
Charleston, SC
09 December 2012